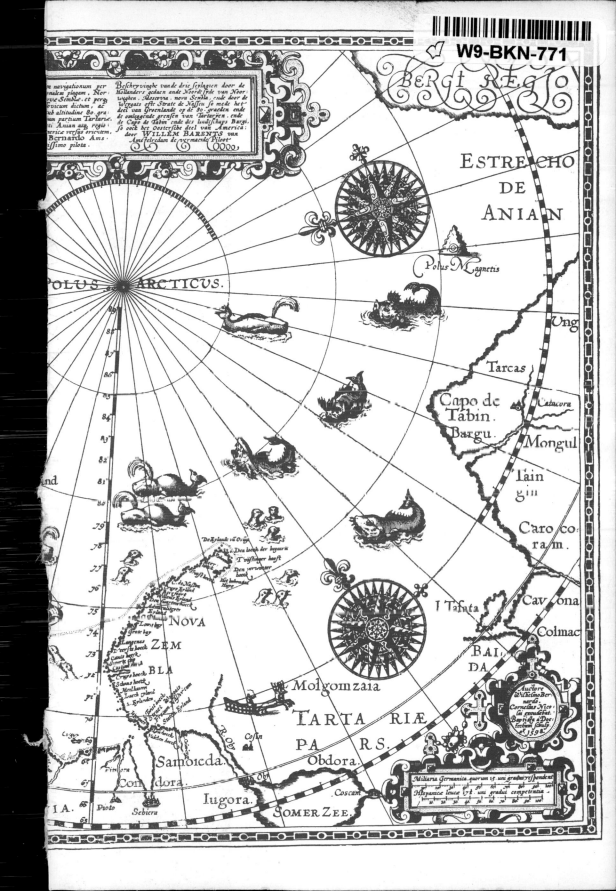

Peter Freuchen's

BOOK OF ARCTIC EXPLORATION

PETER FREUCHEN'S

Book of

Edited and with a Preface by

Arctic Exploration

DAGMAR FREUCHEN

COWARD-McCANN, Inc. *New York*

This book is dedicated to every Arctic explorer's model, guide, and inspiration, Fridtjof Nansen, who said:

> . . . from first to last the history of polar exploration is a single mighty manifestation of the power of the unknown over the mind of man, perhaps greater and more evident here than in any other phase of human life. Nowhere else have we won our way more slowly, nowhere else has every new step cost so much trouble, so many privations and sufferings, and certainly nowhere have the resulting discoveries promised fewer material advantages. Nevertheless, new forces have always been found ready to carry the attack farther, to stretch once more the limits of the world.

Contents

PREFACE

Peter Freuchen was a man of many parts: writer, explorer, lecturer, politician, television personality, a student of nature and of men. He was also a very good historian and he knew the geography and natural history of many lands much better than certain professors. Once, at a dinner party in Denmark, he amazed many people (including me), by getting up on a chair so as to be seen by everyone present and showing how a walrus eats clams by plowing them with his nose from the sea bottom. "He takes them between his fore flippers and swims up in the water," Peter said, making an upward motion with his arms as the chair began to totter.

"Then," he continued, "the walrus crushes the shells with his rugged flippers and smashes them." Here Peter cut the air furiously with his arms, as if he were himself the walrus bringing the flippers against the hard shells. To my great horror, Peter's chair broke just as he stepped to safety! I expected everyone to gasp, but there was not a sound in the room. No one noticed that the chair had broken. Every-

11

one was looking at Peter, waiting for the end of the story. "The shells," Peter concluded, "sink to the bottom, but the flesh stays on top. That is how the walrus gets the clam flesh, and why no one ever finds shells in his stomach."

Peter stepped down to his place. Everyone clapped for him and asked for more stories.

This incident was typical of Peter. He loved people and people loved him, and nothing could distract them from what he had to say. They loved to hear more and more of his stories.

Why was this? I cannot be sure what others would say, but I know what I believe. Peter Freuchen was a man with a large heart for everything living. His humanity, we could say, never slept, but was always impulsively searching for people he could help, cheer on, amuse, or investigate. It is always wonderful to meet such a person! Whenever I go to Europe I hear people speak about Peter's brave exploits in the Danish underground during the Second World War. He had the courage to do anything he wanted to do for people, and the fear which made others halt only drove him on.

After the war, when Peter and I went on automobile trips, I was surprised to discover that he *always* picked up hitchhikers, even if the car had no room for another passenger. "Peter," I would say, "I do not like this. The police are against it too." "Let us pick up the poor fellow," Peter would reply. "He doesn't have the money for the bus. Besides, I want to find out where he is going. Maybe there is something interesting up ahead!"

Something interesting up ahead! Here we have the clue to Peter's great explorations, his constant travel all over the globe. He was one of those people of whom he gives a very good description in this book. He had to be outward

12

bound all the time in search of his dream's fulfillment. He was truly an unusual man. And when he could not travel for adventure, he imagined adventure all around him.

I recall what used to happen when he returned home after mailing some letters or purchasing a newspaper. In the ten minutes he was away, a great adventure had taken place on 57th Street! There was always an exciting story to tell me—he would have talked to somebody, seen or thought or heard of something either amusing, sad, or dramatic—but never dull. Or else (I recall it very clearly) he used to soak his heavy turtleneck sweater in cold water, then put it on wet and let it dry slowly on his body. He wanted to give himself the feeling of being in the Arctic again, he wanted to have the impression that he was in his real home.

I mention all these things to tell you why I believe this book is one of Peter's greatest writings. His love of people, his search for adventure, his love of the Arctic winter, his passion to make the world a better, happier place for all—these are the things that are written on every page of this volume. They are encased in the thousands of stories Peter used to read about the explorers, which he treasured up, told and retold, and finally put into the form which I edited for presentation here. I want to thank Tom Coffey for helping me prepare this book, which has been one of the most satisfying things I have ever done. I hope you will like it.

—DAGMAR FREUCHEN

January 15, 1962

INTRODUCTION

FROM THE JOURNALS OF PETER FREUCHEN

MEN WORTHY of their nature have never been unstirred in the face of the unknown, the dangerous and the mysterious. All through history large numbers of them have set out into different parts of the world causing new values, undreamed-of possibilities, and magnificent achievement to dot the record of man's stay on this earth. In many places of the world animals and plants were once the only living things. One day men came there. They established what they knew of civilization, culture, and science. From that time on, man not only had a wider but a richer and better world in which to live.

Let no one say that it was always greed for money, political power or simple ambition which sent men out into the wilds, the deserts, the mountains, the prairies, or the extreme poles of the earth. It was the unknown, the dangerous, and the mysterious which in most cases beckoned men, which fascinated them even when it frightened them, which summoned them to undertake the difficult, even the heroic, so that the world could be a better place.

This is particularly true with exploration of the Arctic.

15

From far-distant ages the Arctic lands have fired men's imaginations in a way that no other place has ever done. The darkness, ice and cold have terrified the heroes just as they have frightened other men. But they have fascinated the largehearted—and to such an extent that those men could do nothing else but go forth. I agree that such largeheartedness has been subject to the winds of various vices as well as cultural or political influences of different times. It is nevertheless true that great men create history —not collectives, communes, wealths, tools or environment *but great men*—and when society does not interfere with their greatness they create it well.

The history of polar exploration has passed through strange phases and reflected the changes of society itself. Mythology, science, mercantilism, the desire for living space, and the need of nations to understand and control the cosmic order—these are only a few of the factors which have impelled countless men to set their course ever farther and farther north. In this sense polar exploration should be studied as an inseparable part of general history.

But since exploration is an enterprise that has a literature of its own, since a great tradition lies behind it and since great names stand out in it on account of genuine daring or outstanding achievements, it can be isolated and examined on its own account. In this respect exploration is nothing else but travel raised to the level of significant discovery, and it is in this light that I undertake to treat it with regard to polar regions.

For I have not only spent the best part of my life traveling in and out of the Arctic. I am a Dane and I come from a country where ever since ships have sailed and foreign lands been accessible, travel has been the highroad to happiness and adventure. I would like to say a little more

16

about this at the outset of this book, but not just to establish my credentials. I also want to make more clear than I have ever done before my ideas about travel and exploration in general, since they are basic to an understanding of this book.

In the age of the Vikings Denmark was overpopulated. Agriculture was restricted by the large forests that covered the countryside as soon as you got a little way in from the coast. And as hunting and fishing could not provide enough to feed the growing number of mouths, people were forced to be off and away outward bound in search of what they could not find at home.

The joys of travel and the chances travel gave of proving one's manhood and ability appealed to the imagination of those young Danes. Once they had left, many of the Vikings stayed away. Not merely the few who fell in battle with their enemies, that is, those whom they tried to deprive of their property, but also the many who found life easier in foreign lands. Reports of their good fortune and success would reach their homeland and set the young lads dreaming and send the young men forth to follow in their path. Soon to "go off as a Viking" acquired almost the significance of passing an examination. The able ones went, those with energy and courage, who were prepared to risk the fate that awaited them. A safe return, or death, or emigation was their lot. They ventured and they experienced adventure; they won fame; they created tradition.

The lazy ones stayed at home, the stupid and the pusillanimous, those in whom ambition evaporated the moment they were required to hazard anything to accomplish it. That unfortunately was the beginning of my country's decline, for those stay-at-homes were our forefathers, the ancestors of those who live there today. Now, it is only in the individual that the urge to journey forth is still sufficiently strong to make him break his ties and set off, outward bound.

Denmark, however, is not alone in this respect. Wherever I go I come across people who want to hear about travels and far journeyings and who themselves say that they personally have always had an extraordinary desire to go to foreign countries and see strange peoples and visit distant climes. After listening to their confessions for a while, you involuntarily ask: "But then why don't you travel?" And always the answer is that one has a family, another an examination to pass, one's mother would not allow it, another is afraid of not being able to stand up to it, etc. There are always excuses enough and they merely show that that person's urge is but vaguely felt, or at any rate not felt so strongly as to make him indifferent to all other considerations.

Another explanation that is often given is that the person cannot afford it. It's only the money he lacks, so he says. Yet those who *want* to travel, who live life more intensely on a journey, never wait till they have the money in their pockets. They earn it as they go along, making travel a livelihood. There are many ways of doing that. Think of sailors, of businessmen, and of the host of people science sends to the outermost bounds of civilization and beyond the pale of urban bourgeois ease. Women travel as stewardesses both on the seas and in the air: nurses, secretaries, all young girls with that restlessness in their bodies that means that the true traveler will still be up and away. And people do find their way to all the different parts of the world: it can only be the travel urge that drove them there, that mystical joy such people take in the unknown and in the not-yet-tried.

For such people a life of travel is never empty or dead. They have their dream and it keeps them young.

Many have found themselves forced to journey out into the world. Migrations were but seldom due to mass suggestion, to the tales of others that beyond the frontiers within which they had been born lay fortune and happiness. In earlier times, kings, princes and great leaders often had to follow suit and be up and away, taking their followers with them. Most often, however, it was the search for food or other necessities that drove people from their lands. Overpopulation meant that people had to struggle for their livelihood and that made them anxious to move on to other parts. Often to penetrate elsewhere it was necessary to overcome the resistance and drive out the occupiers —people who had themselves previously done the same when they occupied the lands the newcomers now wished to inhabit.

The scientists tell us that the Lapps of Northern Scandinavia once lived on the shores of the Caspian Sea. That tough little people has been constantly on the move, that is to say, in continual flight, and today they are still subject to the pressure of farmers moving northward into places which the Lapps had hoped to have for all time as a refuge for themselves and for their reindeer. Today, the Lapp is as far up in the North as he can go. He can go no farther. His journey is at an end. He won happiness and enjoyed it for a few centuries. Now, his feeding grounds have shrunk and shrunk; political frontiers have set barriers athwart the path of his moves from place to place. His journeys have grown shorter and shorter. The sweeping prospect over unknown expanses that once was his alone, is so no

19

more. The Lapp's travels were forced upon him, but each time he broke camp and moved on, he hoped that he would reach his goal, and so long as he was on the move, the prospect was bright. Now his dream is over, its light extinguished.

But the Lapps, like other travelers, can still perhaps take pleasure in movement itself and in the adventure of seeing what is new. The Jews are the most famous wanderers in the world. Some have told me that it lay in their blood to feel at home wherever they were, no matter what language was spoken around them—whether they had come down into the plains or gone up into the mountains. But even the Jews strove for two thousand years toward the goal that they have only recently reached, however modest. They wanted a country of their own.

It is different with the gypsies. They journey and wander haphazardly. Their mentality is that of the born artist. Be they great musicians or talented in other directions, they still delight in the vicissitudes of the road and its ever-changing public. Most gypsies I have known were content with a wagon fitted out as a dwelling, with a wretched screw to pull it, and a few baskets to weave, knives or axes to grind, or fortunes to tell for their livelihood. They might even live by begging, but seldom were they thieves or dishonest. They knew, of course, that dishonesty was punished with incarceration—the terror of any gypsy. They are lovers of freedom whose joy it is to be ever on the move, preferring to starve as a knife grinder rather than to take a permanent job with a wage every week, a pension after thirty years, and never a day's excitement.

It is the excitement that drives men out on their travels, when happiness is what they are after. It makes the eternal quest for what one suspects to be there all the more tempting, because everyone harbors within him the hope of something better, though he knows not what it is. He merely knows that he could not see it there at home, where the Great Adventure came to none. It was only in the fairy tales of childhood, which we all would so gladly have happen to us, that the unexpected happened.

I have felt all this myself. My family were seafarers on the one side and merchants and farmers on the other. It was the fate of the seafarers that captured my imagination. My childhood's best friend became apprenticed to a saddler, another friend became a postman, yet another went into the office of the mayor of our little town—which was a great stroke of luck. Later, I saw them as self-satisfied people interested in the doings of that little town and with a respect for each other and for themselves. Whenever I come home and look up these friends of my childhood, they look at me with gentle compassion. "We've managed better than Peter," they seem to say. "We haven't had to travel all about the world just to get our daily bread."

And they are right, for they are the settled type of person on whom a government can depend. They never long for anything revolutionary or world-shaking, and one knows that they will never shake any worlds themselves.

There were others of my friends who went with me to the university. When they graduated they became clergymen and magistrates, some doctors or engineers, and nearly all of them good citizens who have been a credit to their country. Nor did they suffer so badly from imagination that they were always requiring a new stimulus for it. Their lives went the way of officialdom: each time a superior died, they moved one step up. In the end they will move on and out to the cemetery and, if they have been sufficiently long in the service, their graves will be given a fine smart headstone.

Other people are driven out into the unknown. It is not just travel that lures them out, though they are not all of the same kind. Some go out into the world to find a job. If they arrive in the right place and find one, that is the end of their travels. Such are the majority. Others journey forth so that they may come back home and show that they have achieved what they would have been unable to get for themselves had they stayed. Others again never find peace in their own minds; they always have some new goal in sight, are always setting forth again on some new journey. Naturally no sharp distinction can be drawn between these groups. They inevitably overlap. And the stay-at-homes follow all their doings. There is something inside even the saddler that gives a tug, but he forgets it when it is time to knock off and he washes the blacking from his fingers and sits down to his evening meal that never fails to appear on his table to the minute. "Thank God for order and comfortable slippers," he says.

And yet those whose whole life is a journey are also happy. They know nothing else. It is because they must follow the animals they hunt that the Eskimos in Thule, the most northerly people in the world, are continually on the move from place to place. One year they will live on Melville Bay to get bearskins for the men's trousers. At other times they must go north to hunt the whale which provides the thread with which their women sew. Or they must live for a while by the birds' breeding grounds to get bird skins for shirts, or they must winter there and catch foxes in their traps so as to have warm furs and something to trade in the shop. Always they are on the move, traveling. Early in the spring the whole tribe gathers up in the north to catch walrus on the new ice. They live in tents, in houses of snow, or in their permanent cabins in the ground during the short autumn before the ice is passable and during the dark winter night that is four months long. During that time they are unable to hunt, yet they travel far to visit each other, making visits which are occasions for tremendous banquets at which they enjoy themselves and listen to news from distant settlements.

No sooner have the first shafts of light from the sun forced their way in through their gut windowpanes than they are all thinking of being off again on their travels: just to see lands emerging over the horizon and to feel the motion of the sledge.

Once distemper came to the Polar Eskimos and when the epidemic was over that little isolated community had only four dogs left. That was before I ever came to Thule, but the old women would tell of how long their journeys took in those days when they had had to march and drag their own sledges.

"And we had more enjoyment out of our trips then, for we kept warm and walked and walked; now you just sit and freeze on the sledge while the dogs pull it."

That was all very well, I told the old woman who had said that, but with dogs to pull your sledge, you travel farther than when you walk. "Does that matter?" replied old Arnaluk. "All travel is just moving on and away from a place where you have spent too many days at rest!"

With my late wife, who was born up in those parts, I once went hunting musk ox in Ellesmere Land with a sledge and dogs. Another family had been across there and had had the misfortune to lose most of their dogs, and so they all had to walk behind the sledge and were making but slow progress.

23

We came across the tracks of their sledge at a place which they had passed a few days previously. In the snow we could see the tracks of the man and his wife, of their half-grown sons and daughters, and the impressions made by the boots of children of four and six years old. I told Nava-rana that I hated to see small children being forced to walk all those hundreds of miles and suggested that we should turn around and go after them and offer to take some of them on our sledge.

"No," said my wife, who was both wise and good, "for don't forget that these small children are brought up from the time they are quite small to travel and to surmount difficulties. Our life here is one continual journey and it is better to begin as early as possible."

And that evening when we had built our snowhouse and the lamp was alight, she told me a tale of a real life of travel.

Once upon a time there were two married couples who were the greatest friends. Always they chose the same place in which to live and the two men always went out hunting together, while their wives helped each other with their household duties and to prepare the skins. Eventually people began to laugh at them and to tease them, saying that neither could catch a seal unless the other were with him. And so the two young couples decided to part company for a while, each going his own way.

It was agreed that they should travel around the world in opposite directions and that they should go on till they met again.

And so they set off. Things were often difficult when they came to places where the hunting was bad, but even though they often had to stay over the summer or spend a whole winter in the one place, they never forgot that they had promised to travel on till they met the friends of their youth.

In the end they became so old that young people had to support them when they walked along, but they would not die, nor rest either, until they had met their friends.

In his hand each held the cup he used to dip water up from the streams when he was thirsty. These were carved out of musk-ox horns, and each of the men had carved two cups and given them to the other couple as a keepsake. Now they were so old and had dipped up so much water that only the handles were left. So worn were those drinking cups of theirs.

Finally, one day they came to a dwelling place at which another aged couple had just arrived. And that couple too was unable to walk unaided.

And so it was that the friends met at last having been all the way around the world.

"You two seem to have aged a bit. We others have lasted well," said the one man, for he and his wife really did believe that they were still like the young couple they once had been.

"Those are words that should have been spoken from my mouth," said the other man, for he and his wife had had the same idea.

"Did you experience anything worth the telling?" asked the first man.

"Each day we hoped to experience strange things never yet seen. That kept us on our feet as we journeyed. That and the hope of reaching our goal," said the man and so died.

The other then said that it had been the same with him. And then he too died.

And that is the end of the tale of the two aged couples

who spent their lives traveling and never saw what they
hoped to see.

Several years passed and then I went to Alaska. I was
there with some film people from Hollywood. They were
able men in their own jobs, anxious to do what they had
come to accomplish, and accustomed to travel in many
lands.

We wintered there and our ship was frozen in by the ice
and they used her as a background for the story of the film
they were making. A number of the people who lived in
that place where we were, were given employment with us.
Among them was a friendly old fellow called Billy Geisler.
He was very old, so old he could remember all the famous
gold rushes and he would tell us quietly and dispassionately
of all the times he had run or driven behind a team so as
to get "there" among the first. Always he had been on the
move, and he still was, even now that he was an old man,
for the dream of his youth was still within him. His journey
was not yet ended.

Billy had a hard time of it that winter, so we had him
come aboard and give us a hand with different things.
Billy was the sort of person to whom there is nothing
unusual in the unexpected, so he accepted our offer with
the condescension that comes from being uninterested in
everything but your own plans.

One day I was standing on deck when Billy came out
from shore across the ice to his work. There was a ladder
from the ice up to the ship's rail and this we all used. Billy,
however, who was eighty-four, went on up to the bows and
clambered up by the hawse.

"What's the meaning of this, Billy? Why don't you use
the ladder, it's perfectly good."

"No thanks, not for me, Captain," said Billy. "My grand-father was eighty and he fell off a ladder and killed himself. My father was a hundred and three and he fell down a ladder and killed himself, so I'll keep away from ladders, thanks. I don't want to die yet!"

Billy told us of his own desire for travel. We came from Hollywood and he knew these parts well. He and his father lived in Los Angeles once, but then so many people had come there that Billy ceased to like it and so he had moved on up north. How many people were there there then? we asked.

"Oh," said Billy, "Los Angeles was already a large town. That was in 1873 and I don't think I'll be lying if I say there must have been about a thousand people there. It all became far too ordinary, so I left."

With the coming of summer Billy disappeared. Then one day a gold digger came down for provisions. He had been several days on the way and he had come across Billy Geisler.

Billy was up one of the creeks washing for gold with a "Long Tom," and he was quite alone. Unfortunately he was stricken with gout and had a job to get up in the morning. He had asked the other to bring some liniment on his return so that he could rub his painful old limbs and rid them of the rheumatism.

The gold digger did not want to go back at once, and as I had to take the motorboat up the lake I offered to take the medicine with me and walk up to Billy so that he could have his gout remedy as quickly as possible.

We anchored at the mouth of Swan Creek and I walked up the stream until I found my old friend. It took me several hours to reach the place, but there he was, standing waist-deep in the water. He had dug himself a large pool

27

from which he shoveled up gravel and washed it. He was evidently getting a little "pay dirt" every now and again.

When I called to him, he straightened up and waded in to the rock where I stood waiting.

Billy complained of his pains which made walking difficult, but there was his little tent properly pitched and with his tools outside it. You could see that there was work being done. But all the same he was in pain, and it was all he could do to get up to me.

"Now listen," I said to Billy. "Why do you insist on slaving like this? You've done enough in your day. Surely you can come down now to the Pioneers Home in Sitka and live in peace and quiet. You've not the slightest need to labor away at this."

Billy managed to force a grin on his face that was twisted with pain.

"Well, you see, Captain, I just want to wash here for four or five years to get some cash. When I've got enough to buy some machinery, I'll get going properly at a place up in Alaska that I found forty years ago. It's the best spot in all Alaska and just right for large-scale mining, gold from the roots of the grass down."

"That's all right, but what will you do with all that gold, Billy?"

"Well, you see, Captain, I had a girl back there in Connecticut. I couldn't get her then because I was poor. So I went off on my travels and I've been at it ever since. But one day I shall go back to Connecticut and show her something that will make her eyes pop out of her head. And then she may well think that Billy Geisler's good enough for her!"

I was younger then than I am now, and a bit of an arrogant fool, for I began trying to talk sense into Billy.

28

"Listen," I said. "You've told us that you left home in 1871, so perhaps your girl's dead by now. Either that or she's a great-great-grandmother. Anyway, she's not the same girl you left. You'd much better go to the Pioneers Home."

The moment I had said that I regretted it, for it made Billy great and me very small.

He took my medicine bottle and smashed it against the rock. He roared with anger and swore in heartfelt contempt.

"What the devil do you think? Do you imagine that I don't know it's all a dream? But it is *my* dream, and it is what I have lived on these many years and it has brought me through such bad times as none of you can ever conceive. You young puppies are so damned clever. But you don't understand what it is to live alone with an idea and a dream. Go to hell out of here and mind your own business!"

With that, Billy waded back out into the stream that he had widened into a large pool so that he could dig out the gravel which he washed to get the gold he wanted for the girl he had loved in 1871. And I walked shamefacedly back to my motorboat and sped away. I never saw Billy Geisler again.

Billy was one of those who kept their dream. His life was decided from the moment he was unable to win his girl. He had managed to get it into his head that it was only the money he had lacked. Perhaps, deep inside of him there had been a doubt, but he had silenced it and had clung to his dream. That was why Billy had had to be continually on the move. Had he settled down anywhere, ordinary, everyday life would have grown up around him and demolished his dream.

I have met others with the same hope. As a rule, they are young men who have met with some disappointment at home. One had been unable to buy the farm that had been his father's and his father's before him; another had been refused by the girl he loved; some had been unable to get a start in life, others had just felt a longing to get abroad.

Those I am thinking of were dreamers, often people who took a delight in nature and loved plants and animals, which made them experts in many things that belong to open-air life. They had been disappointed and, as was right and reasonable, had looked for something they thought they would be able to tackle.

They decided to go to Canada or Alaska and become trappers in the immense forests there. Behind that choice as often as not lay the books they had read in their boyhood—books in which the trapper's life is described as a series of adventures and wonderful experiences, where hardship always ends in a great junketing or is rewarded with due applause for the courage, ingenuity and kindness of heart that they all believed themselves to possess.

As they were also all familiar with guns and had spent many an hour waiting for birds or beasts and had filled the time of waiting with daydreams, it seemed merely natural to try to take up as a career what had occupied their free time so pleasantly. So they set out for the forests of the North and became trappers. During the months, or years, needed for their preparations, they would read all they could about the life they had chosen. Some would stick to novels, others got hold of magazines and periodicals for "hunters, fishermen and those interested in furs," all unknowing that most publications of this kind are written by people who have never seen a pine marten, fox or otter except in a zoo. Some of these would-be wanderers went further and studied the biology of the animals in learned books and made their appearance in the townships on the fringe of the forests ready to start.

Their aim is always to trap skins to the value of a million dollars a year. And they are going to show that this can be done; they know it can be done, they have their methods.

And they all do the same thing: they get their equipment and go off into the woods. They have all been dreaming of having a cabin and they know that they must have a dog or two, that they must catch whitefish to dry for them, and they know exactly what provisions they must buy. And so they start with high hopes and plenty of courage. They are free men, kings in the forest, and now at last they will be able to live just as they have always wanted to live all these years; yes, it will suit them down to the ground.

Then the snow falls and the hunting season begins. They spread out their traps and snares and their life soon becomes a routine. The real trapper sets out on the Monday morning with his dog which pulls a toboggan. He himself walks the soft snow of the forest on special shoes, a rifle slung over his shoulder and the dog following in his tracks. In the evening he camps, felling a couple of trees for his campfire, and so he sleeps in the open until the next morning when he is up and off again. His traps are so arranged that in his wanderings he describes a great loop and returns home on the following Thursday or Friday. Then the animals he has caught must hang up in the cabin to thaw. On Saturday he skins them and stretches the skins. Sunday is his day of rest which he can devote to rejoicing at the open-air life, and pitying his friends at home and wishing they could see him. And on Monday he starts all over again.

The upshot for them all is that at the end of the first year they come to the trading post and have to admit that they haven't quite had the success they had expected.

"But, of course, you have to learn first. There are certain things where you need experience. You'll see next year. I'll make you gape."

And what he has caught brings in just enough for a little rest, that is ten days' or a couple of weeks' hard drinking, after which his money is so reduced that it just suffices to fit him out for another year—ammunition, flour and tea, sugar and salt, some dried fruits and vegetables. He has to get back while it is still summer, for he must catch whitefish in the river and dry it on long racks if he is going to feed his dog during the winter. That done, the long winter can begin.

Next spring he reappears out of the woods.

The trader can see at once how little he has brought.

"Yes, there were two ways of setting about it. I chose the wrong one. Not that my method isn't all right, but it has proved unsuitable for these parts. But next year, you'll see. I've got the experience and now I'm going to reap the benefit."

And so a third year passes and the result is still as meager as ever.

"Yes, of course, there are years when there just isn't anything in the woods. We all know that. And this last winter was one of them, at least in my district. I can assure you, I'm surprised that I've caught as much as I have; for I don't believe there was one more living creature in the woods than these I got. But luckily, as we know, a bad year like that is always followed by one of the really good ones. So I won't miss the boat again."

And so it continues. Year after year. As he goes his solitary round he has plenty of time to discover why it is he doesn't catch more than he does. It is too late when he realizes, as so many have before him, that the only way to make money out of skins and furs is to trade in them. He who sets the traps can make no more than suffices for his daily fare and a rest of two or three weeks before he must return to his woods.

He never achieves the huge catch he expected. But his life is spent in constant movement, eternally traveling even though merely in the one forest. He has adventures and he dreams dreams. Assuredly he wins peace of mind, for I have visited such trappers in their cabins and know that that is so. Calm, friendly people they are, men of few words. They are glad to see a strange face, but never seek one out themselves. And always they have their daydreams. What they think about, I don't know. But perhaps by traveling out and away from the place of their birth they have developed into truly "decent" people and have acquired real peace of mind.

I came once to a trading post up in Canada where people were talking about a trapper who hadn't been seen for a couple of years. At first they had thought that he had moved farther east and so was trading at another post. But when they got in communication with it he hadn't been heard of there. Another year passed, and then the matter was reported to the Royal Mounted Police, the finest force of its kind in the world. A patrol went out to look for the man. They found his cabin in ruins; his bones were scattered all over the place and had been gnawed by foxes and wolves. That has been the fate of many who have disappeared in the deep forests. No one heard of their journey's ending, but it may well be that their travels brought them to their goal and that they had found peace with themselves.

You must not confuse these men whose desire is to get away from all others, with the ordinary emigrant, the person who moves with his family to America, Australia, or some other country, just to get away from the narrow pettiness of life at home.

That was an expression we often heard in Denmark when I was young. This "narrow pettiness" was something indefinite, but a thing to which we couldn't submit. And it was always the best who went away. I can remember how, when I was a child, agents from the shipping lines or railway companies in the U.S.A. and Canada used to go around the country districts. They would tell tales of the huge fortunes that could be made, of how there were new towns growing up over there, and that whoever went could not fail to share in the growing prosperity. These men appealed to the imaginations of the young people and it was those who were the most daring they won over. Plenty of young men and girls decided to get away and go there.

It was often difficult for them to collect together the necessary money for the journey. I can remember many who spent years scraping every penny together. They spent nothing on amusements, never went to fairs or markets in the towns, never came to the pigeon shooting or to the cattle shows, but put their money in the bank. And one fine day they would leave.

Later, I used to come across them out in the prairie. Many of them were well-to-do, others had had nothing but toil and struggle, from which only their children would benefit. They who had left home and country to make a better life for themselves would have their proud hopes fulfilled at least for their children. I have seen old men who were rusted and bowed, and their wives too were marked to show that they had in truth borne their share of all that labor.

I remember a young couple from my boyhood days. A fine couple they were and so confident that they would get

34

on. They saved up for three years there at home in our parish. I remember how they would sit together in the servants' hall poring over their savings books, and how they gathered together their kit for the journey. When one of them, as though it were his greatest task in life—which perhaps it was—carpentered two wooden chests and covered them with yellow wax cloth fixed with brass-headed nails arranged in the shape of their monograms, we all came and admired the masterpiece. An old cowman who was my hero and a man whose word carried great weight in the village because he could show a huge scar from a saber cut dealt him in the 1864 war, gave the young emigrant a few words of warning.

"Those chests will catch the eyes of the Indians and robbers. They're the first thing they'll pull off the post wagon."

Those mystical words and the fatal significance behind them gave me a great deal to think about.

Some fifty years later I met the two again. They were both aged and looked quite different from what they would have had they lived in Denmark. The fierce summer heats had dried them up, and hard work had bowed them. They talked about the market town at home, the cattle shows and the old people in the parish, most of whom were then dead. The two chests had long since been broken up and burned.

They had never had enough money to be able to afford a trip home to see their families. And, besides, they had given way to the same temptation as so many others, and in their letters painted too rosy a picture of their life and circumstances. But at least they had had the satisfaction that their one son was still farming the land they had brought under cultivation; one daughter was a doctor, and

35

two other children were in good positions but so far away that their parents had not seen them for many years.

Whether those two got anything out of going abroad is an open question. They themselves would say that they had achieved what they had aimed at, but one must always remember that ideals and goals are constantly changing. They were happy after their own fashion and in all probability had never realized how the fires of their youth had been gradually extinguished by their struggle to tame land for the benefit of their offspring.

I have met many emigrants and seen the many different lives that have been their lot, but the truth of the matter is that once they had reached their destination they stopped traveling just as effectively as though they had gone back home.

There are individuals who retain the feeling of being on a journey. I have come across many of them, too. The majority stint and save to be able to travel back and visit their family. As a rule such a trip is a disappointment.

The emigrant, of course, just saves enough for the fare. At home, they say to themselves, we can stay with nephews and with brothers and sisters. We know so many who have been missing us all these many years, for haven't they said so in their letters? Then homesickness makes them set out a little before they really should, but all the same they buy their tickets and home they go.

And so the news reaches Denmark that at last they are on their way: "The rich uncle from America is coming." And the nephews and others buy tickets to Copenhagen to go and meet him. Not return tickets, of course, for Uncle can pay the fare home, and also for the hotel and all the rest of it. Money means nothing to him.

It's not that they are intending to sponge on the returning relative, but they just assume that he can buy a pair of new horses, pay off a mortgage, or have a new roof put on the house without its affecting his pocket in the least. Gradually both parties discover that things aren't at all as they had imagined, and when the trip is over, the emigrant is the poorer by a dream; for he had dreamed of that trip home, dreamed that he would find happiness through it.

All his travels have been without foundation, that necessary realization of where he should go and how, and what he was aiming at in the trip.

However, emigration can scarcely be called "travel," and that only until one has made up one's mind where one can live and settle down in that new community. The day that happens, there is an end to traveling and it is only resumed when the emigrant makes the trip back home either for good or on a visit to impress people that he had been right to leave home. On these trips many discover that the "narrow pettiness" of conditions at home could have been overcome. If they had but put as much hard work into that as they did into the prairie, they would no doubt have achieved the same.

And then there are the eternal wanderers. Are they happy?

Those who traveled extensively between the two World Wars will remember the desperate young Germans who could never settle anywhere. These were young people born during or just before the First World War. During the four years of blockade when Germans were severely rationed they were kept alive with "ersatz" foods of all kinds. I don't know whether it was lack of vitamins, or just that they didn't get the right stuff, but whatever it was, that generation was neurasthenic from childhood. They were thin and looked undernourished, and either need or unconscious restlessness had driven them from their country. I came across them in many places in South America, I met them in Alaska, in New York; everywhere you would find these poor wretches always traveling and taking small jobs of any kind but never staying long at anything. As workers they were not conscientious, and they were always having to be off again.

They just traveled on and on toward a goal without knowing what it was, and always they died young. They are of little interest to us here, because from one point of view they were travelers by necessity, forced to journey by their troubled minds.

Is travel a cure for that? Yes, there are perhaps many who feel a certain pleasure in moving, or being moved, from place to place. You can see many queer people traveling and what their quest is, is usually difficult to discover. Economic conditions have changed greatly all over the world, but there once existed a certain class of Englishmen who traveled without any obvious motive, at least as far as others could see. I have met them, too, all over the world, both men and women. As a rule they were tall and thin. They were always most pleasant to those with whom they had to deal, and although there was a certain contemptuousness in their manner, none could take offense at it, for it was really no more than their way of saying that any place which could not provide them with their eggs and bacon in the morning, just as they were accustomed to have them in England, was to a certain extent uncivilized. They were no doubt in search of something, but now you will meet them no more.

Some years ago a French count went on an expedition to the north coast of East Greenland. He told his polar skipper to make for the most northerly bit of coast possible and there they wintered. He had no dealings with any of the crew and himself was never once ashore or even on the ice. He spent the entire winter in his cabin playing cards. He had people to wait on him; he was kind and pleasant, seldom seen and never had much to say. His cards engrossed him.

What he wanted up there, no one has any idea. For him the pleasure in his travels consisted in playing cards while wintering in the Arctic. A queer man! Was it delight in travel, or an attempt to experience something and so acquire knowledge of the world?

I don't know.

I have spent my whole life traveling. I began before I went to Copenhagen University. I suppose I was born with the urge to tackle the new and untried.

I had noticed early in life that those who had spent a good many years abroad had a certain advantage over us others. It was as though they could see the outlines or main features of a person behind his many small details.

I heard a bit of gossip and talk in our village at home: tales of others' little failings and interest in their private lives and alert watchfulness that none overstepped what in that part of the world was the accepted behavior. Those who had been abroad overlooked that sort of thing. They knew that you could have different table manners and still be a decent person. They understood that even though you dressed quite differently from others, it was still no proof of mental deficiency, nor even meant that you were impudently contemptuous of your fellows. And these people had my sympathy. Since then I have learned those who take a narrow interest in their neighbors are often charitable and helpful in both small things and big. Now I often feel uncomfortable when I find myself driving past thousands of my fellow beings and realize that I am indifferent to how they are faring. However, I went off on my travels. My first expedition to the polar region taught me that I was of the right type, that the life there suited my temperament. To leave that and go home and to the university seemed far too tame, for I was neither clever enough nor sufficiently imaginative to find in books and studies the great adventures my heart desired. Instead, I went off again and I have never regretted it since.

Chance took me to the most northerly inhabited place in the world, and there I settled down. I married into the tribe and became a Polar Eskimo myself, for—that was during the First World War—I was alone up there and was forced to live in the old-fashioned Eskimo manner. A harpoon and a spear were the weapons with which we hunted. We traveled from place to place and were very happy in our lives.

In the first place I had the great luck to succeed Dr. Knud Rasmusson, a man who had known how to combine the superior cleverness of the white man with the Eskimo's ability to shift for himself. We were young and poor, so we had no goods to sell, in fact we didn't even have provisions or equipment. But we got them. We traveled up and down that tremendous coastline following our game. We undertook trips of a length that none before us had covered with dogs and the same equipment. We lived by hunting, and we crossed the Greenland icecap at a speed that none before us or since has been able to equal with a dog team. That was a life of travel and a carefree life as well. My wife, Navarana, was the finest person I have ever met. With no other qualifications than her understanding of herself and her fellows, and her intimacy with

40

nature, she helped me during the eleven years we were married as no other wife has ever helped her husband. She taught me the fundamentals of travel so well that although I learned them under those special conditions, I have been able to base all my other travels on them, wherever I have been. She taught me the joys of being in a new place every day. We saw a promontory ahead of us, we had no idea what lay behind it. There was adventure and excitement in that, and it never left me.

Navarana died while we were on a trip. Our children were both born while we were traveling. Traveling became my life. But it was only later that I understand the danger there was in that. I had believed that mine was an honest and an entirely conscious desire to get away from civilization with its—for me—too circumscribed regulation of everything and its predetermined methods for every one of our actions. Yet that civilization, I discovered, was after all the result of the experience of generations, and every man I have come across who had done as I did, began at once to introduce just those things he himself had abandoned.

I myself taught "my" Eskimos. I introduced new instruments and tools. I sold them things to make daily life easier. In other words, the primitive forms of living by which I felt attracted were the very things that I immediately set about reforming. Of course, I never thought out properly what I was aiming at, but it can only have been to get life in North Greenland to resemble that of Europe. And it was from just that, I realized even at the time, that I was trying to get away.

There is this great difference between travel in North Greenland and life in Europe, that up there your job is at the same time a struggle merely to maintain life. When things are like that, life can't be dull. If you slacken off, if you take things too easily, it won't be long before you are a dead man. There is no need to say that excitement and absorption in what you are doing are never absent from your travels. And up there your whole life is travel.

But there were many other dangers in living among primitive people. Remember that I was alone up there, the only white man, and being white I knew a little more about many things than any of the others. I was, besides, the possessor of a number of commodities that were greatly desired. Every year, except during the war or when the ice would not let them through, ships would bring me things that for the Eskimo were treasures of hitherto unimagined worth. That gave me an exceptional position and it lent weight to my words. Because of that they listened to me, and because of that my every wish was fulfilled. My requests were law.

Possibly I am a person of weak character, but in any case I succumbed to that, and when I came home to Denmark after spending ten years in Thule, I was at first astounded, then filled with righteous anger, when anyone even began to contradict me. I had certainly not been accustomed to that. Soon, however, I was forced to accept the possibility that not everything I said was right. That went a long way toward breaking me in.

Life in the Arctic regions, "far from the madding crowd," is not without its dangers. Many people suppose that the period of darkness is burdensome to people there, especially to whites. I have never felt that, because I always had plenty to do. The worst thing about the Arctic is its monotony. It provides excitement and novelty of new conditions for a few years, but then things begin to repeat themselves. It is not easy to learn to drive a dog sledge, but it can only produce a certain number of situations and when you have been through them all, there comes repetition and that gradually makes you more and more sure of yourself, till you begin to feel the lack of novelty even here. Walruses, polar bears and seals are big animals to hunt. They can be dangerous and at any rate have acquired a certain notoriety, but they do not have large brains and their ability to think is restricted. They know only a certain number of tricks, and when you have seen these and know them, the hunting of them calls for little more than the physical effort involved. It can become monotonous and those who cannot bear a little monotony ought to go home in their first year. For them polar life will not be the right one, if only because it is a wandering life and not everyone is born to that.

And yet it can completely fill your mind, become part of your very nature. I realized that when I thought that I had lost it all. That was when I had the bad luck to become buried under the snow during a snowstorm. When I had dug myself out one foot was frozen and later had to be amputated.

I was more unhappy then than I ever have been in my life. I thought that was the end to all my travels.

I was so distressed and beside myself that I began to write novels. My great worry was that all my experiences would go for nothing. The great travels I had planned could never be carried out, or so I thought. And that was why I took up writing. I knew that no one except the specialist can be bothered to read tedious travel journals. But I knew too that if you put real travel experiences into novels, the reader can feel whether they are genuine or not. The reader is sufficiently sensitive and perspicacious to do that. He will notice at once when a novel about the backwoods has been written by a country schoolmistress who has never been abroad. So, I gathered together all my experiences and all that I had seen and heard and I put them into novels which have had a good sale all over the world.

And then I discovered that a man who only lacks one foot can travel just as well as anyone else, provided he himself wants to. Since then I have done long and arduous trips. I have lived to see new ways in which man lives his life and have known the joys of being able to set off, outward bound, and of coming back again.

The time came when my books had sold sufficiently for me to go on writing, so that I was able to continue both forms of excitement. Thus, I became both traveler and author, and I daily feel how close to each other are these two forms of emotion.

Through this I have been brought into contact with numbers of people. For many years I have lived with very, very few, knowing exactly what they would say to me and exactly what I would say to them. The contrast of seeing and being able to talk with many was so great and wonderful that it made me discover the charm of contrast. That is why I go out on my travels and come home again. I live my travels over again in my lectures, articles and books. Life has arranged itself rather wonderfully for me.

When I lived in Greenland my best friend from my student days was my "neighbor" for several years. He was doctor in a district some five hundred miles from Thule, and each winter I went down and visited him. He himself drove around seeing his patients and hunting bear, and he loved the life.

After that he took a practice in Denmark. He lived in the country and visited his patients in a motorcar. Not even he came across anything very new. He had been too long at it and life was just a succession of repetitions. It was a godsend to him when during the war he was able to help English parachutists and hide them from the Germans, and to take part in the underground struggle against the Nazis. But, before that, he had been feeling the need of change and variety, and he had to get out and away.

So, one fine day, he called in another doctor to replace him. He took a job as a ship's doctor. And there he was, outward bound. He went around the tropics, out East, and he experienced all the joys that a bath in new worlds always is for those who are wide awake. Not everybody has the courage to do what he did; nor the strength of character to realize that there are things more important than doing what others can also do, and equally well.

But, to travel in search of happiness, is there anything unusual in that now? I don't think so, nor that those who cannot help traveling come to misfortune by it. It makes me think of that huge section of mankind that travels in thought, those who read the tremendous travel literature that exists in all languages. What do they experience? Personally, I can't say, for when I have read such books, it has always been as the professional traveler. For me they were reference books, books I needed in making my preparations and to get to know contrasts.

It is a lamentable thing that so many—how many!—of the great travelers are such bad writers. Their imagination led them into the great fields for travel, but it did not always put a pen in their hands. You can often see how they have set about their writing with a certain reluctance, at any rate without inspiration. The result is a collection of dry facts that the reader must himself clothe with flesh and blood before he can get anything out of it. And he does it! It is unbelievable how well people travel in armchairs.

45

Perhaps they come to the land of happiness while they are about it, but then it is such a short time before dinner is ready or they must go to bed and leave off. A great deal of imagination is required of these people, for when a book is dry their personal contribution is quite different from what is required of them when an author has the talent to make a situation real and to describe the background and setting.

The armchair traveler has at least the advantage that he is not disgruntled with the life, government or cooking of his home. He only knows that he can well imagine himself going off traveling, but he just can't bring himself to incur the trouble of breaking up house, nor does he dare risk such a leap into the dark, for he is not the type to risk his own person. All his dashing about is done in imagination. There are many like that.

Let me name some of the great travelers who were also inspired writers: Fridtjof Nansen, the famous Norwegian polar explorer; Knud Rasmussen, the great Danish student of the Eskimos; Stanley and Livingstone on Africa; Humboldt about South America. Yes, there really have been many whose writings could capture the imagination. This is not the place to discuss whether they have kept people from traveling or have invited them to do so. That, too, depends on whether their readers feel the urge to emulate or surpass them, or merely come to realize that the joys they themselves are seeking can be found in other parts of the world, and through that they escape from the tedium of their lives in which there is no excitement. We humans differ, if in nothing else, at least in this, that we have the strangest conceptions of how one can best and easiest live happily.

I once had a young secretary. He was quick and efficient. Then I went off on one of my trips and he took a job in an office. I didn't see him for several years. When I returned home the young man came to see me. He wanted to borrow some money. "What do you want it for?" I asked.

It appeared that he had a mighty thirst for adventure and he badly wanted to travel. He had been offered a job in an office in Buenos Aires.

I asked him whether he thought he would find more adventure working in an office in Buenos Aires than in an office in Copenhagen, and his reply was: "Well, at any rate they speak Spanish!"

In Denmark we are rather far away from Spanish-speaking peoples, but one's boyhood literature with its pirates and Indians and pioneers in the virgin forest always speaks Spanish, so that young clerk felt that in itself should be enough to give romance and mysticism to his new surroundings. He got his money and he overcame his family's tears and lamentations. Then I had another visit from him to warn me of the impending call of some relative who intended to come and curse me for helping him and generally for giving him the urge to travel in the first place.

I came across him later in the Argentine. He was not living a life of great adventure, for he was working in a dairy, but he was satisfied and his pleasure lay in writing home and portraying his life out there as full of dangers and privations. He figured in these letters as a hero, the unvanquished fighter of countless battles with brigands, cattle thieves and fearsome beasts. He, I am sure, had achieved happiness.

Later on he will quiet down, his ideals and ambitions will change, but he will still be able to surround himself with a mystic glow in the eyes of his friends and relatives at home. And herein lay much of his happiness, that he wanted to go

47

on being the great man in the eyes of his people at home.

Yes, but that is in no way different from what you can find in circles much higher and among those much more famous than he. I have met Danish and Norwegian artists who had achieved great success abroad—singers, actors, authors and others. They had their public in America or elsewhere about the wide world, but their real happiness lay in having it known in dear little Denmark or Norway. They dearly loved a mention in a Copenhagen or Oslo paper, while any report of a fiasco in the same place would make them fly into a rage. That shows how impossible it is to travel away from oneself and one's origins. That is why emigrants are never entirely happy, as long as they can remember the joys of childhood in their home, the friends and spirit of their youth in the land they have left.

It is only physical travel that can fully absorb people, for while journeying they forget what it is from which they are fleeing. Some feel indignant at the wickedness of people in the place where they are living, forgetting that people's re-actions are often the result of their own clumsy behavior—often they leave home and go abroad because their business is not doing so well, or because their harvest was worse than their neighbor's. It is so easy to find excuses, but what is usually overlooked is that the person whose shop has the most custom, or who harvests the best crops, is the one who in everyday language is the "most capable."

For failure there is always an explanation to be found. In this man inventiveness is enormous. He can go on and on finding reasons just why things went wrong, but he who is unlucky once, twice or ten times, or always, the world calls incompetent. Yet perhaps a person who has once been un-successful may find it is difficult to make his neighbors realize that he is turning over a new leaf. The mere accus-

48

toming of one's immediate fellows to the idea that henceforward things are going to be different can cost all too much effort. The answer is to get away—away from those things and persons which are making life difficult and keeping you back, away to new conditions where you will be able to make good. However, it is only the few who do that. You always take yourself with you however far you go; you may be outward bound, but your brain and body go with you.

Traveling also helps one to forget. There was a man in Thule whose three small children were playing a game he himself had played innumerable times when he was a child, for his father had taught him it. The game was to slide down a steep slope of snow on a sealskin. The real excitement came at the bottom of the slope when the one who was guiding had to turn to one side, for below was roaring water. There was a violent tiderace right at the foot of the mountain there, where the sea was never covered with ice, and that was what made it so exciting and alluring. The boy was steering for the two small girls and what happened no one knows. All three disappeared into the roaring sea right in the middle of winter. The parents heard a shriek and that was the last sign of life from them. Their bodies were never found.

After that, Golugtangua journeyed south down to the civilized Greenlanders. He traveled alone, just with his dogs, making for the bad hunting grounds, for he wanted a spell of difficult conditions to help him forget his grief.

As he said, travel was the only thing that could offer you new thoughts. Life had taught him that.

Golugtangua was away a whole year. When he came back he moved in with his family. The children were never spoken of again. His grief was forgotten.

49

There is something in that of the mentality of the Vikings. They went on expeditions to strange lands, some because they wanted renown, others because they were resentful of some little wrong suffered at home.

Travel has cured many who have been persecuted by their thoughts. It puts things in new lights and transfers responsibility to other shoulders. Such people should travel. They are the ones who will find happiness in it—perhaps. At any rate they do not have it at home.

I often think of the line from that wise Icelandic sage:

"God punished him for his evil deeds most grievously, for He gave him a bitter mind."

That is true and, if nothing else helps, a man or woman whose heart is full of bitterness ought to go off and travel. It can't make things worse and it is at least easier to live where you are unknown. All over the world man adjusts himself to his place. I have been in Alaska and met many capable people there. Many were hardened by the tremendous difficulties of those grim winters, but they were all wonderfully understanding and all were tolerant of others' habits, broad-minded and gentle in their criticism.

It took me some time to get to know them, for I was a stranger, but one day a wise old gold digger told me that one of the most important rules in Alaska and elsewhere on the fringe of the world's circle, was never to ask anyone about his home, family, name, or why he was there. Observe that rule, and you will become friends with many of them, he said. If anyone wishes others to know more about him than he himself has told them, leave it to him to tell it.

That was because in those days there was no one in Alaska who was not a traveler. Now there are farmers there. The Arctic has been opened up to those with quite differ-

50

ent intentions from what the old adventurers had. Alaska still has its travelers, but it also has its settlers, people whose journey is at an end.

Many have found happiness there, where they were beyond the reach of the .curiosity of neighbors which they had found irksome. It requires strength of mind and character to be transplanted, yet surprisingly many stand it successfully. However, the mere fact that they broke loose shows that there was something in them that they never got from their homes. Travel stimulated their minds. They sought happiness, and even though they often did not themselves consider that they had found it, the thing that mattered was that they searched. Our task after all is to develop the man in us, as a person, and I never saw anyone who had become less of a man by traveling. But that is no reason to regard those who travel as better than the others who stay at home.

Everyone knows that large class of people, the amateur yachtsmen, who spend half the year sailing about in fine boats. They have excellent equipment and handle their craft with such efficiency and ingenuity in making the most of conditions as few professional seamen can equal. For them sailing is a sport and there is a tremendous gulf between them and the poor devils who do it for money. Both have a deep contempt for the other, yet both try to imitate the other. Are not these amateurs all dreamers? Do they not, I wonder, daydream of mighty voyages to distant seas during which they will encounter and, of course, overcome endless dangers and unexpected difficulties? I know them only from the tales they tell ashore. They will describe how they weathered the most dreadful storms; how they escaped that uncharted rock. In their talk they relate over and over again horrible things that we others

51

with a greater respect for ease and comfort are only too glad not to have experienced. Yet those are just the things that for them gave the summer its charm. It is the sea they love, and they miss it all through the winter. These people are travelers at least in spirit. Their bodies never get very far away from their elegant cabins or out of their well-cut clothes, but they do have adventures and experiences, they take an active part in moving from place to place, and are far nearer to being "travelers" than the general run of tourists.

Let me say here and now that to be a "tourist" has always seemed to me the worst fate that can happen to anyone. I have only tried it on few occasions and never for long. The last time was in my own country, Denmark, in company with a number of famous authors. We were led around by a guide who in a furious gabble gave us much false information about many of the places we saw. We forced him into a church about which he had no patter prepared, and inspected the skeletons of some old kings. They were in glass cases and each had his name on a plate, so that he couldn't go wrong there. But he wanted to tell us something more about them, so that he could show off his languages. So, pointing with a long finger at the skeleton of one of Denmark's rulers, killed in 1086, he said: *"Il est mort!"*

And no one protested.

I have seen tourists in many countries. They are hounded in herds from castle to church, from church to picture gallery, and on to famous views. After a few days they surrender to their grim lot and trudge along apathetically without a word to say, or the desire to look, their mental faculties so low and depressed that they cannot even remember their delight in traveling, their faith in the adventure that would come their way and the things they had hoped to learn, nor even all the money they had wasted on that ghastly enterprise. Tourism is not travel.

And yet you cannot define the difference between them. At least not in a few words. There is too much, too many things and too great a distance separating them.

Some have set off outward bound in order to win honor and renown, as in the days when kings wanted colonies. Then there were scholars whose happiness consisted in knowing more than others about the earth and distant places. There still are, and their numbers grow from year to year. Every returning expedition breeds with its results the germs of others. The purely adventurous excursions to places that "had never before been visited" are now no more. There are so few places like that left. The airplane has revolutionized discovery. The camera, films, wireless, and competition have put an end to the exciting fairy tales that used to curdle the blood and inflame the imaginations of the young and inexperienced. I remember my boyish, almost adoring admiration for polar travelers who came back and told tales of starvation and suffering, of pitiless frost and menacing death. A little later, I began to wonder how it was that they always wanted to go back up there. Then, when I myself was able to sample polar life, I never encountered any of their great sufferings. Or if I did, I never thought much about it. I have lived a happy life traveling, and I will never settle down for good.

A certain frugality is also necessary in the traveler. Do not think that happiness lies in having much money, fame whether scientific or military, or in having an unsurpassed traveling technique. Happiness is to be found abroad and at home in the worth of what has been achieved. That will vary according to the goal you have set yourself, the point of view you have taken.

A scientist can return home after several years travel abroad and be happy because he has found a hitherto unknown northern limit for a single flower. Others aim at unraveling the geological complexities of some mighty chain of mountains. Others have even greater aims. Happiness does not lie within the limits of the definable. Happiness dwells inside us, though it is also necessary to realize that those who go out and those who remain at home are part of the same society essentially.

There is one point about this book I should make clear right now: no one really knows the names of all the great explorers, particularly those of the Arctic. How many have striven with nature up there, we will never know. Expeditions in search of new trade routes, whalers after new fishing grounds, men after adventure—all these added to our knowledge of the cold North and have helped exploration in the fullest sense. But we have no complete record of who all these people were. We don't know what they did exactly, or how they added to the body of knowledge of their time.

We have often been told that nothing changes in the Far North. Time stands still, people frequently say, and nature obeys different laws in the Far North—laws unlike anything we know. But this is no longer true. The pattern of life followed in Arctic countries today has changed even the laws of nature and would make them as unfamiliar to the old-time explorer as to a man who simply followed the expeditions of former days from the comfort and security of armchair reading.

Little of our earth now remains undiscovered. In the Arctic, great stretches of coastline have been chartered in detail and made familiar even to schoolboys. But beyond actual territories, lakes, and oceans, not too much is known. Nor could it be known until now. We stand now on the threshold of an era in which the Arctic is to be discovered *intensively* as opposed to the simply territorial or *extensive* exploration of past ages. It is for this reason that the story of past explorations and adventures in the Arctic has its place—it can teach us to stand on the shoulders of those giants who have gone before us and thus better appreciate their work.

I myself am an Arctic explorer of the old times. I have fought my way, dog whip in hand; I have paddled kayaks, and I have trudged long, lonely distances, dragging my sledge. I and the men with me were sometimes absent for years at a time, while those dearest to us were ignorant whether we were alive or dead. Such things happen no more. Wireless has done away with these long periods of uncertainty, with the isolation which the scientist in the Arctic once had to endure.

The Arctic is now an integral part of the world. We have reached a point in history where we can collate the experiences of individuals, like the separate blocks of stone on a great building, and so enrich man's empire of the world. How science and economics, art, adventure, and all the talents of men work together toward this end, I will attempt to show in this book. The Arctic world is no less thrilling for the loss of its mystery, and no less interesting for our better knowledge of it. We are still able to share in the triumphs of the men who work there, and are made more hopeful of what is yet to come.

Yet even when all this is said, we must still acknowledge

that the Arctic remains under the dominion of the midnight sun and of the crushing winter darkness. Nature's variety there is and it remains infinite. For every riddle answered, a thousand more present themselves, and research continues to demand men of courage—men with brains but also with plenty of heart and strength. I have learned that we veterans did not work in vain, that our discoveries have contributed to the discoveries of today, and that we too have our place in the glories and splendor of tomorrow.

BOOK ONE

The Great Explorers
of the Arctic

The Age of Heroes

Mercantilism and Nationalism

The Race for the Pole

World War I and After

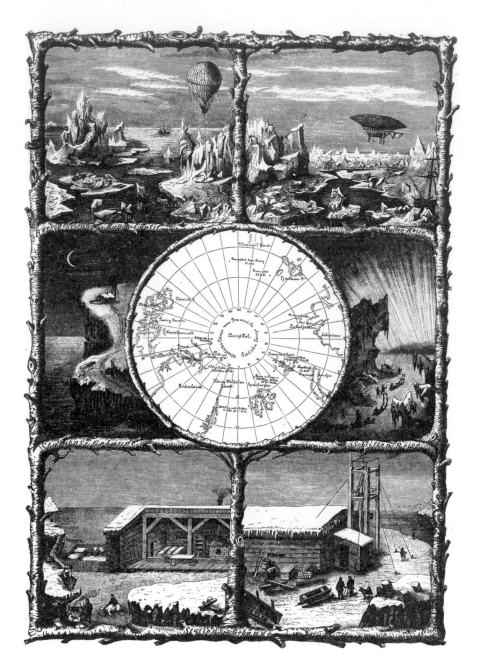

I. The Age of Heroes

1. *Pytheas*

EACH AGE has its daring explorers and adventurers. But of all ages and all explorers and adventurers the Greek Pytheas was the greatest. Once and for all time, more than 2,000 years ago, Pytheas set the pattern of discovery, adroitly combining the best of the science, art, and other human talent available in his time.

Who was Pytheas and what did he do?

Though Pytheas was practically unknown when I went to school in Denmark, historians since that time have gradually uncovered his achievements, and in the last few decades he has been emerging as a towering figure in exploration and in early science as well as in what the Greeks called philosophy. Pytheas in fact is now regarded as one of the greatest figures not only in exploration and science but in human history generally.

It was Pytheas who discovered that the tides are controlled by the moon. It was he who first found out how to apply astronomy to geography so that people could locate a place on the earth by the light from the stars. And it was he who laid the basis for the science of accurate map making, as we know it today.

You might think that was enough achievement to satisfy anybody. But in addition to all that, Pytheas between 325 and 330 B.C. made one of the greatest voyages of all time. He sailed from his home town of Marseilles, which was then a Greek city, through the Strait of Gibraltar toward the Far North. On the way he stopped in Britain, the northern end of Scotland, perhaps Ireland, and then Iceland beyond which he sailed a distance of about 100 miles. Further progress was stopped by the slushy edge of the drifting pack ice, by a shortage of supplies, and by fears of the crew. So Pytheas returned to Marseilles, but not without examining once again the coast of northern Scotland and, again for the first time in history, studying the Baltic Sea as well.

Strangely enough, as Polybius tells us, Pytheas was in poor circumstances, and we may therefore conclude that the enterprise was a government expedition or a commercial enterprise of which Pytheas was placed in command. The nearest approximation we can get to the date of his trip is by contemporaneous reference to Alexander the Great and Aristotle—about 330 B.C. We may well suppose that the object of the trip was the discovery of the countries whence came rare and valuable products like tin, which reached the Massalians by a long overland route and descent of the Rhone.

Pytheas prepared for his perilous undertaking by carefully fixing the latitude of Massalia as a point of departure. His pre-eminence in his own day will be obvious when we recollect that he lived before the principal Greek astronomers, Eratosthenes and Hipparchus. None of his predecessors had ever dreamed of the methods which he adopted

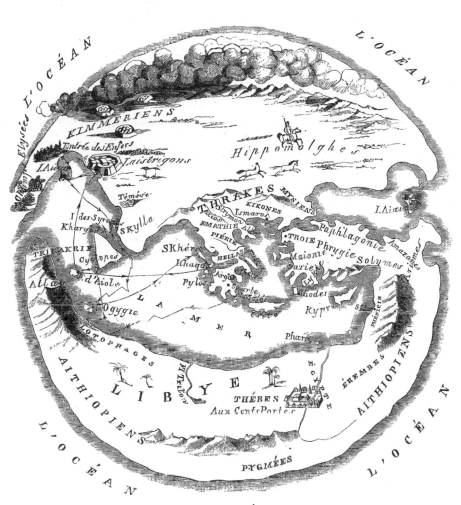

MAP OF HOMER'S WORLD

and which he demonstrated in their daring use.

The earliest way of calculating the distance of a place from the equator was by observing the length of the longest and shortest days. The ancient geographers divided the earth into parallel zones, within which the longest day had a certain length, generally an hour: one zone from twelve to thirteen hours, the next from thirteen to fourteen,

61

and so on. The zones were called "climates," from the Greek word *klima*, "slope" or "inclination." They were unequal in width, the zone in which the longest day was from fourteen to fifteen hours being 600 miles in width, while the zone in which the longest day was from nineteen to twenty hours had a width of only 125 miles.

Pytheas used this system which was to be later discarded during his voyage. But in fixing the latitude of Massalia he adopted a more accurate method. He erected a large gnomon or sundial at Massalia, and divided it into one hundred and twenty parts. He observed its shadow at noon on the day of the solstice, and found that its length was forty-two of the parts on the gnomon, less one-fifth—that is, forty-one and four-fifths to one hundred and twenty, or two hundred and nine to six hundred. This proportion gave him the altitude of the sun at Marseilles—70 degrees 47 minutes 50 seconds. And the length of the longest day there was fifteen hours fifteen minutes.

Another important point was to fix upon the nearest star to the Pole as a guide for steering the ship. Through long months of study, Pytheas found that there was no star on the Pole, but that there were two very close to it. These would have been Beta Ursae Minoris and Alpha Draconis, as they are called in these days. And Pytheas used one of these, probably the second, as his polestar.

It is probable that there was no other man, in the days of Alexander the Great, who could have prepared for a voyage of discovery by fixing the exact latitude of his point of departure, or by selecting correctly the specific star by which he was going to plan his entire course.

His countrymen were well able to furnish him with a serviceable vessel made to his own design. A large Massalian ship was a good sea boat, and able to make a voyage into the northern ocean. But Pytheas demanded something special—a boat from 150 to 170 feet long, with a depth of hold of 25 to 26 feet. The tonnage of this vessel was probably about 400 to 450, so that Pytheas' ship was larger and even more seaworthy than the crazy little *Santa Maria* with which, eighteen hundred years afterward, Columbus was going to discover the New World. But the comparison with Pytheas should not be carried too far. For in the days of Alexander, a voyage of discovery beyond the Pillars of Hercules was even more bold and daring a conception than a voyage in search of the Indies by the western route in the days of Ferdinand and Isabella.

We have seen that Pytheas, the first of the great explorers. like the illustrious Genoese of later times, prepared himself for his difficult task by long and patient study of the astronomical bearings of the question. He provided himself with all the knowledge, skill, and technique available in his time. With that he raised his anchor, and began his coasting voyage toward the Sacred Promontory (what is today Cape St. Vincent)—the western limit of the known world. The Grecian ships were supposed to make an average of about 500 stadia, or 50 miles, in a day's sail, but Pytheas' ship was, as we have seen, specially equipped and might have been able to do twice what other ships did, at least under favorable conditions.

Coasting along near the shore, Pytheas would first have come to the Massalian settlement at the mouth of the Rhone, and then to Rhoda and Emporium (the modern Ampurias) in the beautiful bay of Rosas, at the base of the Pyrenees. Next he came to the temple of Artemis, crowning the lofty promontory now dedicated to Saint Martin, where the Massalians had their *hemeroskopion* or lookout station. There the Greeks built a settlement called

63

Artemisia (the modern Denia) at the foot of the heights—a place where explorers could anchor and find rest. And after that, the last friendly haven would be at Maenaca, the modern Malaga.

Sailing through the Straits of Calpe (now the Strait of Gibraltar), the Greek mariners would never dare to stop at the Carthaginian Gadeira (Cadiz), although in previous times the native ruler of the country had been on cordial terms with Phocaea. So Pytheas did not linger but sailed slowly on to the Sacred Promontory, the end of the known world—very slowly, indeed, for the 48 leagues from Cadiz to Cape St. Vincent took him five sailing days.

Pytheas continued his coasting voyage to the north as far as Cape Finisterre, the probable farthest point of Himilco. Then he turned eastward along the north coast of Iberia, and went around the Bay of Biscay. Though his log is lost, we gather that he described the coasts of Iberia, made observations on the tides, and prepared a book describing the best way of passing from Iberia to Celtica, or Gaul. His first recorded observation on the voyage determined that the longest day was fifteen hours, and this would place him in latitude 40 degrees 59 minutes off Oporto.

Pytheas found that the northwestern part of Gaul formed a long promontory called Calbion, the country of a tribe called the Ostimii, which stretched far to the westward. He even thought that it extended for 2,000 stadia to the west of Cape Finisterre of Spain. But great allowances must be made for errors in longitude at a time when no means other than guesswork were available for estimating it.

Pytheas mentioned an island off the coast called Uxisama, evidently intended for Ushant. A second observation is given to sixteen hours for the length of the longest day, equal to 49 degrees North, a reading that is within 30 miles of the latitude of Ushant.

The explorer left the north coast of Gaul, and shaped a direct course for a part of Britain which he called Cantion —the Cantium of which Caesar would write in later years. This must have been the route, because he reported that the coast of Gaul where he left it was some days' sail from Cantion.

The Cantion of Pytheas was undoubtedly the modern Kent, although the explorer may have intended to include additional territory to the north. There Pytheas stopped, and we are told that he not only landed, but traveled over a part of Britain on foot. He probably went westward to collect information about the tin trade—a kind of grass-roots study. In those days such a trip would have entailed a very difficult and perilous journey, and he probably had with him at least the nucleus of a war party.

Britain in the third century before Christ was almost in a state of raw nature. The valleys were covered with primeval forests, their lower parts were occupied by vast swamps, and it was only on the downs and hill ranges that there were any *gwents*, or open clearings.

The Celtic tribes had been in possession of this land for several centuries, and had made some advances in civilization. They brought domestic animals with them from the continent, raised wheat and other cereals, and had iron tools and arms, wooden chariots with iron fittings, as well as ornaments of bronze and gold. Pytheas saw all these things and made notes about them. In addition, he analyzed the farming operations and way of living among the natives of Cantion.

Between this southeastern district and the *gwent* now comprising the downs of Wiltshire and South Hampshire, there was the great forest of Anderida, extending from Hampshire to the Medway. Pytheas would have to pass this forest on his way to the western part of Britain (or present Cornwall), which was then called Belerion. Here he found the country of the tin, which was dug out of the ground in mines and, even then, carried through elaborate shafts and galleries.

Pytheas found the people very hospitable, their commerce with foreign merchants having civilized them and softened their manners. The metal was carried by them in six days' journey to an island called Ictis (St. Michael's Mount), whence the traders from Gaul conveyed it across the Channel, and down the Rhone to Massalia.

Pytheas' visit no doubt gave a stimulus to the trade with Marseilles and he was probably the first to introduce coined money into Britain. Philip of Macedon, after the discovery of the gold mines of Crenides (or Philippi) in 356 B.C. had about a half million dollars' worth of gold coin made each year. His beautiful stater, which was generally diffused through the Mediterranean from where it circulated inland, was possibly what Pytheas introduced in Britain, since its use seems to date from the time of his visit. The staters were afterward roughly imitated by the natives. But no British coin can be dated earlier than about 200 B.C.

Several pieces of information have been preserved from Pytheas' observation on the people of Britain.

In consequence of the rain and absence of sun, he said, the British did not use open threshing floors, but threshed their grain in large barns. They stored this raw produce in pits underground, and the part that had been longest in store was brought out daily and prepared for food.

66

He also told how they made a fermented liquor from barley, which they used instead of wine. It was called *curmi*. As Columbus was the discoverer of tobacco, so his great predecessor, Pytheas, discovered beer. Pytheas also says that the Britons made another drink from honey.

Their houses, he wrote, were of wood and thatch, and he mentions the war chariots, but adds that the chiefs were generally at peace with each other. He believed the people to have been *autochthones*, or aborigines.

When Pytheas returned to his ship, in some haven of Kent, he proceeded northward along the coast of Britain; and his next observation gave seventeen hours as the length of the longest day. This would be in latitude 54 degrees 2 minutes North, somewhere in the neighborhood of Flamborough Head.

Still coasting to the north in his great voyage of discovery, he reached a point at the northern end of Britain where the length of the longest day was eighteen hours. The corresponding latitude is 57 degrees 58 minutes 41 seconds North, which is that of Tarbett Ness, in Ross-shire (northeastern Scotland).

As he advanced to the Pole he found that the cultivated grains and fruits, and almost all domesticated animals, gradually disappeared. As a result the people in the Far North were forced to live on millet, herbs, and roots.

The intrepid explorer still pushed onward to discover the northernmost point of the British Isles. Coasting along the shores of Caithness and the Orkney Islands, he finally arrived at a land where the length of the longest day was nineteen hours. This was in latitude 60 degrees 51 minutes 54 seconds North, in Burra Fjord (Firth), on Unst Island, the northernmost of the Shetlands. Pytheas gives the name of Orcas to this extreme point of the British Isles—a name which in later times was transferred to the Orcades, or Orkney Islands.

It was at Orcas that Pytheas received information of an Arctic land called Thule—a place that was a distance of six days' sail, and which (he learned) was near the frozen ocean. It was probably here that he made his great decision to press on and "see what he could see."

What was this "Thule"? Scholars have engaged in long debates whether it was Norway, the Orkneys, Shetland, or Iceland. There is no doubt in my mind that it was Iceland. I say this not only because of the statements that have been preserved, or at least by strong presumptions seem to have been preserved from Pytheas' own writing, but by the total witness of other writers who tell us what Pytheas did. Strabo, for instance, reports Pytheas' view that "Thule is by ship six days away from Britain toward the North" and Pliny, Solinus, and Servius concur in the statement. Then there is a consensus of witnesses (including Cleomedes, Pliny, Strabo and others) to what Pytheas saw in astronomical references—movements of the sun, the equivalent of our latitude determinations—as well as to the fact that he must have circumnavigated Iceland. Finally there are numerous references to the way Thule looked from the sea, and its relation to ice flocs or, as the ancients said, the congealed seas. "After one day's sail from Thule," says Pliny, "the frozen sea is reached—a place which some call 'Cronium.' "

The name of Pytheas comes first in the annals of Arctic discovery, not only in terms of time but also greatness. He was a good and brave man as well as a perceptive student. And in some of the long nights I spent in the Arctic I realized that he had to be all this and more to survive the perils of that first trip to the top of the world.

Pytheas was also a writer of genuine talent. His most important book, *The Ocean*, was lost in the course of history, as was another earlier volume, *The Periplus* (perhaps the first "do-it-yourself" book, since it was a series of directions for sailing and navigation). Both these volumes were, however, known to the ancients, studied everywhere, and were much commented on. It is in fact through commentaries on them that we know about them today. Unfortunately the fragments of quotations and paraphrases which have been saved from Pytheas' writings were mostly chosen from a point of view that tends to neutralize their value. For Pytheas' journeys and reports were so staggeringly great that his contemporaries, as well as many so-called experts since his time, referred to them only with disbelief and for purpose of ridicule.

It would seem nevertheless that when Pytheas first returned from his exploratory voyage to the Arctic and published his book, his report was received in good faith. The first reaction of people was to believe what he said. This was particularly true, no doubt, along the south shore of what is now France where Pytheas lived and was known as a truthful man. And in fact Pytheas' fellow citizens at Marseilles were already in touch with at least the North Sea and the Baltic by overland commerce and by tribe-to-tribe hearsay. So Pytheas' reports fitted in with what the people already knew from other sources.

In the rest of the Greek world the book was also received in a favorable way, at least in the beginning. The earliest of the writers who quoted or paraphrased him treated him with respect. They openly revealed their admiration for his accomplishments. About 200 B.C., for instance, the mathematician Eratosthenes expressed his belief in Pytheas' narrative and he accepted it at face value for what it said. He showed no skepticism whatever about the voyage—and this, more than a century after the publication of *The Ocean.*

This situation, however, was reversed in the centuries to follow. Strabo's *Geography,* in the third decade after Christ, rejected Pytheas as a liar, mainly on the grounds of "the doctrine of the Five Zones"—a geographic concept that dominated Greek thought after the time of Pytheas' voyage. That concept insisted that there were five zones on the earth, of which three were uninhabitable—the equatorial because of the heat and the two polar zones because of the cold. Historians tell us that such thinking originated in the sixth century B.C. But its influence over Greek geographic thinking developed, they say, very slowly and did not become a tyranny until some two centuries after Pytheas. Thenceforth, history has rewritten by the Greeks in the same way that the Communists have generally recast European history in our time. And so Pytheas began to go into decline, and his great voyage was viewed as poppycock!

Strabo's skepticism regarding Pytheas' voyage was, then, based on the dogma that the Arctic, the southern edge of which was thought by Strabo to lie just north of Scotland, was uninhabitable by any living thing—human being, plant or animal. Pytheas, in defiance of such a dogma, maintained that he had sailed six days north beyond Scotland and that there he had found an island of reasonable climate —one which he called Thule but which we know as Iceland, even beyond which he had sailed a full 100 miles.

To Strabo the ocean would cease being liquid beyond Scotland. No one, he thought, could sail through it, and the weather would be so cold that no one could live in it. Necessarily, then, Pytheas was a liar. This is what Strabo called him, and so Pytheas remained in the minds of scholarly Europe until modern times. Pytheas' rehabilitation and his restoration as a great polar hero dates from less than fifty years ago. Around the turn of the century, textbooks were still under Strabo's influence and called him the greatest liar of antiquity. But today they put him down as one of the most outstanding discoverers of all time.

Fridtjof Nansen, himself one of the foremost explorers and students of history, concludes that Pytheas is the greatest explorer that history reveals, if for no other reason than that he pushed back the limit of the learned world's knowledge from the south coast of Britain to the Arctic Circle—or about 16 degrees farther north. This, as historians readily agree, is farther than any other man has ever done. (Perhaps I should mention that since Nansen's time, it has been shown that Pytheas went a day's sail, or about 100 miles, even farther.)

As Sir Clement Markham has said, the more we learn about Pytheas' voyage, the greater he becomes. There does not appear to be any limit to what Pytheas estimated about polar exploration, or to the way in which exploration since his time remains but a modification of his first and mighty voyage.

2. *Irish Monks and Norsemen Pirates*

IT IS NOT surprising that the Age of Aristotle, on fire with the restlessly inquisitive spirit of the Greeks, should have seen the birth of the first and perhaps the greatest polar explorer. That first contact with the new world of ice and snow was followed by later travelers—but not until the early centuries of the Christian era. The discoveries of Irish monks and Norsemen pirates also marked a step forward in Arctic exploration, but they were seldom the result of deliberate exploration like Pytheas' trip.

The Irish monks were not, first of all, concerned with adding to geographical knowledge. They only wanted to find remote islands to the north and east of Ireland to which they might escape from a too gregarious community life and enjoy one of solitude and contemplation. Sailing in hide-covered coracles or curraghs, they were flung about on the tumbling seas until they found refuge in the western islands of Scotland. From there, when they were eventually driven out by the Norsemen, they spread to the Orkneys, Shetlands, and Faroes.

Some who were hardier and more adventurous seamen than the others had a more ambitious plan. They lived in monasteries around the mouth of the Shannon and each year at the first sign of spring they saw flock after flock of wild geese migrate northward to summer breeding grounds. If the birds could live up north, they could do so too, they thought. And so they set out. By following the flight of those spectacular and noisy geese the Irish monks reached Iceland. And when the Norsemen or Vikings reached Iceland about 870 A.D., they found, the Sagas record, monks

and priests, "papar" with their "bells, books, and croziers," already there.

The Norsemen discovered Iceland when the long ship of the Viking chieftain Garda was blown off its course on a journey from Norway to the Faroes and driven westward. Discovery led to settlement, and settlement to colonization. Year after year the Vikings, making landfall by releasing ravens and other shore-sighting birds, spread their stone farmsteads and churches all over the island. On what eventually became regular voyages from Norway, the Norsemen experienced all the hazards and dangers that bewildered and exhausted and often destroyed the Arctic navigators through the ages: impenetrable fogs, the menace of ice floes and flaming water, the blustering, freezing squalls and violent storms. On one Norse voyage twelve ships, conveying colonists, their wives and children, their cattle, and all their possessions, sank out of a fleet of twenty-five. During one of these storms, in the tenth century A.D., a Norseman, Gunnbjörn, was swept past Iceland to within sight of the Greenland coast.

Gunnbjörn's discovery led to the first landing on Greenland by a great Viking chieftain, Eric the Red. Eric had been outlawed from Iceland as the result of a blood feud. So he set out with twelve friends and their wives and children and landed near the modern Angmagssalik, on the southeast coast, about 985 A.D. But this coast was (and remained for many centuries until now) too barren and too icebound for settlement. So the Norsemen moved around to the west. And in the deep fjords—so like the fjords of their native Norway—they made their homes. Farms of stone and peat multiplied as new colonists arrived from Norway and Iceland. In a climate much milder than today, they appear to have flourished. In summer there was deep green grass for the cattle. Rabbits and reindeer and foxes were hunted. And it was not long before the Norsemen began to trade with the "Skraelings" or Eskimos—exchanging corn and iron from Norway for walrus ivory and the skins of bear and seal.

The present inhabitants of this very spot are a couple of families of Eskimo settlers. Their houses are good and well built, they have fenced in some of their fields, and they own cows, horses, and many sheep. The patriarch of them all is Otto Fredericksen, whom I have seen many times. He always greeted me with dignity, and I could never help thinking that old Eric the Red must have been a good deal like this man—with his great red whiskers, his strong, heavy body, and his wide, assured stance.

Otto Fredericksen and his people were in the midst of their haying when I last saw them. None of the grass was being wasted. They had even brought in some from a small field up in the hills, carrying it down on horseback. These horses were their greatest pride, and so anxious were they to impress me with the animals that Otto arranged a sort of rodeo to display their horsemanship.

Frankly, I have seen more expert riders in my time than those Eskimos. The peak of their skill was that they could make the horse go in the direction they wanted. Some of the young people rode them away from us and then back. The most daring of the lot actually was able to sit on his horse backward and stay with the animal, but this feat was beyond the others.

Our applause was too much for their discretion. Some of them prodded their animals into a trot, and two of the riders promptly fell off. They explained to us that it was very, very difficult to sit on a horse's back when the animal

76

NORSE SHIP

was moving, and totally impossible if the creature was "jumping." But they will, I think, master even that art in time. That was the first year that Otto Fredericksen had owned any horses, and they had not of course had much practice.

To return to our narrative: It is not easy to elicit from the stark and enigmatic language of the Sagas the precise extent of Norse exploration in the Arctic. In their search for hunting grounds, the Norsemen undoubtedly voyaged far up the west coast of Greenland. From there they set out, we should note, for the great Norse discovery of the New World. From there they sailed on epic voyages to Wineland and Markland, on the voyages of Bjarni Jerjulfsson, of Leif Ericson (the son of Eric the Red), and of Thorfinn Karlsefni which carried the high-prowed and grotesquely figured ships of the Vikings to Baffin Island, to Nova Scotia and Labrador, and even as far south as the coast of Maryland.

In 1261 A.D. the Norse settlements in Greenland became a crown colony of Norway. But already this Arctic prelude was drawing to a close. The milder climate which had enabled farming to flourish in Iceland and Greenland in the Viking Age began gradually, and unaccountably, to change. The cold returned. Ice closed slowly in over land and sea.

At the same time, Norwegian sea power began to decline in the face of the thrustful competition of the growing northern seaports of the Hanseatic League. Oppressed by the new harshness of the climate, deprived of the resources of the mother country, the Norse farmers in Greenland in 1345 A.D. were excused payment of tithes by the Pope. Ten years later, alarming (but unwarranted) rumors reached Norway that in their desolation they had forsaken Christianity for the pagan beliefs of the Eskimos. So missionaries were sent to their rescue.

But the sight of the sails of a ship off Greenland was now a rare event. In 1492, a letter of Pope Alexander VI declared that the Norse settlers in Greenland were eking out a miserable existence on dried fish and a little milk and that no ship had reached them from either Norway or Iceland for eighty years. And, indeed, excavations of the Norse cemetery of Herjolfness in South Greenland show vividly to what straits the abandoned Norsemen had been reduced. Their bodies, mummified by the ice, were found to be emaciated, diseased, and deformed by years of intermarriage. Many had obviously been the victims of Eskimo attacks. Beneath the ice encasing their rough wooden coffins were traces of happier days in the form of tree roots and plants, relics of the warmer climate which their ancestors, the early colonists, had once enjoyed.

A few survivors may have lived on until the early sixteenth century, for about 1550 A.D. there is a record of a ship bound for Iceland, but blown off her course, whose captain landed on one of the small islets or skerries off the Greenland coast which the Viking Gunnbjörn had first seen six centuries before. Clambering over the ruins of an old stone farmhouse, he came suddenly upon the body of a Norseman wearing a hood and cloak of coarse wool and sealskin. This man was the last of the Norse settlers of Greenland to be seen by a European.

Iceland and Greenland and the eastern fringes of the Canadian Arctic were not the only Arctic lands to be discovered by the Norsemen. About 880 A.D., soon after the first Norse settlement in Iceland, a Viking named Ochtere, then living in northern Norway, sailed from Helgoland on a voyage of exploration and trade in walrus tusks. He made his way around North Cape and eastward around the Kola Peninsula into the White Sea. The exploits of the Norsemen of Iceland and Greenland were for generations recited annually at Scandinavian festivals and were not usually committed to writing until long after the event. The story of Ochtere's voyage, however, with details of the tribes he encountered along the north Russian coast, has survived as a contemporary record. On his return he told it personally to King Alfred of England, who inserted it in his history of the world written in the ninth century A.D. It is the first contemporary record of an Arctic expedition which has survived until today.

Knowledge of those early Arctic wanderings has survived mostly in verbal tradition, since medieval and Renaissance learning dealt with the affairs of Greece and Rome. But there are, fortunately, some ways of tracing the penetration of the Arctic made in early times: law, histories of whaling and the merchant marine in those times, and in the poetry and song preserved in folk tradition, mostly in northern Scandinavia.

Whaling particularly; for it was an increasingly profitable luxury trade as a source of blubber oil for lighting, for perfume (ambergris) and for whalebone used by the ladies of the court. What geographical discoveries those whalers and fishermen made is unrecorded. There are, however, two Arctic voyages of the fourteenth century of which some contemporary record has survived. One was by a young Franciscan minor friar, Nicholas of Lynn (mentioned in Chaucer's essay on the Astrolabe). Fragments of his works were preserved by sixteenth-century writers.

From those writings it appears that about 1360 A.D. Nicholas, sailing from Norway, reached a sea "far to the north which froze in winter." He was in a land whose inhabitants were no more than four feet high and where along the coast timbers of ancient wooden ships and the ruins of ancient homesteads could be seen. This strongly suggests that Nicholas reached southern Greenland, met the Eskimos, and saw vestiges of the old Viking settlements we have already mentioned. On his return, he drew up a scheme for the broad geography of the Arctic. The Pole he pictured as glistening black magnetic rock standing in the midst of a whirlpool. The whole thing, he wrote, was surrounded by a circle of mountainous lands divided by numerous channels through which the sea, sucked toward the central whirlpool, rushed so swiftly that no ship could survive.

Another Arctic voyage, reputed to have been made in the fourteenth century by two Venetian brothers, Niccolo and Antonio Zeno, was published with a map by their descendants in 1558. This voyage, which must be considered highly dubious, has a unique place in Arctic history, not for its alleged discoveries but for the way in which the Zeno map, a maze of fact and fancy, was to mislead future generations of Arctic explorers. On it, in deference to the cherished medieval theory that civilization sprang from one center, all lands are closely linked together. Greenland is shown swinging around to the east and south to meet the northernmost coast of Norway. Enclosed within this great bend of land lies Iceland and other islands. And far to the west numerous islands are strung about, carrying a variety of fanciful names and shapes. It was disastrous that so much of this ingenious piece of map making should have been incorporated in the maps and globes of the great Flemish cartographers Mercator and Ortelius in the sixteenth century. For centuries the latter were accepted as a sort of bible for Arctic exploration. And yet the lives of many men depended on their accuracy.

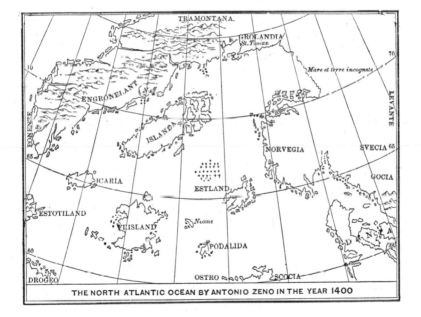

THE NORTH ATLANTIC OCEAN BY ANTONIO ZENO IN THE YEAR 1400

THE ZENO MAP

83

3. *The Norsemen Discover North America*

IN 999 LEIF, one of Eric the Red's two sons, crossed from Greenland to Norway by way of the Scottish islands and, as was usual with chieftains, was invited to spend the winter at the court of the king, that dauntless proselytizer Olaf Tryggvason. Before spring the monarch had convinced the young Greenlander that he had better get baptized. So he did. Then the king asked him to take missionaries back home with him and Leif agreed to do so.

It seems that with the clergymen aboard, Leif was anxious to get back early in the season, perhaps so as to be in time for the Greenland Festival of that year. So he did a very risky thing for those days—he may in fact have been the first to attempt it: he sailed direct from Norway for the south tip of Greenland instead of going by way of Iceland. Leif steered too far to the left, however, for he missed Cape Farewell. The first land he struck was Labrador, around Nova Scotia or Newfoundland. Realizing he must have overshot his mark, Leif turned northeast and proceeded to Greenland.

In the eleventh century the Scandinavian countries were ecclesiastically a part of the Archbishopric of Hamburg. The famous *History of the Church of Hamburg,* finished around 1070, was the first medieval book to tell Europe about the mainland of North America under the Norse name that Leif gave to it: Wineland. Its author, Adam of Bremen, had been up in Denmark some years before, at the court of King Svein Estridsson, who, Adam found, "knew the history of the barbarians by heart, as if it had been in writing." At the court, and especially from the

84

king, Adam heard much concerning Iceland and Greenland. He heard of Vinland, too:

"Moreover he [the King of Denmark] mentioned yet another island, which had been discovered by many in that ocean, and which is called 'Wineland,' because vines grow there of themselves and give the noblest wine. And that there is abundance of unsown corn we have obtained certain knowledge, not by fabulous supposition, but from trustworthy information of the Danes."

Thus was North America introduced to the literature of Europe. It had to be an island, for according to the geographic concepts of Adam as revealed in his book, there were only three continents: Europe, Asia, and Africa. It did not occur to him that Vinland could be a part of one of these, or could be part of another continent hitherto undiscovered.

Numerous Icelandic sagas mention or describe the discovery of Vinland. As information passed by father to son they date from before 1070, but they were not written down until a half century later than Adam's book, some of them a hundred or more years later. During that interval a good deal of embroidery had had time to develop—which, as the critical historians usually think, did not so much replace or alter facts as confuse them.

One of the developments was a certain jealousy between Greenland and Iceland, or perhaps rather the growth of a tendency in Iceland to give more credit to Icelanders than to Greenlanders—this partly because these traditions were most likely to be preserved by the descendants of men who had taken part in the Vinland adventures. Each scribe had a tendency to magnify somewhat the role played by his ancestor, and occasionally transferred credit from one character to another.

It was perhaps in this way that there appeared in Iceland a variant of the story to the effect that it had not really been the Greenlander Leif, the son of Eric the Red, who found Wineland the Good, but an Icelander named Bjarni; and that other men had later sailed in search of the land seen by Bjarni, somewhat as Eric had sailed a generation before in search of the land seen by Gunnbjörn.

II. Mercantilism and Nationalism

4. *So Resteth This Way of the North*

IN THE fifteenth century, a fresh impulse to Arctic exploration appeared. It swung on a new and very simple objective:
the search for a northern route to the Indies, to China, to
Japan—to the kingdoms, as they were then called, of Cathay.
Marco Polo's desert caravans had returned with news of
the unimagined wealth of those places and had dazzled the
civilized European world of the thirteenth century. In the
vision of these lush and opulent lands, the fifteenth-century
adventurer saw fortune. And the governments of the time
found the answer to all their economic ills.

For many years Cathay was regarded by men of learning
to be unapproachable by sea. The Scriptures taught that
the earth was not a globe as the Greeks believed, but a flat
disk—four square, centered on Jerusalem, surrounded by a
continuous and impassable ocean which divided mankind
from Paradise. Sailors of the time disagreed with this view,
but their view counted for nothing. Cathay, people believed, would be reached only by land—over the mountains
and the torrid deserts which Marco Polo had crossed. But

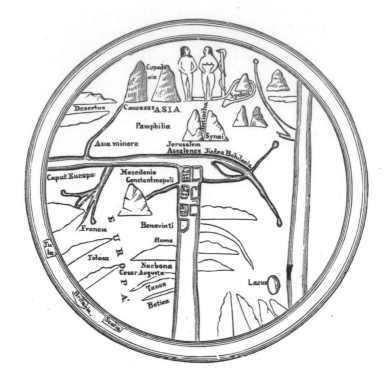

EIGHTH-CENTURY WORLD MAP

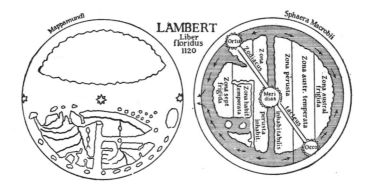

LAMBERT'S MAP

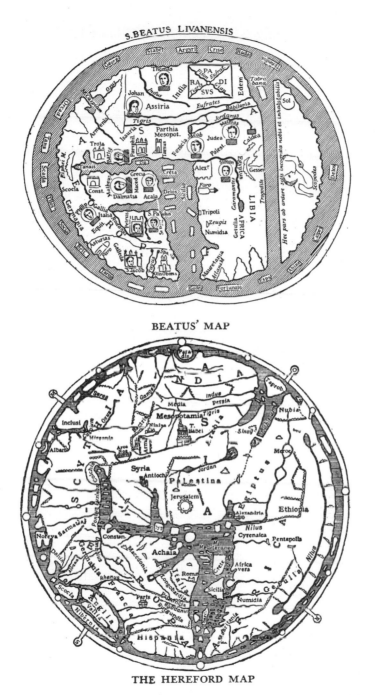

S. BEATUS LIVANENSIS

BEATUS' MAP

THE HEREFORD MAP

89

these routes were barred in the fifteenth century by the warriors of Islam.

Gradually the idea of the sphericity of the earth was generally accepted. And then in 1462, a development which transformed geographical thought and cosmographical ideas occurred: the translation into Latin of Ptolemy's *Geography*. With its tables of longitude and latitude, it provided cartographers with a basis for the fixing of positions on the terrestrial globe. Rudimentary as navigation was bound to be until the solution of the problem of longitude in the eighteenth century, the Age of Discovery could now begin in the long sea voyages of Western history. With globes in use and charts and maps beginning to take modern shape, voyages of circumnavigation of the world were considered possible. And seamen, sailing under the rival flags of Portugal and Spain, embarked on a host of great voyages to east, west, and south, to seek a seaway to the Orient.

To the south and east of Africa the explorations promoted by Prince Henry the Navigator and to the west those of Bartholomew Diaz led in 1497 to the rounding of the Cape of Good Hope by Vasco da Gama. Here, everyone thought, was one seaway to Cathay.

In the west, too, there was hope. There the discovery by Columbus of the so-called West Indies—territories in a region where, it was thought, wealth must necessarily be created by the life-giving rays of a perpetual sun—suggested that these were close to Cathay and that in this westward direction a way through to Cathay would be found. This hope, however, was short-lived. Then Genoese John Cabot sailed from Bristol west and north as far as Newfoundland and Labrador but found no way through. Indeed, from Cabot's voyage and from those of others searching for a

LATE FIFTEENTH-CENTURY WOODCUT MAP

western passage to Cathay it soon appeared that not islands but an entire continent barred the way.

With this westward route closed, the three principal mercantilist nations had several alternatives confronting them. There was the way south down the Atlantic, and thence eastward around Africa or westward around the southern extremity of America. Or, as could be seen from the globe, there was the possibility of a northern ice-infested route across the summit of the world. This last was of course viewed as a poor alternative to the temperate and torrid waters of the South Atlantic. But those waters lay within the domain of Spain and Portugal, whose relative roles in their exploration were defined by the Treaty of Tordesillas in 1491.

A line of demarcation running south along the meridian through the center of the north Atlantic Ocean was drawn by the Pope, who ruled all of Christendom. The right to exploration and discovery on the west of it was granted to Spain, and on the east to Portugal. For these seafaring countries, this division was not unsatisfactory. But for the merchants and seamen of other countries, excluded from their monopoly, only the northern routes to Cathay, through the ice and fogs and blizzards of the Arctic, remained.

"Out of Spain," complained Robert Thorne in 1541, "they sail all the Indies and seas occidental, and from Portugal they sail all the Indies and the seas oriental, so that between the way of the Orient and the way of the Occident they have encompassed the world . . . also by way of the meridian there is a great part discovered by the Spaniards. So resteth this way of the north only for to discover. . . ."

So resteth this way of the north: here was the great call to polar exploration, even though for Thorne and many others it appeared to be a dismal prospect. Dismal or otherwise, however, it was thus that the search for a northern passage became the dominant motive behind the English, Dutch, and French explorations of the Arctic for two centuries and more. These nations did not intend to discover but to penetrate, to pass through to the riches on the other side. But like the man in the poem who came to scoff but stayed to pray, they certainly changed their minds.

5. *Chancellor, Willoughby, and the Brave Elizabethans*

RICHARD CHANCELLOR, a great Arctic voyager of the Elizabethan Age, once explained the reasons which first impelled his countrymen to search for a sea route to Cathay.

"At that time," he said, "our merchants perceived the commodities and wares of England to be in small request with the countries and people about us, and near unto us, and that those merchandises which strangers in the time and memory of our ancestors did earnestly seek and desire were now neglected, and the price thereof abated, although by us carried to their own ports, and all foreign merchandises in great account and their prices wonderfully raised, certain grave citizens of London and men of great wisdom and careful for the good of their country began to think with themselves how this mischief might be remedied. Neither was a remedy (as it then appeared) wanting to their desires. For seeing that the wealth of the Spaniards and Portuguese by the discovery and search of new trades and countries was marvellously increased, supposing the same to be a course and mean for them also to obtain the life, they thereupon resolved upon a new and strange navigation."

In such circumstances, the first English voyages into the Arctic and into the New World can be seen as part of the general expansion of overseas enterprise. This we call mercantilism.

Like the voyages to discover and colonize the New World, the Arctic voyages were no haphazard, impetuous adventures. On the contrary, they were most carefully planned. The men behind them included not only the Court, the city companies, the rich merchants who were the principal investors of funds, but a highly efficient group of technical advisers, specialists in economics, in navigation, and in the geography of distant lands. Many of them were also shrewd men of business.

Outstanding among these planners was Richard Hakluyt, author of the great collection *The Principall Navigations, Voiages, and Discoveries of the English Nation,* whose publications filled the minds of Englishmen with thoughts of adventure and of profit. A perceptive geographer, Hakluyt was admirably qualified to sift from a great mass of picturesque but often fictitious travelers' tales the geographical and economic facts essential to his plans for exploration. His cousin was a lawyer and an expert in dyes and oils and in the woolen goods which were England's principal export. No less important, in planning the new Arctic voyages, was the training of seamen in the theory and practice of navigation, in which England lagged so far behind her main rivals, Portugal and Spain.

New textbooks had to be written, new instruments devised. And professional pilots had to be instructed in the latest navigational developments. In this field, the leading adviser was a brilliant young Welshman, John Dee, a mathematician from Cambridge who had studied at Louvain with the great European cosmographers and cartographers, Gemma Frisius and Gerhard Mercator. John Dee became the principal instructor in astronomy and navigation to almost all the Arctic captains and pilots of his day.

The first question confronting the planners as they studied their globes was in which direction the first expedition should be sent. Should they search for a northeast or a northwest passage to Cathay?

Until the year 1558 when the famous map of the Venetian brothers Niccolo and Antonio Zeno was published, the northeast appeared more hopeful. As far as the North Cape of Norway, the seas were familiar to English ships and had been found to be ice-free. Even beyond North Cape, Russian fishermen were known to sail frequently as far as the River Ob. The northeast route, moreover, offered some compensation if an expedition failed to reach Pacific waters. Along it, along the shores of the Old World, "civill people," prospective customers, were known to live, while beyond the Ob—if the cartographers who showed Tartary and Scythia joined to northeast Asia were correct—there were possibilities of an even more lucrative trade with the outlying kingdoms of the East.

To the west, by contrast, the outlook was less hopeful. John Cabot, probing northward in 1497 as far as Labrador, found no trace of any passage or strait to Cathay. Nor could the two Basque brothers Miguel and Gaspar Corte-Real in 1500 A.D. find any limit to the northward-stretching coast of the American continent. If the discovery by the Breton seaman Jacques Cartier of the mouth of the St. Lawrence had been known when he returned from his voyage in 1536, those who argued in favor of a western route might have been more encouraged. For thirty years later when Cartier's Canadian discoveries first appeared upon the maps, it looked as if here at last was the opening of a northwest passage. As so often happens, however, publication lagged far behind geographical discovery. The northeast, therefore, was the direction chosen.

The next problem for the planners was finance. They had a host of powerful friends at Court and in the City, and with their help "The Mysterie and Companie of the Marchants Adventurers for the Discoverie of Regions, Dominions, Islands, and Places unknowen" was established on the 12th of December, 1551. Its first Governor was Sebastian Cabot, son of the John Cabot who had explored the coast of Labrador at the end of the previous century. This Company of Merchant Adventurers became the focus and hub of all the earliest activities directed toward the search for a northeast passage. One of the Company's first acts was to appoint the leader of their first expedition, and to recruit as his second-in-command a professional chief pilot. As Captain-General they chose, according to custom, a distinguished soldier, a courtier, Sir Hugh Willoughby, who knew nothing of navigation. His second-in-command was a professional seaman, Richard Chancellor, who was

SEBASTIAN CABOT

97

known throughout England as "the odde [i.e., outstanding] man of his time for matters touching the sea."

Willoughby, who was to sail in the "Admiral of the Fleet," the *Bona Esperanza* of 120 tons, had William Gefferson as master of his ship, while Chancellor in the *Edward Bonaventure* carried as master a man destined to become famous as an Arctic pilot, Stephen Borough. The third ship of the Arctic squadron, the *Bona Confidentia,* had a Dutch master, Cornelius Durforth. These men, with the merchants who hoped to trade along the route and in Cathay, and those generally known as "the ignorant and unruly mariners," comprised the expedition.

All Willoughby's ships, armed merchant ships, shallow enough in draft to be able to navigate the great rivers which some maps showed flowing into the Arctic from central Asia, were specially strengthened. A sheathing of lead was, for instance, devised to protect their bottoms against the attacks of a particularly virulent and piercing worm which was said to infest the torrid waters off Cathay. It was a precaution characteristic of the robust optimism with which these Elizabethan seamen, in sailing ships of a hundred tons or less, set out on a voyage through the Arctic to the Far East, along a route heavily encumbered with ice, obscured continually by fog and mist.

It is most interesting today to reread the instructions given to the leaders of polar expeditions in those times. The instructions drawn up by the Governor of the Company for the use of Sir Hugh Willoughby (and preserved by Richard Hakluyt) are worth recording if only because they give a vivid picture of what was expected of a sixteenth-century expedition voyaging through Arctic and other unknown regions. But they also throw light on some of the problems confronting the leader of an Arctic expedition at that time.

One of the great problems, evidently, was the preservation of discipline among the crew, and there are strict injunctions that "no blaspheming of God, or detestable swearing, be used in any ship, nor communication of ribaldry, filthy tales, or ungodly talk to be suffered in the company of any ship, neither dicing, carding, talking nor other devilish game to be frequented, whereby ensueth not only poverty to the players, but also strife, variance, brawling, fighting and oftentimes a murder. . . ." It is no wonder that not only in the oaths, *juramenta*, taken by each man to the Captain-General, but throughout the Instructions, which were to be read aloud each week, "unity, love, conformity, and obedience" are constantly enjoined.

More important, because so revealing of the shrewd and practical attitude of those who drafted them, are the clauses laying down rules of behavior for the expedition on its arrival in a new land. The use of force was forbidden except in the last resort. Women were to be respected. Courtesy combined with caution were to be the watchwords of the landing parties. And tolerance, especially in religious matters, was to be maintained at all times. "If the people," Willoughby was told, "shall appear gathering stones, gold, metal or other like on the sand, your pinnances may draw nigh, marking what things they gather, using and playing upon the drum or such other instruments as may allure them to harkening, to fantasy, or desire to see and hear your instruments and voices. But keep you out of danger, and show to them no sign of riguour or hostility." Only so could these Arctic navigators of the sixteenth century expect to obtain what the Company wanted—a full account

THE PERSISTENT
BATTERING OF
SHIPS BY THE
ICE FORCED
MANY
EXPEDITIONS TO
LEAVE THEIR
BOATS AND SEEK
SHELTER ON
SOLID GROUND.

of the new peoples and countries, detailed information about natural resources, and opportunities to develop trade.

In May 1553, through the warm air of an English summer day, the three ships of Willoughby's Arctic expedition moved slowly downriver from Deptford. The Court was in residence at Greenwich at the time, and as the ships of the Arctic expedition came in sight, there was great excitement. "The courtiers," an onlooker relates, "came running out, and the common people flocked together, standing very thick upon the shore. The Privy Council looked out at the

100

windows of the Court, and the rest ran up to the tops of
the towers." The ships, in response to this ovation, fired
a salvo in salute "in so much that the tops of the hills
sounded therewith, and the waters gave an echo," and the
sailors "shouted in such sort that the sky rang again with
the noise thereof. One stands on the poop of the ship, and
by gesture bids farewell to his friends . . . another walks
upon the hatches, another climbs the shrouds, another
stands upon the mainyard, and another in the top of the
ship." After "divers gentlemen and gentlewomen" had

101

come aboard to drink the health of ships and crews (to whom they gave "right liberal awards"), Sir Hugh Willoughby's Arctic fleet made for the open sea.

For Willoughby the expedition ended in tragedy—a personal tragedy of the kind which was to darken many another expedition to the polar regions. Off the west coast of Norway, a great storm swept the ships apart, and Willoughby's ship, the *Bona Esperanza,* after days of wandering, got crippled in the Barents Sea. It made a landfall on the north coast of the Kola Peninsula, somewhere in the neighborhood of Murmansk. There, because of the weather and the battered state of his ship, Willoughby and his men were forced to winter, and there, one by one, they died; probably of scurvy, the enfeebling and eventually killing disease which was to be the scourge of generations of polar explorers.

In 1554, a year after they had sailed from Greenwich, their bodies were found in this desolate spot by Russian fishermen, and with a note in Willoughby's own hand, describing their adventures—the seals, the deer, the bears and the foxes they had seen, the unceasing storms of snow and hail which they had endured on their voyage, so violent that they would have been expected only in the depths of winter. Day after day, Willoughby wrote, they had searched the bleak and snowbound coast, to the east, to the west, to the south. But they found no human being.

Richard Chancellor, meanwhile, in the *Edward Bonaventure,* had managed to put in at Wardhouse (Vardö) in Finnmark, and there met some Scottish merchants. When he told them of the object of his voyage they did their utmost to dissuade him from so insane an enterprise. But Chancellor was adamant. "Nothing at all discouraged with the speeches and words of the Scots," he sailed and held on his course until "he came at last to a place where he found no night at all, but a continual light and brightness of the sun shining clearly upon a huge and mighty sea. . . ." At length, the *Edward Bonaventure* put into a great bay, a hundred miles wide—the bay in the White Sea at the estuary of the Dvina River, where Archangel now stands.

The rest of the story of the Willoughby-Chancellor expedition is one of Russian rather than of Arctic discovery, for not far from where he landed Chancellor was met by emissaries from Czar Ivan the Terrible, who invited him to return with them by sledge on the fifteen-hundred-mile journey to Moscow. For the merchants and for the government of England, it was a momentous journey. It led in 1555 to the foundation of the Muscovy Company for the development of the highly lucrative Muscovy and Persian trade by way of the northern Dvina route. And it led three years later to the foundation of the famous port of Archangel. In the realm of Arctic exploration, however, Chancellor's voyage added little to geographical knowledge. Indeed, it carried the search for a Northeast Passage no further than the Viking Ochtere had done in the days of Alfred the Great.

6. *The Quest for the Northwest Passage*

THE SEARCH for a Northeast Passage was now taken over
by the newly established Muscovy Company, and Stephen
Borough, former master of the *Edward Bonaventure,* was
invited to follow up the explorations which Willoughby
and Chancellor had begun. Like Chancellor, under whom
he had served, Borough was a professional seaman, an
expert at his trade, trained in the latest practice of navigation by John Dee. In 1556, after a banquet with music and
dancing given at the Sign of the Christopher at Gravesend
by the aged Sebastian Cabot, Borough sailed in the *Search-
thrift,* a tiny ship, smaller even than Chancellor's *Edward
Bonaventure*. He had better fortune than Chancellor, and
reached as far east as the Kara Sea. But at its entrance, south
of Novaya Zemlya, his way was blocked by a mass of ice
churned up by the winds—an impenetrable barrier which
was to be the despair of many an expedition during the
sixteenth and seventeenth centuries.

For twenty years, the new and immensely profitable trade
with Russia wholly preoccupied the merchants of the City
of London. Nevertheless there were many, among the no-
bility, among the landed gentry and in the learned world,
who were not so concerned with immediate gain. These
were men for whom the study of geography, of cartography,
and of navigation had become a fashionable intellectual
pursuit. They were prepared to support a further search.

In Elizabeth's reign, however, the direction of the search
was changed. The quest was now for a Northwest Passage.
There were reasons for this change of policy. On the one
hand, the publication in 1558 of the Zeno map showed

SIR MARTIN FROBISHER

Greenland swinging eastward, thus barring the eastern
route; on the other, was the incorporation in the Flemish
geographer Ortelius' map of 1564 of Jacques Cartier's discovery of the mouth of St. Lawrence River. The year 1569
saw a great event in the history of man's mapping of the
world: the publication of Gerhard Mercator's world map
on the new Mercator projection. This finally decided the
direction of the new explorations. It showed in its outline
of Arctic geography not only the start of a passage to the

105

west but a formidable land barrier to the east, thus lending the great weight of Mercator's authority to the fabrication of the Zeno map.

For twenty years thereafter Arctic exploration was directed westward. And in the spring of 1576, Martin Frobisher, a bold and practiced seaman who was to win fame during the Armada—a man who was the quintessence of the Elizabethan adventuring spirit—sailed with two pinnaces, each of only twenty tons, on another Arctic enterprise. Frobisher's first landfall was the southern tip of Greenland. But since Greenland was far away to the east

ESKIMO IN KAYAK BY SIR MARTIN FROBISHER

on his maps he called his new land West Friezeland, identifying it with one of the many islands dotting the western Arctic on the Zeno map.

From Greenland, Frobisher sailed westward until he reached a "strait" now known as Frobisher Bay, at the southeast end of Baffin Island. These are the "straits" or "streights" to which Richard Hakluyt refers in his account of Frobisher's voyage: "And that land upon his right hand as he sailed Westward he judged to be the continent of Asia, and there to be divided from the firme of America, which lieth upon the left hand over against the same. This place he named after his name, Frobishers Streights."

As Frobisher and his men approached the coast of this new Arctic land, they saw an astonishing sight. Darting out from the icebound shore, came a fleet of skin-covered canoes, the kayaks of the Eskimos, the first they had ever seen. The appearance of these small men excited them. With their pronounced Asiatic, Mongoloid features, surely these, they thought, must be men from Marco Polo's Cathay. As proof that here was Cathay at last, or at least an outlier of it, an Eskimo and his kayak were hauled aboard and brought back in triumph to London.

Martin Frobisher's arrival in London with his "Pyknean" or "Strange Man of Cathay" caused a considerable sensation. "And so," said a contemporary, "they came to London with their ship Gabriel the sixth day of October; and they were joyfully received with the great Admiration of the people, bringing with them their strange man and his Bote, which was such a wonder unto the whole city, and to the rest of the Realm that heard of it, as seemed never to have happened the like great matter to any men's knowledge. . . ." The Eskimo (who died of a cold soon after he landed) was not the only, nor indeed the most sensational, prize

107

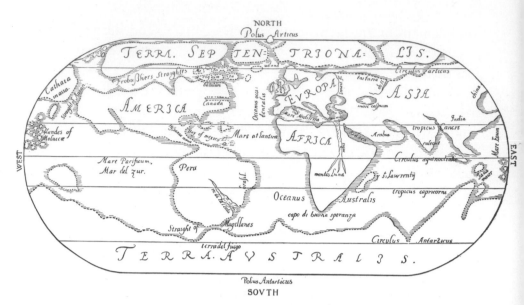

MAP SHOWING FROBISHER'S STRAIT

brought back by Frobisher's men from the Arctic. Some brought back Arctic flowers, and some green grass. One brought a piece of black stone. It looked like coal, but when thrown into the fire, according to Humphrey Gilbert, the author of *Discourse of a Discovery for a New Passage to Cathaia,* "It glistened with a bright marquesset of golde."

Martin Frobisher was convinced that, in his westward-heading "strait," he had found the entrance to a Northwest Passage. His charts and the Mongoloid appearance of the Eskimo convinced even his instructor in navigation, the learned and discriminating John Dee. But when rumors spread that the black stones of Baffin Island had been identified as gold, all thought of the Northwest Passage was forgotten.

A Cathay Company was formed. The Queen bought

108

shares. Miners from the tin mines in Cornwall—the mines which Pytheas had sought in Aristotle's time—were hastily recruited, and Frobisher and his officers, after kissing the Queen's hand at Lord Warwick's house in Essex, sailed in 1577 on a second expedition to the Arctic.

This time, on his outward voyage, Frobisher landed in Greenland, the West Friezeland of the Zeno map, to which he gave the homely name of West England, and there he established friendly relations with the Eskimo inhabitants, trading "bells, looking-glasses and divers of our country toys" for their dogs. He noted, too, among objects the Eskimos brought him that some were of iron; evidence of contact with "civill people," relics of trade or plunder, perhaps, dating from the days of old Norse colonies, or proof of more recent contact with whalers or fishermen whose voyages had

109

never been recorded. Frobisher took possession of this new land of West England "to the use of our sovereign lady the Queen's Majesty." He was optimistic about the prospects for further exploration. It was a country, he said, which promised "good hope of great commodity and riches, if it may be well discovered." He then sailed for Baffin Island and returned with two hundred tons of the black ore.

Frobisher's third and last voyage to Baffin Island was in 1578—the year in which Drake, in his ship the *Golden Hind,* was the first to round Cape Horn.

110

This time it was a colonizing and not an exploring expedition, the first of its kind in the Canadian Arctic, and the fifteen ships which sailed from the Port of London carried miners, settlers, massive planks and timbers, and a large prefabricated wooden house to establish a mining settlement in Frobisher Bay. But no sooner had they entered the so-called "strait" than disaster overwhelmed the fleet. A storm arose, sweeping down upon the ships a mass of churning, grinding ice floes which sank most of the supply ships and ended the whole enterprise. When the remnants of the fleet, scattered by Atlantic gales, arrived at a number of different English ports, they were confronted by another and quite unexpected catastrophe. The famous ore, identified by an unscrupulous Italian assayer as gold, proved to be worthless iron pyrites. The Cathay Company was bankrupt. Martin Frobisher was disgraced. And his discoveries, his claims to have found a Northwest Passage and to have reached the very frontiers of Cathay, were utterly discredited.

"The passage to Cathay," commented sourly a contemporary, "is left unto us as uncertain as at the beginning, though thereupon hath followed great charges to the Company."

Only from Russia was there any comfort for the disgraced explorer. In January 1579, the Russians protested violently to the English Government. Frobisher's Eskimo, the "Strange Man of Cathay," they declared, was none other than a Russian Asiatic subject, kidnapped by a pack of English adventurers.

The bankruptcy of the Cathay Company put an end for some years to expeditions to the western Arctic. The planners now turned eastward again, and in 1580 two sturdy and experienced English mariners, Arthur Pet and Charles Jackman, sailed in the pinnaces *George* and *William* to try for a Northeast Passage. But just as Stephen Borough had been held up a quarter of a century earlier, so their way was barred by the same impenetrable wall of pack ice which loomed up out of the fog at the entrance of the Kara Sea. It was the last English attempt to seek a Northeast Passage during the sixteenth century.

7. *The Lively Geography of John Davis*

THE FROBISHER fiasco, however, had not robbed the northwest of all its protagonists. There were still some geographers and courtiers who felt, like Frobisher, that only in the northwest lay the solution to the problem of Cathay. In 1584 they obtained from the Queen a charter for a new North-West Company and selected as the leader and chief pilot of the new enterprise a remarkable man, John Davis.

Davis, a splendid seaman was a quiet and modest man with no gallant flourish to his name like Frobisher. But he was by far the most accomplished navigator of his day, with an intimate knowledge of new and ingenious navigational instruments, of the new techniques of navigation at sea which the Age of Discovery had compelled the English to invent. In providing the first detailed descriptions of Eskimo life in Greenland, moreover, he showed a power of acute and meticulous observation, a capacity for vivid description—something which in polar literature is hard to match.

Frobisher had been optimistic about the prospects for exploration in Greenland. So Davis, on his first voyage in the *Moonshine* and the *Sunshine* in 1585, determined on a systematic exploration of the coasts. He landed first in southwest Greenland, near the modern Godthaab in Gilbert Sound. He then sailed across Davis Strait to Cumberland Sound in Baffin Island, north of Frobisher "Strait." The following year, 1586, Davis divided up his four ships for simultaneous voyages along the eastern and western coast. The southeast coast, against which the pack ice is swept and massed by southward-flowing cold currents from the Arctic Sea, presented a formidable and frightening sight. "The loathsome view of the shore and the irksome view of the ice," Davis wrote, "was such as to breed strange conceits among us, so that we supposed the place to be wast and voyd of any sensible or vegitable creatures whereupon I called the same Desolation. . . ."

The east coast of Greenland, indeed, as many later expeditions were to find, proved both desolate and unapproachable and the two ships working there were forced by eastward-branching currents toward the coasts of Iceland. After failing to land on the southernmost promontory of Greenland, Davis made for his old anchorage on the southwest coast, in Gilbert Sound. The Eskimos, remembering the music and dancing with which Davis' sailors had delighted them the previous year, welcomed the Englishmen enthusiastically. They were, Davis found, a gay and simple but also a mischievous and "thievish" people, who cut the ships' cables and stole the *Moonshine*'s boat and pilfered anything in sight. Davis made some curious discoveries in Greenland. Like Frobisher, he saw many relics of trade with Europe, iron objects which the Eskimos greatly prized, and was shown "a grave with divers buried in it, only covered with sealskins having a cross laid over them," the grave of a Viking colonist, or of some Eskimo family converted by the Norsemen to Christianity.

Davis took careful note of everything he saw in southwestern Greenland—the trees, fir, spruce, and juniper, birch and willow. He noticed too the great swarms of seals wallowing in the sea or basking sleepily in the sunshine on the islands off the coast. He explored the deeply cut fjords along which the Viking colonists had built their farms; fjords so numerous, penetrating so far to the east, that he thought the land must be "a great number of islands stand-ing together." Inland, along this western coast in summer, he found "a plan champaign country, with earth and grass, such as our moory and waste grounds of England are . . . but found nothing, nor saw anything, save onely grapes, ravens, and small birds, as larks and linnets. . . ."

John Davis, on his return, was optimistic about pros-pects for the discovery of a Northwest Passage. On October 3, 1585, he wrote to a government official: "Right honor-able most dutyfully craving pardon for this my rashe bold-ness, I am hereby, according to my duty, to signyfy unto your honor that the northwest passage is a matter nothing doubtfull, but at any tyme almost to be passed, the sea navigable, voyd of yse, the ayre tollerable, and the waters very depe." It was therefore with high hopes that in 1586 and 1587 he made two further voyages westward from Greenland, venturing northward on one occasion into unexplored waters of a bay to which a great English ex-plorer of the early seventeenth century was to give his name. Twice he crossed over toward Baffin Island but was swept southward by drifting ice beyond Frobisher Bay. On the second of these voyages, drifting south, he found his small ships caught up and spinning in "a might overfall," probably the turbulent waters at the entrance to Hudson Strait.

In 1587 John Davis returned to England, having con-tributed to geographical knowledge of the Arctic more than any of his predecessors. But as far as the English were concerned Arctic exploration was now at an end. In July of the following year, the Armada of Philip of Spain was sighted from the English coast and Elizabeth's seamen—Martin Frobisher, John Davis, all in fact of those tested

CORDIFORM WORLD MAP

BY PETRUS APIANUS, 1520

and trained in great voyages of discovery—were needed for more vital and immediate tasks than Arctic exploration or a search for an Arctic passage to Cathay.

John Davis, in *The Seaman's Secrets,* admirably summed up sixteenth-century views about the polar regions, bringing all his own personal experiences to bear in his remarks about the Arctic. "The frozen zones," he wrote, "are contained within the polar circle, the Antarctick frozen zone within the Antarctick polar circle which are also reported not to be habitable by reason of the great extremity of colde supposed to be in those parts because of the Sunnes far distance from those zones, but in these our dayes we find by experience that the ancient Geographers had not the due consideration of the nature of these zones, for three times I have been within the Arctick frozen zone, where I found the ayre very temperate, yea and many times in calme wether marveilous hot; I have felt the Sunne beames of as forcible action in the frozen zone in calme neere unto the shore, as I have at any time found within the burning zone; this zone is also inhabited with people of good stature, shape and tractable conditions, with whom I have converced and not found them rudly barbarous, as I have found the Caniballs which are in the straights of Magilane and Southerne parts of America." Davis' observations—the observations of an active and not a professorial geographer—serve as an encouraging if optimistic preface to the Arctic explorations of the seventeenth century.

118

8. *Barents and the Bold Dutchmen*

LATE IN THE sixteenth century, the Dutch, under Spain, emerged as rivals to the English in the search for an Arctic route to the Orient. They were bold and adventurous seamen and their success had turned Antwerp and Amsterdam into the treasury of Spain. So it was only natural that their merchants wanted to expand their trade. Since 1555, when the English Muscovy Company was established, the merchants of the Netherlands had looked with growing envy at the riches flowing into the coffers of the City of London from Russia and lands farther east. But to the Dutch, the kingdoms of Cathay were closed. The Spanish-Portuguese monopoly had barred them from the South Atlantic routes. So they too began to look to the north, for a northeast sea or land passage to Asia, which might let them at least share the intermediate Russian trade.

In 1565, on the eve of the great revolt which was to liberate the Netherlands from Spain and lead, under William of Nassau, to the rise of the Dutch Republic, the Dutch White Sea Trading Company was formed. It was under a most enterprising manager named Oliver Brunel. Brunel had already established a Dutch trading post on the Kola Peninsula and with Russian fishermen, whose contributions to Arctic exploration were probably far more extensive than has ever been recorded, had not only reached the islands of Novaya Zemlya which enfold the Kara Sea but after a remarkable eastward journey overland had traveled as far east as the River Ob.

In an attempt to find the Northeast Passage, however, Brunel did no better than the English who had preceded

119

him. He was forced back by the ice barrier at the entrance
to the Kara Sea. He had nevertheless high hopes for another attempt—one to be sponsored this time by the rich
merchants of Amsterdam.

The outstanding figure in this first Dutch Arctic enterprise was, however, not Brunel but Willem Barents, the
chief pilot on three successive voyages. These were voyages
(according to Gerrit de Veer's account, published in England in 1609) "so strange and wonderful that the like hath
never been heard of before; done and performed in three
years, one after another by ships of Holland and Zeeland
. . . towards the kingdoms of Cathaia and China. . . ."

A sea has been called after Willem Barents, and a fine
big sea too, but the thing that makes him more important

121

than many other navigators is the fact that he was the first European who learned how to winter in the Arctic. After more than 350 years, this amiable Dutchman seems much closer to the Arctic and Antarctic explorers of our own day than he does to Columbus or Drake or Magellan who were much more nearly his contemporaries.

We aren't sure about the date of his birth, but it was at or a little before the middle of the sixteenth century on the island of Tershelling in the North Sea. He went to sea as a cabin boy and rose to the command of an Amsterdam merchant ship. Then he became a seal hunter and learned more about the waters of the North than almost any other navigator of his day.

A stocky fellow with a square beard and a great reputation for good sense and good humor and for taking good care of his crews, he was more or less retired when the merchants of Amsterdam set out to find a trade route of their own to the Indies.

As subjects of the Spanish King, they had trafficked with the East along the routes pioneered by Magellan and da Gama but a long quarrel with King Philip had culminated in 1561 in a Dutch declaration of independence. By 1594, it looked as if they would win it. From that time on, however, Dutch ships were not very safe if they had to put in at ports where Spanish officers were in charge, and even before their rebellion they had been restricted in their trade, so that they were all the more ready for a free route of their own—free, that is, from the tolls and exactions of Spain, for they knew they would never get one free of risk and danger.

The city employed its best captain to find such a route, speculating that if it was possible to go south of Africa to the East, it should be equally practicable to go north of

122

Europe and around to China. This was the Northeast Passage Barents was to find.

He sailed in June, 1594, in a ship not very much different nor any more seaworthy than the ones in which the great Spanish and Portuguese had achieved their great successes. But he ran into such heavy pack ice before he had gone beyond territory already known that he could not get through. He returned to Amsterdam, counseling an earlier start next time, and the city prepared for him over the winter an expedition of seven ships.

In 1595, therefore, Captain Barents led his flotilla around the top of Scandinavia, past North Cape, past the present site of Murmansk, and around the Kola Peninsula into the White Sea. This turned out not to be a passage reaching down toward China, but the expedition encountered some friendly hunters who were dressed in strange skins—

SPITSBERGEN

123

reindeer hides. These hunters were no encouragement in the quest for a water passage to China. They said the sea froze in winter—froze so hard that men could pass over from the peninsula into Russia. So Barents went no farther than the White Sea for fear of being trapped in the ice, and then sailed back to Amsterdam.

In 1596, the city fathers equipped two ships, and for some reason, decided they wanted another commander, perhaps a man of more gentlemanly ancestry than Barents. Anyway they selected Captain Jakob van Heemskerk, an experienced sea captain of a family so influential that usually it did not send its sons to sea. He had, however, a good scientific education for that day, and was much interested in the Arctic. He and Barents proved to be congenial shipmates, for van Heemskerk treated the older man as the real head of the expedition. Barents actually was called navigator and chief pilot. There was a second smaller ship commanded by Jan Corneliszoon de Rijp.

The story of this expedition comes down through the doctor, or barber-surgeon as he was called in the ship's crew list, a very cheerful young fellow who in some things was ahead of most of his profession. He was Gerrit de Veer, and his story of the year on which he now embarked was one of the most popular books of its generation.

The two ships sailed in May, but at North Cape, instead of sailing straight east as Barents suggested, van Heemskerk and de Rijp decided they should proceed farther north first. After struggling through ice floes for some days, they came to an island, which no one had ever suspected before, and a party of men went ashore to search for food. They met a lean, fierce polar bear which killed two of them before Barents led rescuers to shoot the animal. The place has been Bear Island on the maps ever since.

124

Still holding on the northerly course, the expedition discovered Spitsbergen, which means "jagged mountains." These, Barents supposed, were part of Greenland. However, the Dutchmen solved one age-old mystery, for they saw wild geese nesting in the crags of Spitsbergen, and no one ever had known before where these birds came from. At last Barents got his way, and he and van Heemskerk headed toward the east. But the smaller ship of de Rijp was sent back to Amsterdam to report progress that far.

In July, the explorers sighted the long island of Novaya Zemlya about halfway along its western shore. They followed the coast north and east but after they rounded Cape Mauritius and entered the Kara Sea, the weather turned bitterly cold, while the sea was full of icebergs and large, menacing floes. It was only August, but already the Arctic winter was approaching. "The wind blew so uncertain that we could hold no course but were forced continually to wind and turn by reason of the ice and the inconstantness of the wind," de Veer wrote.

They made little progress toward their goal, therefore, and were still on the northeast coast of Novaya Zemlya in September when heavy snowfalls began. Barents suggested that they take refuge in a snug little harbor, which later they called Ice Harbor, in the hope that after the storm passed they could beat their way east into what he hoped would be warmer waters. But in the morning their ship was frozen fast in the ice.

There was nothing for it except to plan to winter here, the first Europeans faced with the prospect of surviving through the long Arctic night, and they went at it with good sense and good spirits enough, according to de Veer's account.

Fortunately, Barents and van Heemskerk remained always in cordial agreement, for some of the men were sick and none of them quite sure what was best to do. However, under the guidance of the ship's carpenter, they began to construct a sizable house of driftwood, of which they found plenty lying about on beaches and rocks, and some timbers from their ship.

The carpenter was the first man on Novaya Zemlya to die, and the floor was not yet laid, but they carried on the plan he had made, although many of the men were barely up to the task of hauling heavy timbers around. They had no trouble getting the walls up, but when it came to a roof they were stumped for a while. Then they hit on the trick of covering their house with one of the ship's sails and weighing it down on the outside with sand. This made a very snug roof indeed, because it soon was covered by a thick layer of ice and snow—which is fine insulation, as every Eskimo knows. To keep warm they burned wood in a ship's stove set up in the center of the house—it was just one big room—and let the smoke out through a hole in the roof, using a barrel with the bottom knocked out as chimney. Bunks were built along the walls, and all the ship's supplies they could handle, including the trade goods of the Amsterdam merchants, were stored around and between them.

Barents was one of those who got sick before the winter was very far advanced, and the men rigged up a special bed for him near the fire. Young de Veer tried to keep them healthy by making every man take a hot bath once a week; he contrived a bathtub out of half a barrel, and melted snow on the stove. He insisted that they take regular exercise, and those who were strong enough got plenty going outside through snowdrifts to collect wood for the fire.

Food, of course, was not very good, but they had plenty

of biscuits and pancakes and some wine. They caught a great many foxes in traps, and had fox stew (not very tasty). They used the skins to make coats and caps and shoes. In spite of blizzards and some depression, they celebrated Three Kings Day on January 6th with as good a party as they could. De Veer furnished music and everybody enjoyed such skits as electing one man King of Novaya Zemlya for the day. In spite of all de Veer's efforts, one of the sailors died in January.

As the sun came back and the ice began to break up in March, Barents and van Heemskerk consulted on how they might make their way back to Holland. Their ship was smashed up in the ice, but there was enough left of her timbers to make two open boats in which to sail along the coast of the island, across to the Russian mainland, and back along the route of Barents' 1595 voyage. It would be a hard trip for open boats, but there was no other hope for them.

The voyagers did not start until June, and even then the ice was so thick that they had trouble forcing their way through the floes. Once they were frozen in for a little while. Before they left, Barents wrote out an account of their experiences and left it hanging in a powder horn on the wall of their hut. If all of them were lost, perhaps someone else would explore that way and find their record.

Barents was too weak to walk, and he was taken down to one of the open boats in a sled. Once in a while the men landed and built fires to warm themselves and cook a meal. But Barents grew worse all the time, and on June 28, 1597, he died "with a sudden qualm," de Veer wrote. The boats were off the mainland just south of Novaya Zemlya.

127

For three months the survivors struggled westward. The boats sprang leaks, but they were afraid to land because of the savage polar bears which would attack them on sight. Mostly it was cold, but one summer day when they came to a small island which was not inhabited by polar bears, van Heemskerk made the sailors unpack all the boxes of trade goods which they were carefully carrying back to the merchants in Amsterdam. The cloth was taken out and aired and dried, and everything well packed up again.

At last they reached some fishing villages inhabited by Russians, and there to the intense surprise of both parties they were found by de Rijp and his men. Their ship had been blown down from the Arctic into the White Sea, and the men had wintered there comfortably enough with the help of the Russians, and now the two parts of the expedition were reunited. At the end of October, they got back to Amsterdam.

There is a curious postscript to the story. Nobody, so far as can be told, went to Ice Harbor on Novaya Zemlya for the next 274 years. But then in 1871, a Norwegian hunter passed that way and found the hut of the Netherlanders just as they had left it, preserved by the cold and undamaged. The bunks looked as if the men had just left them. There was the half barrel which de Veer had made into a bathtub, a musket in one corner, and hanging on the wall the powder horn with Barents' last letter. Today, all those relics are in the Naval Museum at The Hague.

These Dutch expeditions which had achieved not only access to the Kara Sea but the discovery of Bear Island and Spitsbergen and a reconnaissance of the unknown western coast of Novaya Zemlya came to an end with the return of the Barents expedition. The reason lies in the course of Dutch history. The year 1597 when Barents and his men escaped from their winter quarters in Novaya Zemlya marked a great event—the liberation of Holland from the Spanish Army by the son of William of Orange. The Dutch in their war of freedom from Spanish rule had already defied Spain in the East. A Dutch fleet had visited China and Siam. Dutch factories had been established in the Spice Islands of Cathay. Now, in open defiance of the Spanish monopoly, the liberated Dutch established their own East India Company. They were, in consequence, no longer much concerned with an Arctic route to Cathay, and it was left to the English to resume the search for a northern passage in the persons of two great Arctic navigators and discoverers, Henry Hudson and William Baffin.

9. *Hudson*: *Tragedy at Sea*

THE DISCOVERIES of Hudson and Baffin in the western Arctic exceeded all those of previous expeditions and laid the first foundations of Canada's Arctic territories. Hudson, a professional seaman, had already gained a high reputation with the Dutch as a navigator and pilot in Arctic waters. As an employee of the English Muscovy Company, he had made an historic voyage in 1607, the first directed toward the North Pole. On this, in the waters of Spitsbergen, he reached a latitude of 80° 23′ N., a latitude not exceeded by any ship until the voyage of Captain Constantine Phipps in 1773.

Homeward bound from this voyage, Hudson rediscovered Spitsbergen, calling it Newland (though he carried copies of Barents' charts), and southwest of Barents' Bear Island, added another territory to the Arctic map—a small island which he called Hudson's Tutches. This was soon to be rediscovered by a Dutchman, Jan May, and named Jan Mayen Island. On this first voyage Hudson carried with him not only Barents' charts but—as Barents himself had done—a translation of the sailing directions for a voyage from Norway to Greenland. These directions had been compiled by a Norse colonist living in Greenland toward the end of the fourteenth century. Nevertheless, though Hudson sighted the east coast of Greenland more than once during his exploration of the waters west of Spitsbergen, each sighting he identified with one of those numerous islands which had decorated the western Arctic on the Zeno map.

On September 15, 1607, Henry Hudson returned to

131

"Tilberie Hope in the Thames." His employers, "certaine worshipfull merchants of London," were not too disappointed, for he had advanced northward farther than any man before him. He had, moreover, confirmed Barents' reports of the rich fisheries waiting to be exploited in the waters around Spitsbergen and Bear Island. They had reason enough, therefore, to support another voyage—a voyage this time farther to the east, in the waters explored by the Dutch north and east of Novaya Zemlya. Its main object was to achieve what the Dutch had failed to achieve: the navigation of a Northeast Passage.

For this voyage, in the *Hopewell*, Henry Hudson had choice of three possible routes into the Kara Sea: by way of the north of Novaya Zemlya, past Barents' old winter quarters at Ice Harbor; by the channel called Matochkin Shar which, as Barents discovered, separates the two islands of Novaya Zemlya; or finally, by way of the Vaigach Strait, which, like the adjacent Kara Strait, leads directly into the Kara Sea from the west. But he didn't succeed by any of these. Between Spitsbergen and Novaya Zemlya, Hudson found that the sea was a mass of ice stretching to the horizon. He had missed the narrow channel dividing Novaya Zemlya. As to the Vaigach Strait, Hudson might have had some luck, but the crew resolutely refused to proceed. The incident is important only that it provides the first evidence of a fatal weakness in Hudson's character—a weakness in leadership which was to end in his death. Mutiny, not the ice of the Kara or Vaigach Strait, forced Hudson to bring the *Hopewell* back to England.

Hudson's failure discouraged the Muscovy Company from suporting another venture, and he sought employment elsewhere, first in France, then with the Dutch and the newly established East India Company of the Chamber of Amsterdam. With them, on January 8, 1609, he signed a contract undertaking "to search for a passage by the North, around by the North side of Novaya Zemlya." At the last minute, however, the directors of the East India Company changed their plans from an eastward to a westward voyage, to explore not the Northeast Passage but, in rivalry with the English, the North American coast.

There were good reasons for this change. In 1609, the year in which Hudson signed his contract with the East India Company, Holland forced Spain to grant her full rights to trade in Eastern waters. The Company thereupon abandoned the now needless Arctic adventure for a very much more lucrative project: colonization in the New World. This third voyage of Hudson's therefore belongs to the history of the discovery of North America rather than of the polar regions. It is the story of trading and fighting with Indians, of landfalls off Maine, off Cape Cod and in Chesapeake Bay, and of Hudson's penetration of the great Hudson River as far as Albany—a discovery which led to foundation of the colony of New Amsterdam, later named New York. This voyage, however, made one negative contribution to a great unsolved problem of Arctic exploration. Hudson was convinced as he sailed up the Hudson River that such shallow and narrow waters as these could not possibly lead to a northern passage.

The merchants of the City of London, determined that so brilliant an English explorer should not again be employed "to the detriment of his own country," now themselves commissioned Hudson "to try if, through any of those inlets which Davis saw, but durst not enter, any passage might be found to the other ocean called the South Sea." This last voyage of Hudson's, which led to the discovery of Hudson Bay and to the explorations and Arctic trading of the Hudson's Bay Company whose stations dot the map of the Canadian Arctic today, led also to his death.

From the day Henry Hudson entered Hudson Strait and sailed on into the waters of the "great and whirling sea" which was Hudson Bay, he was convinced that he had discovered the western route to Cathay.

He contrived, despite the fog and drifting ice in the strait, to explore Ungava Bay and the north coast of the Ungava Peninsula, and during early autumn he struck out into Hudson Bay to the west and north. He then turned south to James Bay and the mouth of the Rupert River. It was now November, too late to turn back, for "the nights were long and cold, and the earth covered with snow," and his ship was soon frozen in, beset for the winter. Hudson's men had already witnessed omens of approaching disaster: a savage sacrifice of "fowles hanged by the neck" on Digges Island, a thunderstorm which broke

HUDSON'S BAY

over the jagged cliffs as they landed. During the winter, the carpenter died; scurvy broke out; supplies, it became tragically clear, could not last the homeward voyage, and by June when at last *Discovery* weighed anchor, suspicion, mistrust, accusations of hoarding food, led inexorably to the final tragedy: the marooning of Hudson, his son and five loyal men, without food, without weapons, at dawn off Charlton Island.

The mutineers had been led by Robert Juet, mate of the *Hopewell,* and Abakuk Prickett, servant of Sir Dudley Digges, author of *The Circumference of the Earth or a Treatise of the North-West Passage,* who had been a patron of Hudson's expedition.

On their return they were brought before the Masters

135

of Trinity House and the High Court of the Admiralty to answer for their crime, but were saved from the gallows only because of their foresight in bringing back Hudson's charts which recorded the great discoveries of the man whom they had so callously condemned to death. Somewhere along the northwestern shores of Hudson Bay, they maintained, "by a great flood or billow" which swept in from that direction, lay the entrance to the Northwest Passage. Their arguments were so convincing, their optimism so infectious, that the mutiny on the *Discovery* was forgotten.

So in 1612 a new expedition under Sir Thomas Button, consisting of the *Discovery* and another ship, the *Resolution,* was launched by the Governor and Company of the Merchants of London, Discoverers of the Northwest Passage. Its object was "to search and find out a passage by the north-west of America to the Sea Sur, commonly called the South Sea." Bylot, mate of the *Discovery* under Hudson, was the chief pilot of the new venture, and in the course of two voyages, in 1612 and in 1615, Button explored the western shores of Hudson Bay as far north as Southhampton Island.

Sir Thomas Button was followed four years later by Jens Munck, a Dane, who wintered where the town of Churchill now stands, at the mouth of Churchill River. In 1631, Captain James, following in Hudson's wake, gave his name of James Bay, and another Englishman the same year, Luke Foxe—"Northwest Foxe" he called himself—explored the waters around and north of Southhampton Island and is commemorated in Foxe Peninsula and Foxe Basin.

Further gaps in the great work of exploration of Arctic Canada were filled in by British voyages to Hudson Bay in the middle of the eighteenth century. Needless to say, no exit from the bay to the west was ever found, but in the perspective of history, that is relatively unimportant.

The discoveries by Hudson and his immediate successors in the first half of the seventeenth century had led to the founding in 1670 of the Hudson's Bay Company. Just as in the central Arctic the discoveries of Barents and Hudson had given rise to the whaling and sealing industry, so in the west a great fur trade was developed by men—hunters, trappers, traders, voyageurs, pioneers—who in the succeeding centuries were to be primarily responsible for expanding the land frontiers of the Canadian North.

10. *Baffin and the Art of Navigation*

IN 1616, WHILE the coasts of Hudson Bay were being explored, a very remarkable English navigator and explorer, William Baffin, came nearer to solving the problem of the Northwest Passage than any until the nineteenth century. It is one of the misfortunes of polar history that only the bare outline of Baffin's explorations is known. For he was a highly accomplished navigator with experience of both Hudson Bay and Spitsbergen waters. He was also the first to take a lunar observation at sea. His detailed maps and journals, if they had ever been preserved, would certainly have shortened by many years the search for a Northwest Passage.

Baffin knew from his own experiences of Hudson Bay that there was little prospect there of any outlet to the west; tides, currents, the movement of ice, were all in keeping with the conditions of an enclosed sea. He decided therefore to try farther north and to follow Davis' tracks up the west coast of Greenland and into the strait where Davis had thought there were a number of possible directions for entrance to a Northwest Passage.

Baffin's ship was the same *Discovery* which Hudson had navigated into Hudson Bay and his mate was Bylot, one of the mutineers, a man who, whatever his part in the murder of Hudson may have been, appears to have played an important part in a number of these Arctic expeditions. Keeping to the Greenland side of Davis Strait, Baffin anchored the *Discovery* near the present Danish station of Upernavik, and then forced his ship, of only fifty tons, northward through the pack ice to Melville Bay and beyond. In this region and westward, Smith Sound, Jones Sound, as well as Lancaster Sound, were all discovered—the last two leading, if he had but known it, westward through the Canadian Arctic archipelago to the open waters of the Beaufort Sea.

Near Smith Sound, Baffin noted the greatest variation in the compass known at that time, and must then have been in the vicinity of the ever-shifting North Magnetic Pole.

Baffin returned to England in August 1616, with news of discoveries which were greater in extent and importance than any in this part of the Arctic until the nineteenth century. But unsupported by maps or journals, it was not long before they were discredited or forgotten. Neither Smith Sound, nor Lancaster Sound, nor Jones Sound, nor even Baffin Bay, appears on the maps of the Arctic which were published in England after the Napoleonic Wars— maps which unfortunately had to serve as the basis for the great revival of British naval exploration in the Arctic in the first quarter of the nineteenth century.

No further progress in the navigation of the Northeast Passage was made during the seventeenth century, nor any attempts beyond a futile and farcical expedition led by two drunken Englishmen, Wood and Flawes, in 1676. These in their foolishness served only to discourage further effort. In the eighteenth century, however, Arctic explorations were renewed, though less by English or Dutch ships than by the new Imperial Navy of Peter the Great, czar of the expanding empire of Russia.

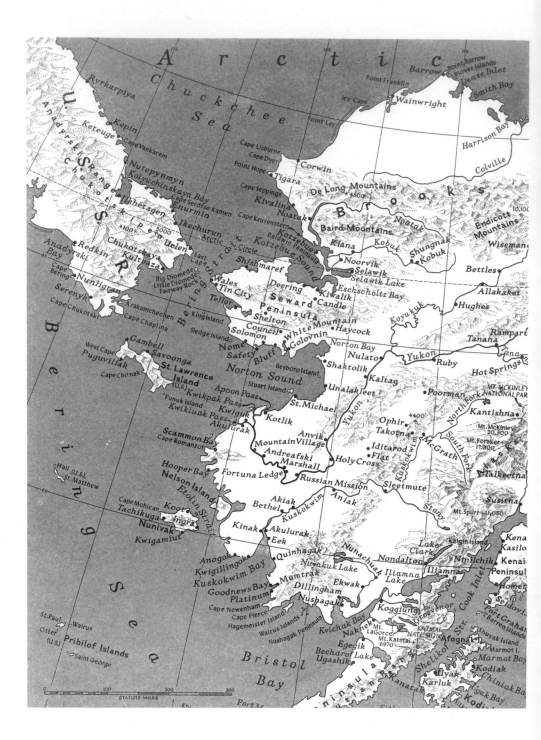

11. *To the Bering Strait*

THE EIGHTEENTH CENTURY was principally a century of Russian achievement in the Arctic. It witnessed the culmination of Russian colonial and trade expansion through the forests and across the great waterways and prairies of Siberia to the Bering Strait and the north Pacific Ocean. In grandeur of scale and range, these Russian expeditions were characteristic of the physical and intellectual energy and ambition of their principal architect, Peter the Great—a ruler determined to match and outstrip the West by "the finding of a passage to China and India through the Arctic Sea," and a Northeast Passage leading into the Pacific Ocean.

The first problem confronting the Russian explorers was whether Asia and America were joined by land or separated by sea. Though an answer was not known until the second quarter of the eighteenth century, this problem had already been solved three quarters of a century earlier by a Siberian Cossack, Simon Dezhnev, one of a band of Cossacks fleeing to the east to escape serfdom. In 1644, Dezhnev reached the Kolyma River, which flows into the East Siberian Sea. Four years later, in flat-bottomed boats, Dezhnev's party set out, following the coast toward the east until he reached East Cape (Mys Dezhneva) overlooking the Bering Strait. This was the land of the warring Chukchi tribes. Only Dezhnev and his boat's crew escaped, and, rounding the Chukotski Peninsula, they reached the mouth of the Anadyr River. Some vague and unconfirmed reports of this first discovery of the Bering Strait may have reached the Imperial Court. A map presented to Peter the Great by a Swedish prisoner of war in Siberia was said to have recorded a Russian penetration of the Bering Strait and even Russian penetration as far south as the Kamchatka Peninsula. It is indeed possible that such rumors may have stimulated the grandiose project which Peter the Great was about to launch.

The first great Russian Arctic expedition was as different from earlier efforts as were the British expeditions of the eighteenth century from those of the Merchant Adventurers. In planning and execution it was a national enterprise. It combined with national strategic motives, as in the West, objectives of geographical and scientific discovery. And the ships used and the leader appointed, Vitus Bering, belonged to the new and progressive Imperial Russian Navy.

Six months before his death in 1725, Peter the Great put the finishing touches to his great Arctic plans. To Vitus Bering and his men they must have presented a formidable prospect. They entailed an initial overland journey of 5,000 miles across Europe and Asia to Okhotsk on the Pacific coast. This meant the transport of men and supplies by raft over the swirling waters of four of the mightiest rivers in Russia. But this was not all. The plan also called for a sea voyage northward around the Kamchatka Peninsula, and a landing on the American coast.

By the summer of 1725, Bering and the twenty-five men of his expedition had reached the settlement of Yakutsk on a curving branch of the Lena river. Already it had been an immense and wearisome journey. Worse was to come. So far they had traveled mainly over steppe land, but between Yakutsk and Okhotsk lay seven hundred miles of country broken by rivers, mountains and swamps and swept by the blizzards of an early winter. Of the two hundred horses in Bering's caravan many died of the cold. Cumbrous loads of equipment and provisions had to be hauled on sleds to the coastal township of Okhotsk.

There Bering soon found himself tangled in the web of petty officialdom whose procastination and corruption and secret maneuvers were to prove throughout his explorations a great barrier to progress. One of the ships for the northern voyage, however, was built and in the summer of 1727, two years after leaving St. Petersburg, the sea route to Kamchatka was explored. In the following summer the second ship was finished after intolerable delays and in the summer of 1729 Bering was able to circumnavigate the Kamchatka Peninsula as far as the Gulf of Anadyr.

The Chukchi tribes, from whom Simon Dezhnev had so narrowly escaped, proved friendly this time and their stories of journeys northward across the peninsula to the Kolyma River encouraged Bering to persevere. Sailing out of the Gulf of Anadyr, the ship passed St. Lawrence Island, named by Bering after his patron saint, and entered the Bering Strait. To the west, Dezhnev's East Cape, the farthermost point of Asia, loomed above the sea. But to the east over the Alaskan coast fog hung heavily over the water and no sign of land could be seen. In part, Bering's mission had been accomplished, for a sea passage linking the Pacific with the Arctic Ocean had been found.

But the passage had still to be navigated and the coast followed to the west for the discovery to be beyond all doubt. *To go on, to turn back*: it was no easy decision for Bering to take. Bering Strait was free of ice. But it was dangerously late in the season. Winter and the ice might at any moment close in. In any event they faced a long and hazardous voyage to Okhotsk. Disaster, Bering well knew, could mean disgrace and worse. He therefore turned back.

A fruitless voyage eastward the following summer com-

143

pleted Bering's five years of exploration and he returned in triumph to St. Petersburg to report to the Czarina Ann. But applause quickly turned to scorn as Bering told his story. The charting of the Kamchatka Peninsula, the discovery of new islands, the revelation of a strait separating Asia and America about which the geographers had speculated—all these achievements were submerged in the flood of public accusation of Bering's apparent timidity. It was fortunate that there were men at court who still believed in him sufficiently to support his plea to be allowed to redeem his reputation by leading another expedition.

12. *Bering's Grand Design*

BERING'S NEXT expedition was on an even more majestic scale, and it exceeded in scope and complexity anything that had yet been attempted in Arctic exploration. The whole Arctic coast from the Gulf of Ob to the Anadyr River was to be systematically mapped. Bering was to search for land to the east of Kamchatka across the Bering Sea. South of Kamchatka Martin Spanberg, his Danish second-in-command, was to chart the Kurile Islands and the islands of Japan. This was the plan. But even the Admiralty College, when it took over direction of the vast enterprise in 1733, thought this was more than one man could possibly control. And Bering was left with only the principal exploring expedition, from Kamchatka across the Bering Sea.

When Bering arrived in Okhotsk late in 1734, it was no longer the frontier settlement of his first visit. It was now a township, thronged with the colonists, technicians, the innumerable officials sent out by the Imperial Government. Here he was immobilized for six years, bewildered and frustrated by the procrastination and the intrigues, by the multiplication of dossiers, by the stream of inquiries, of orders, and of counterorders dispatched across the vast expanses of Siberia by a central government determined to exercise remote control over every detail of his operation. Not until 1740, seven years after he had left St. Petersburg, were Bering's new ships ready to sail eastward on the new explorations. One ship, the *St. Peter,* carried as surgeon the German naturalist Georg Wilhelm Steller. Louis Delisle da la Croyère, related to Guillaume Delisle, geographer to Louis XV, sailed with Chirikov, the Russian captain of the other, the *St. Paul*.

Bering's last voyage ended in both triumph and disaster. The broad beaches and dark forests of northwest America were reached and in one day spent on shore, Steller the naturalist found time to make copious notes on fauna and flora and to gather specimens of Alaskan native arts and crafts for the imperial collections.

The plan to winter had to be abandoned, for Bering, among others, was weakening rapidly from scurvy. Both ships therefore put out to sea and made for home. Bering's ship, sailing through fog and storms of torrential rain, was wrecked on the beach of Bering Island, and there the greatest Arctic explorer of the eighteenth century died.

Bering's discovery of the strait which bears his name, and of the islands south of it, his charting of the Kamchatka and Anadyr Peninsulas, and his two landings on the American coast are among the great achievements of Arctic exploration. To them must be added the immense and systematic work of charting the whole length of the northern Russian coast eastward from the Ob. All these complicated and extensive operations, successfully completed despite the hindrances of a highly centralized and often incompetent administration, disposed once and for all of the fantastic ideas about the Arctic geography of northeast Asia and northwest America current in the first half of the eighteenth century.

They were also more indirectly to affect the course of Arctic exploration. In the East as in the West, exploration was followed by trade, and by the formation of trading companies. In the footsteps of the Russian explorers, trade began to spread during the second half of the eighteenth century across the Bering Strait and down the North American coast. By the first quarter of the nineteenth century, Russia—in the form of the government-sponsored Russian-American Company—was firmly established in Alaska. She thus became a strategic factor in the problem of a Northwest Passage around the northern extremity of British Canada. The search for this was to preoccupy the British Navy for more than half the century which followed the Napoleonic Wars.

13. *The Great Tradition*

NOW WE COME to the second period of European enterprise in Arctic regions. The merchants' desire of gain was no longer the driving force, but national interests. Britain's imperial interests got involved in Arctic exploration and it was the English officers' "emulation and desire of fame," which led to the discoveries in the first half of the nineteenth century.

The moving spirit in British Arctic exploration of the first half of the nineteenth century was John Barrow. Industrious, highly capable, widely traveled in his younger days, Barrow served as a decisive and influential Secretary to the Admiralty for forty years from 1804, and became moreover in later years President of the Geographical Society of London. He was born of humble Westmorland stock. As a boy while working in a foundry at Liverpool he managed to be the first in England to make an ascent with the famous Italian aeronaut Lunardi in his balloon. He followed this adventure by a summer cruise to the Arctic in a whaler and from that day he became an ardent enthusiast for polar exploration and a great student of its literature, especially of the Elizabethan age.

When Barrow, after many years in China and South Africa, joined the Admiralty in 1804, he found himself in an exceptionally strong position to influence polar affairs. The year 1817, as he describes in his autobiography, appeared ordained by circumstance to be the one in which the great traditions of British Arctic exploration might be revived. There was little demand on the Royal Navy at the time. The Arctic geography of North America, the dis-

148

covery of a Northwest Passage (on which the Russians had their eyes), even the insularity of Greenland, were all problems yet unsolved. Indeed, how little was then known of Arctic geography despite the explorations of the last two hundred years can be seen from the map accompanying Barrow's own *Chronological History of Voyages in the Arctic Regions,* published in 1818. At the mouth of the Mackenzie River, at points northward of Great Bear Lake, the sea had been reached late in the eighteenth century by Alexander Mackenzie and Samuel Hearne, men of the Hudson's Bay Company. But farther north, except for a vague and shadowy outline of Greenland's west coast, the Arctic map, despite William Baffin's discoveries, was blank.

But there was another and more immediate reason for the renewal of Arctic exploration. Ice conditions, because of some temporary climatic fluctuation, were in 1817 quite exceptionally favorable and as Barrow recorded in his article in the *Quarterly Review,* William Scoresby the Younger, the whaling captain, had that very summer reported the extraordinary disappearance of an immense quantity of ice. "I believed," Scoresby had written to Sir Joseph Banks, "on my last voyage [1817] about two thousand square leagues [18,000 square miles] of the surface of the Greenland seas, included between the parallels 74° and 80°, to be perfectly void of ice, all of which had disappeared within the last two years." This was an opportunity not to be lost. Barrow at once proposed to Lord Melville, First Lord of the Admiralty, a plan for two voyages "for the advancement of geography, navigation, and commerce" and this, with strong support from the Royal Society on scientific grounds, was rapidly approved.

Barrow's plans were on a grand and multiple scale. One naval squadron was to sail northward between Spitsbergen and Greenland and then as close to the Pole as possible and on to the Bering Strait. This was in the direction of Captain Constantine Phipp's expedition of 1773. The second and principal squadron was to search for an entrance to a Northwest Passage along the traditional avenue of Davis Strait while other ships waited off Bering Strait to welcome or rescue any survivors who might get through. This was the plan for the first maritime operations. In addition, there was to be a land exploration of the almost unknown Arctic coast of North America.

In May 1818 the naval squadrons sailed. Captain David Buchan, with orders for the northern journey, commanded two sailing ships, the *Dorothea* and the *Trent*. His second-in-command was an officer whose name was soon to become a household word, Lieutenant John Franklin. This voyage, however, was a total failure. Off the west coast of Spitsbergen a violent gale fell upon the ships, forcing them to make for land. Venturing out again to the north, they were beset for days in heavy pack ice along the edge of the Arctic Sea, then escaped and returned, battered by the ice, to Spitsbergen. A coastal map of northwest Spitsbergen, but nothing else, came out of this first attempt.

The voyage of the second squadron, under the stocky, redheaded Commander John Ross, who had a very remarkable young naval officer, Lieutenant William Edward Parry, as his second-in-command, ended inexplicably. Ross's ships, the *Alexander* and the *Isabella,* sailing up Davis Strait, restored to the map the discoveries of the great Elizabethan seaman, Baffin: Baffin Bay, and Smith, Jones, and Lancaster Sounds, which Baffin had named after his supporters in the City of London. But after arriving on August 30, 1819, off Baffin's Lancaster Sound, the most likely of the three to

150

JOHN ROSS' EXPEDITION

lead to a Northwest Passage, Ross sailed westward for a day, then stopped. Ahead of him, he insisted, he "distinctly saw land round the bottom of the bay forming a chain of mountains connected with those which extended along the north and south side." So convinced was he of their existence that he named them after a Secretary of the Admiralty, the "Croker Mountains." To Parry and his fellow officers, however, the "Croker Mountains" seemed no more than a fantastic optical illusion. They could see nothing. The sea ahead was clear. They felt certain that they were on the very verge of a great discovery. When Ross, therefore, insisted on turning back, he seemed to have made an incomprehensible and most lamentable decision.

Amusing and malicious stories about Ross and his mythical Croker Mountains were soon going around in London. Some found it impossible to doubt the word of so capable

151

and trustworthy an officer. But there were many who hinted slyly that the Croker Mountains were a happy excuse to retreat to safer waters. So damaging was this gossip not only to Ross but to the Navy that the Admiralty decided to dispatch another expedition, one that was to be undertaken by William Edward Parry.

The most illustrious name among the many which dis-

THE TERROR

tinquish those years is that of William Edward Parry. He was famed not only for his geographical discoveries and for his contribution to our knowledge of the northwestern parts of Canada, but also for the excellent organization of his voyages. Before his day it had happened all too often that whole ships' companies were lost as a result of bad food and conditions. Parry realized that if men were to winter in the Arctic, their spirits must be kept up. They must lead a regular life. And they must enjoy a varied diet which should include fresh meat. His winter camps became patterns for all who came after him. Not only did he have cleanliness parades and medical inspections. He also cheered his men by bringing out a newspaper at regular intervals. He even let them produce and act a play which he himself had written, *The North-West Passage,* or *The End of the Voyage.* And what was at least equally important, he taught posterity that crews need not be confined to the narrow quarters on board while their vessel is icebound.

As soon as light permitted, he sent out spring reconnaissance parties in all directions. His little two-wheeled cart, on which his men could stow provisions and equipment to last them for some time, was the forerunner of the sledge, and his journeys with it were the first of the sledge journeys of today.

Parry's voyages took place in the 1820's and were not confined to the Northwest Passage. He visited Spitsbergen too, and with his sledges reached latitude 82° 45' N.

The next most distinguished British explorer is John Franklin. It was in 1845 that the British Admiralty resolved to make a really big effort to win for England the honor of discovering this route. Two ships, the *Terror* and the *Erebus* with a crew of a hundred and thirty-four, were fitted out, and sixty-year-old Sir John Franklin was chosen as leader. The octogenarian Sir John Barrow, who had sent out so many other marine expeditions, was also a moving spirit in this enterprise.

The ships left England on May 10th, and on July 26th

they were hailed by a whaler off Lancaster Sound in Baffin Bay. From that moment no more was heard of them, and at the end of two years such anxiety was felt that rescue expeditions were started.

The following years are characterized by the number of these expeditions. Several attempts were made to send vessels by the same route which Franklin had followed. Search parties made their way up the Canadian rivers, while ships were fitted out and sent through the Bering Strait. In the course of the next twelve years thirty-nine ships and six land expeditions were dispatched. To follow the histories of these different excursions, by which the fate of the Franklin expedition was gradually disclosed, is a study in itself.

It was not until the MacClintock expedition of 1858 and the American Lieutenant Schwatka's voyage in 1879 that it became at all possible to reconstruct the miserable fate which had overtaken Franklin and his men. It was then known that having been icebound for three years in the northern straits, Franklin decided to abandon his ships and lead his men southward along the Great Fish River to the Hudson's Bay Company's stations in northern Canada. The history of this tragic journey, which not one of the hundred and thirty-four men survived, Lieutenant Schwatka was at last able to trace.

Nevertheless, the Franklin expedition, whose history is a source of thrilling tales and a record of tragic incident and brilliant achievement, led to the charting of the great Canadian archipelago and to the discovery of the Northwest Passage.

To sail northward around the American Continent to the miraculous lands of the East was not the rapid matter

RELICS OF THE FRANKLIN EXPEDITION

156

that medieval traders had imagined. On the contrary, the voyage was made in the opposite direction, after years of suffering and hardship.

In the early spring of 1850, Sir Robert MacClure sailed around Cape Horn and right up through the Bering Strait. Continuing eastward along the northern coast of America, he came upon straits which led farther in the same direction. Here he was compelled to winter; nevertheless, in the autumn of the same year he reached with his sledges those sounds which hitherto had been approached from the east alone. He now knew that the Northwest Passage had been found, but it was only after a stay of several years in these parts that he made contact with expeditions from the other side, and not until 1854 did he return to England.

III. The Race for the Pole

14. *Nordenskjöld and the* Vega *Triumph*

THE NEW AND important factor in the expeditions of the latter half of the nineteenth century was the leading part which came to be played in them by the scientists. Observations of scientific interest had of course been made before: it is for instance largely to the ships' surgeons of the Franklin expedition that we owed our knowledge of the conditions and inhabitants of the polar countries. But it was now understood that side by side with geographical research a scientific investigation of these lands should be carried out, with that of their animals and plants, their geology and their climate. It was also realized that this research could be best engaged upon from winter base camps ashore.

This new type of exploration had its first beginnings in the region separating the islands of Greenland from those of Canada; it was here that the great Smith Sound expeditions were made, under the leadership of such men as Kane (1853), Hayes (1860), Hall (1871), and Nares (1875). One of the chief questions occupying the scientific minds at the time was that of the "Open Polar Sea." It was be-

158

THE VEGA

lieved that, thanks to the Gulf Stream, there must be a navigable channel around the North Pole, so that, if only the intervening belt of ice could be penetrated, there would be no difficulty in sailing directly to the North Pole. It was this theory which led to the forming of the Smith Sound expeditions; many years passed before it was dropped, and many men wore themselves out in the attempt to reach the promised water beyond the ice barrier. Nevertheless, observations made by the members of these expditions were most valuable, both in the information about climatic conditions which was gained, and in the field of natural science.

But it is above all the Swedish expeditions which we have to thank for the great scientific knowledge won from the Arctic toward the close of the nineteenth century. These expeditions concentrated chiefly on Spitsbergen, and were begun by Otto Torell, but the most prominent name of all is that of Nils Adolf Erik Nordenskjöld. From 1858 onward he accompanied the Spitsbergen expeditions, and soon took over their leadership. He realized the importance of taking with him scientists of all kinds. It is to him that we owe the first thorough survey of Spitsbergen. He made the first accurate meteorological observations from pack ice, and it was his scientists who gave us a thorough knowledge of Arctic creatures and plants, of geological conditions and many other things. The peak of his brilliant series of successful expeditions was the *Vega* voyage in 1878–80, on which not only was the Northeast Passage navigated for the first time, but also a wide knowledge was gained of the northern coast of Siberia.

Since Nordenskjöld's time it has been an almost invariable rule for scientists to accompany Arctic expeditions, or indeed that these should be carried out expressly for the purpose of solving some scientific problem. European scien-

DR. KANE AND PARTY

tists began to take a greater interest in Arctic questions. Thus in 1881 we had the first International Polar Year, in which a number of countries sent expeditions to the Arctic, in order to obtain correlated, simultaneous meteorological observations from all the regions around the Pole. Of these Polar Year expeditions the one led by the American Greely to Smith Sound is the best known, because of its disastrous ending. Owing to bad ice conditions the relief expeditions arrived too late, and only a handful of men were saved, after appalling sufferings. Greely's account is perhaps the most tragic document in nineteenth-century polar history.

161

It would take too long to relate more of the enterprises of this period. A single name stands out, because it is that of a man in whom were combined the best qualities of an Arctic explorer: a keen scientific brain, a great gift for organization, and a steadfast and heroic strength of character. This is Fridtjof Nansen, to do justice to whom would take not just a chapter but many, many books. To Nansen and to the great explorations preceding and following his own we must now turn our attention.

15. *The Disaster of the* Jeannette

THE STORY of exploration at the top of the world is more than an account of various dashes northward, ending with Robert Edwin Peary's attainment of the Pole itself. Ever since Willem Barents sailed into the Arctic, brave men and, it must be admitted, foolish men too, added to our knowledge about the northern ocean and its lands of ice and snow. Their contributions made the full story of exploration. Each link is essential to the chain. For the full story is one of science as well as adventure.

All the men who lived in Greenland from the very beginning were grateful beyond measure for the driftwood which wind and tide and currents deposited on the shores of that treeless country. Where it came from was no concern of theirs; they were too busy using it to speculate about it. Only later did scientists begin to think about the route it must have taken, about how it got there from Siberia. Then one of the most tragic events in Arctic history prepared the way for an expedition that was to give an entirely new concept to many phenomena of the Far North.

The tragedy began when a young American naval officer, Lieutenant Commander George Washington DeLong, interested James Gordon Bennett of the New York *Herald* in an idea he had for reaching the North Pole. Bennett, who had sent the famous traveler Stanley to find Dr. Livingstone in Africa, was not the man to count expenses if a sensational story for his paper was in the making. He promised to finance DeLong's voyage.

DeLong was full of enthusiasm but not sufficiently care-

THE JEANNETTE

ful in selecting his ship or his crew, although he had some very good men. The three-masted bark *Jeannette,* fitted with an auxiliary steam engine, had come around the Horn into the Pacific. At Mare Island, California, where she was examined, naval contractors and engineers said De-Long was deceived in her, that she would never do for such a trip as he proposed. But Bennett persuaded the government to approve her.

At St. Michael, Alaska, DeLong engaged two Indians, Alexey and Anequin, as hunters and dog drivers, although why he preferred Indians to Eskimos, who are more experienced in this work in the Far North, is not known. There was a great store of provisions and equipment taken aboard, but too little coal.

They did not get very far past Bering Strait when on September 6, 1879, the ship froze fast in the ice east of Wrangel Island. They did not worry, however, for they

164

had found a new island which they named Herald for the newspaper. But when summer came again, they got almost no nearer their goal.

December 1880 found them again in the grip of ice with the temperature at 50 degrees below zero. January brought gales along with the bitter cold; by the end of the month the ice with the ship in it had drifted to 74° 41′ North and 173° 10′ East, north of Siberia. This was no record. In Greenland explorers had been up to 83° North, but De-Long made a number of observations and was satisfied, for he still expected to get out of the ice.

In the summer of 1881, DeLong decided not to use his engine because of the shortage of coal, which would be needed during the coming winter. He relied on sails, but even in June the pressure of the ice grew worse and worse.

The men urged DeLong to leave her and try for shore in the boats, but he refused. Ice actually pierced the hull, but when DeLong went below to look, the pressure eased and the openings in the ship's timbers closed. The ship was heeled over at 23 degrees, but DeLong simply ordered Chief Engineer Melville to photograph her, as it would make a sensational picture for the *Herald*. But that night as they ate, they could hear the ship shrieking and moaning as the ice squeezed her timbers. All that night they watched and when the ice came through the sides, they knew the *Jeannette* was lost.

The crew unloaded boats, sledges, pemmican, supplies of all kinds in a haphazard way. Incredibly, no orderly preparations had been made for abandoning ship, and at the last no one could find the casks of lime juice, chief guard against scurvy in those days, although one sailor even dived into the icy water of the forehold.

165

Thirty-three men gathered around the pile of equipment on the ice. One was too sick to stand, one had been half-blinded some days before in an explosion, and several were suffering from cramps. They had three boats weighing four tons, and three and a half tons of food and supplies. The Lena Delta, nearest mainland point, was 500 miles away, and the temperature ranged from 10 to 25 degrees below zero.

From this moment, DeLong showed himself a different man with a firmness new to his men. For four days they camped on the ice, sorting supplies and nursing the sick. DeLong ordered the three boats with provisions for sixty days loaded on sledges. He firmly forbade the carrying of nonessentials although the men grumbled at leaving their extra clothing. Only the ship's papers and scientific records were added to the load beyond what was essential to life.

On June 17, 1881, as they were about to eat supper, one of the men shouted that they had better look out of their tents if they wanted to see the last of the *Jeannette*. The ship had been crushed by the ice until it did not look like a ship any more, and now the ice seemed to be content. It opened suddenly, and the remains of the vessel sank within a few minutes.

Next morning they began their terrible journey over the ice. Even after stripping the load still more, they made only five and a half miles in eight days, and when DeLong took his bearings he found that the drifting ice had put them twenty-five miles farther north than where they started! He did not tell the men. Soon the drift turned south and by July 28th they had covered 180 miles, and saw land which they named Bennett Island. At Kitelni Island, the largest of the New Siberian group, they wasted time looking for provisions around the long-deserted hut of fossil-ivory hun-

ters. At last they could launch the boats. DeLong commanded in one, Melville in another, and the second mate, Cripp, in the third.

They had not gone far when a gale blew up, and suddenly the second mate's boat failed to top a wave. There was nothing the others could do and soon, on September 12th, they were parted, ninety-two days after the loss of the *Jeannette*. Melville reached the mainland four days later, met some natives, and was saved. DeLong and the eleven men with him did not make it; their bodies were found the following March with the commander's diary beside him. The last entry read: "October 30th, Sunday, 140th day, Boyd and Goertz died during the night, Mr. Collins dying." DeLong could not have survived long after that. He had proved himself a brave man who paid for his errors with his life. More than that, he had provided the impulse for the systematic Arctic exploration of modern times.

16. *Nansen*: *King of the North*

THE INITIAL quiver of this impulse came in 1884, three years after DeLong died, when an Eskimo seal hunter from Frederikshaab in West Greenland, out in his kayak, saw a confused mass of objects spread out over an ice floe. He helped himself to some, which he showed to the manager of the colony. Later the ice floe was located again, and was found to be bearing supplies from the DeLong expedition. They had drifted across the top of the world, and for one daring explorer this was the challenge to solve a riddle of the North.

The man who saw in the *Jeannette* tragedy a key to Arctic mysteries was Fridtjof Nansen. The year DeLong was dying in Siberia, Nansen was twenty years old and had left his studies at the University of Christiania for a voyage on a sealer, the *Viking*, off the east coast of Greenland. That spring of 1881, he gathered specimens of animals and collected scientific data on them, at the same time envisaging what later was his first triumph—a trip across the Greenland icecap.

What sort of person was this twenty-year-old student who was convinced he could conquer where the greatest adventurers and explorers before him had failed? The tall, fair-haired Norwegian, whom Admiral McClintoch called "a true Viking," excelled in daring, in endurance, and in intellectual stature—intellectually, Nansen is without question supreme among all Arctic explorers. He was by training and by inclination a scientist—a zoologist who turned later to oceanography, mathematics, astronomy, and much else. Nansen remained a scientist all his life, even when burdened in later years with grave national and international responsibilities. He was also in a very special sense an adventurer, loving exploration not only for its excitements, or for the satisfaction of physical achievements, but also because he was convinced (with Ibsen whom he so grealty admired) that the key to man's destiny lay in the study of personality and in the development of individual character—in the silence and solitude of the wilds, alone with nature. There was no doubt an element of escapism in this mind-searching Nordic approach, and indeed escape was a necessity for Nansen. Science alone was not enough; it was too cold, he said. But in the Arctic, Nansen wrote, "I found the great adventure of the ice, deep and pure as infinity, the silent, starry night, the depths of Nature herself, the fullness of the mystery of life, the eternal round of the universe and its eternal death." Only in the Arctic could Nansen find relief from the dark and somber imaginings, the doubts and fears with which in the restless, turbulent civilized world he was so constantly afflicted.

After completing his scientific studies at the university, Nansen was able to prepare for this trip. A sportsman as well as a scientist, he proposed to make the youth of the world conscious of the exciting possibilities of skiing—up to then exclusively a Norwegian device for moving across the soft snow. In 1888, he used skis for the first crossing of the icecap, and proved to be right about the boost it would give to skiing all over the world, so much so that it is now, of course, a great international sport.

When Nansen returned, he had ready a plan for a polar expedition which he laid before the Geographical Society. Although it was strongly criticized, the Norwegian

Government agreed to pay one-third of his expenses, if the rest was obtained by private subscription.

Nansen's plan was to seek what DeLong had fought against: *getting trapped in the ice.* The Norwegian proposed to enter the floes at a point where the winds and currents would drift the ship across the top of the world from one side to the other. He expected to pass right over the Pole or very close to it.

For his purpose, he needed a ship such as never had been built before—one that would ride with the ice instead of being crushed by it. He and Colin Archer, a Norwegian shipbuilder who must share the honor of the expedition's achievement, designed and built a vessel of great strength, pointed at both bow and stern and with sloping sides so angled (after figuring and refiguring many times) that ice pressure would lift the vessel out of the water instead of cracking the hull. This ship was named *Fram,* which means "forward."

With Otto Sverdrup, a great explorer in his own right, also on board, the *Fram* left Christiania (now Oslo) on June 24th, 1893. On September 22nd, Nansen made fast to an ice floe at 78° 50′ North and 133° 37′ East, not far from Bennett Island, the same pack ice which had crushed the *Jeannette.*

Now came the test of the *Fram's* ability to withstand the deadly thrusts of the ice. The rudder was hauled up, the engine taken apart and oiled for its long rest. When ice pressure on the ship began, everyone rushed up on deck to see how the *Fram* would take it. Slowly the ship was lifted up, just as her designers had intended. Soon the crew grew so indifferent to the deafening noise of the ice pressure that they did not even get up to look at what was happening, no matter how loud it thundered!

As Nansen had calculated, the *Fram* now started drifting northwest, although she was fixed in the ice with her bow pointing south. Because his expedition was so well prepared, there were none of the usual exciting but tragic stories to tell of it. They just drifted, and after nearly a year and a half she was at 84° North, 101° 55′ East.

This was not fast enough to suit Nansen. By now also he knew that the *Fram* would not drift across the Pole. He realized that he should have entered the ice pack farther east for that, he said later. So he decided to leave the ship and make a dash for the Pole with one companion, Hjalmar Johansen. On April 14, 1895, they got to 86° 14′ North, the highest latitude yet reached by man, and then came home by way of sledge to Franz Joseph Land where they found a ship.

Meanwhile, Sverdrup was bringing the *Fram* safe home and reached Norway only a week later than Nansen. They had drifted as far north as 85° 57′, then west to Spitsbergen and then southward. Sverdrup knew it was no use to stay longer in the ice because the drift from here was too well known. So in June 1896, the engine was reassembled and Sverdrup, an old ice navigator, jockeyed the ship free over a course of 180 miles, and in August the *Fram* passed the last of the floes after being fast in the ice for thirty-five months.

Her voyage stands out as one of the most important contributions to oceanography. Six huge folio volumes on the results were published, and Nansen was hailed as the first man in his line. He had been outstanding in everything he did, and when the Nobel Peace Prize was added to his many honors for scientific achievement, the whole world could see that the hero of the *Fram* was a man of many parts—all of them great.

172

The *Fram* expedition was by no means only a great Arctic journey, created by the vision and genius of an exceptional man. Its scientic work, consisting of long and continuous observations in the highest northern latitudes, mainly in oceanography and meteorology, proved of fundamental importance for polar science, and indeed provided the basis for all future Arctic work. In this respect and in the new attention Nansen paid to scientific principles in such matters as diet and nutrition, the *Fram* expedition raised to a new level standards of polar exploration.

Nansen's subsequent career in political and diplomatic life, as the protagonist of Norwegian independence, as the League of Nations Commissioner after the First World War who organized the repatriation of prisoners and the relief of famine, is outside the scope of this book. In all these diverse activities he showed those same gifts of imagination and vision which he displayed in the realm of scientific exploration. And he had the greatest rewards he himself could have desired, not in the acclaim that greeted him wherever he went or in the numerous prizes he received from all over the world, but in the vision of what he had added to human knowledge, human freedom, and human happiness.

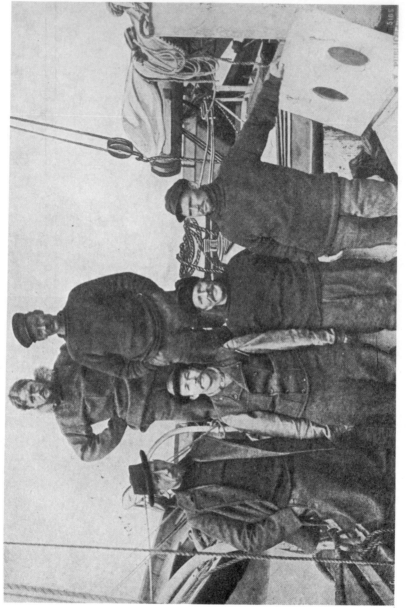

Back row: Godfred Hansen. Anton Lund.
Front row: Roald Amundsen. Peter Ristvedt. Adolf Lindström.
Helmer Hansen.

17. *Amundsen's Fourfold Victory*

THE FACT that Nansen had not reached the Pole, however, left an opportunity for another Norwegian, Roald Amundsen, who already had made a name for himself and was to become the only man to reach all four major goals of the aspiring explorer—North Pole, South Pole, Northwest Passage, and Northeast Passage.

Roald was born July 16, 1872, on a tiny Norwegian farm. His mother, who wanted him to become a doctor, died shortly after Roald entered the university, and he himself told me that she was spared a bitter disappointment, because he would have become an explorer in any case. Nothing could have stopped him.

First he had to go through his compulsory military service, which he enjoyed because it hardened him for his later work. Then in 1894, he signed on as a deck hand on a sailing ship to get experience. While the rest of the crew idled away the time between watches, he studied about the sea and navigation and made a nuisance of himself asking questions of the officers.

After three years at sea he was able to make his examination for ship's officer, and at twenty-five he became first mate on the Belgian Antarctic exploration ship *Belgica* under Captain Franz de Gerlache, a fine man but unfortunately more of a scientist than a sailor. The expedition spent a month at Tierra del Fuego studying marine and land life and mapping the rugged coast. Then they sailed south, and it was here that the captain's shortcomings were felt. At one point, Roald knew they should be heading north out of the ice and forgot himself when Gerlache kept the course south.

"It's a mistake, sir," he cried. "We'll be smashed to pieces."

Gerlache told him to mind his place and go aft. But the mate was right, and the ship froze fast. The captain lost his head and his health, and Roald and the ship's doctor really took over and managed the expedition for the thirteen months their ship was frozen tight. The doctor was Frederick A. Cook, whose future was to be altogether miserable but who was an able traveler and a man of courage.

In later life, Amundsen used to laugh and tell funny stories about this expedition, but at the time it was not so easy. The expedition had not been fitted out for an Antarctic winter, for example, so there was not sufficient clothing for all the men on deck at one time. Amundsen got out his needles and sewed garments for the crew out of extra red blankets. The men were very conspicuous but they were warm. Roald also proved his theory that fresh meat would prevent scurvy—he had them all eat seal, and sick men recovered.

In the end, he and Dr. Cook finally got the *Belgica* out, and Gerlache slapped Amundsen on the back in the presence of all the men and said: "You did a fine job, my boy. I shall recommend you." Back home, Roald set himself to study with several scientists to whom he was recommended by Nansen. What he wanted to do was find the Northwest Passage, which had cost so many lives and taken the best years of many daring men. So while he studied, he worked at odd jobs and saved as much money as he could until he found a little old ship, the *Gjoa,* which he thought capable of the voyage.

Nobody else agreed. The *Gjoa,* forty-seven tons, had been a fishing boat in North America for twenty-seven years. But Roald was happy that his ship was the same age as himself. He washed it and scraped it and worked on it himself for two years, supporting himself part of the time as waiter in a waterfront restaurant. He gathered friends as enthusiastic as himself, willing to toil at getting the ship ready after a day's normal work. They took short cruises to familiarize themselves with their vessel. But financial backing they could not get. In June 1902, his creditors, who had been hounding him for some time, served him with a bailiff's bill, which seemed to mean that he would lose his ship and stores.

But Roald would not give up. He went to some dealers he still had not done business with and got some provisions and gear on credit, then got his crew of seven men together, and in a frightful rainstorm, when even the harbor master's men were not out, they slipped away to sea without saying good-by to anybody.

Amundsen proved on the way across the Atlantic that his ship could take gales and waves. Then he reprovisioned, before he set out to negotiate the Northwest Passage. He thought that other ships had been too deep in the water to find it. The little *Gjoa,* just seventy feet long, drew little more than six feet. Even so, he was grounded once but got off, and in King William Land found good winter quarters. Here he stayed for two years, because he had in mind to locate the magnetic pole, too, which he did after a long sledge trip. (In 1953, when new observations were taken with instruments much superior to anything he had had, the magnetic pole was found to be not far from the place he had put it.) In his long stay, too, he made collections of plants and animals and studied Eskimo life. At last, in August 1905, he started the *Gjoa* on her voyage again, and although there were several points in Simpson Strait where there was only an inch of water under the keel, he saw open water ahead on August 26th. He returned to Norway with cash enough to pay his creditors, but many of them refused to accept it because they were honored to have had a share in so great an achievement.

Amundsen had no trouble getting financial backing now, and he set about preparing an expedition to the North Pole when suddenly a telegram announced that his old friend Cook had reached the Pole. Roald was disappointed for himself but glad for his friend, but then another telegram gave credit for that exploit to Robert Peary, who also denounced Dr. Cook as a fraud. The actual conquest of the Pole was, of course, achieved by Peary on sledge and not by ship.

18. *The Doomed Flight of the* Eagle

ONE OF THE most venturesome of all attempts at polar exploration was that of a Swedish technologist, Salomon Andrée. Andrée, a zealous social reformer, a man who saw in technology the only means whereby the new discoveries of science could be properly applied for the betterment of mankind, was a typical product of the liberal tendencies which accompanied the remarkable industrial and techno-

SALOMON ANDRÉE

logical advance of Sweden in the later nineteenth century. His balloon, the *Eagle,* the instrument by means of which the mysteries of the polar basin were to be revealed by methods less arduous than sledging journeys or the slow process of an Arctic drift, was an elegant affair, manufactured by M. Lachambre of Paris. Its envelope was a double Chinese silk. The car was of wickerwork and Chinese cane. And it was equipped by Andrée with draglines and a steering sail, inventions which he was convinced would make it "steerable to a high degree," even as far as the Pole.

The base for the ascent was Spitsbergen. After an abortive attempt in August 1896 (when Andrée and his companions, Knuth Fraekel and Nils Strindberg, were the first to greet the *Fram* after her drift across the Pole) the journey started in the summer of 1897 in circumstances far from auspicious for this first polar flight. "My comrades," wrote Andrée in his diary, "insist on steering, and as I have no fully valid reasons against it, I shall agree to it, although with some reluctance." The balloon rose, then fell again, then floated northeastward across Virgo harbor, the trailing draglines furrowing the water. Halfway across the harbor, in full view of a crowd of tense spectators, the *Eagle* began to sink and its car to skim the surface of the water. Then as ballast was hurriedly thrown overboard, it bounded up like a great ball, leaving two-thirds of the draglines, an essential element in Andrée's vaunted steering mechanism, lying along the beach. They had now lost all power of retarding the balloon in relation to the wind. The steering sail set above the carrying ring had no longer any power of steerage! Thus freed from all contact with the earth the *Eagle* soared a thousand, two thousand feet, floating high above the edge of the ice pack, so high that the men in the car felt the heat of the sun. The air was still; only a melancholy whistling

ANDRÉE AND THE EAGLE

from a balloon valve broke the silence. As he watched the dark shape of a bird, perhaps a fulmar, gliding serenely on their starboard bow, Andrée reflected, "It is not a little strange to be floating here above the polar sea. To be the first to have floated here in a balloon. How soon, I wonder, shall we see successors? Shall we be thought mad or will our example be followed? I cannot deny but that all three of us are dominated by a feeling of pride. We think that we can well face death, having done what we have done. . . ."

In ten hours the *Eagle* traveled four hundred kilometers toward the northeast. Then loss of gas and cooling by cloud brought them down. The wind failed and the *Eagle* came to rest for an hour or two, then the wind rose again from the east and they traveled westward into an icy fog and threw out knives, ropes, an anchor, scientific instruments, anything to gain height. Even so, the *Eagle*'s car began to hit the ice, and continued bumping, rising, falling, bumping, so incessantly that they could get no rest and were were forced to descend and anchor to an ice floe for twelve hours or so. Then they were off again. But almost immediately the sun vanished into the clouds, ice began to coat the envelope, and a fine drizzle froze on the ropes. On this stage of the journey, in twenty-one hours they made five hundred miles but were only two hundred miles northnortheast from their last starting point. On July 14th, though they were sailing high at the time, Andrée for some unknown reason brought the balloon down and anchored to the ice. It was the last flight of the *Eagle*.

Then began the long march over the sea ice by three men who were probably less well equipped to counter the ferocious advance of an Arctic winter than any in polar history. They had three choices of destination: Cape Flora on Franz Josef Land where Frederick Jackson of the

Jackson-Harmsworth Expedition had left supplies; the Seven Islands off Nordaustland; or Mosselbukta. They chose the first though it was twice as far away and spent twelve days marching to the southeast, making little headway against the contrary drift of the ice of which Andrée seems to have had little knowledge. Andrée then turned toward the Seven Islands. But still the drift was against him. Eventually, after journeying at an average speed of three miles a day, they reached White Island utterly exhausted. It was then September 17th and White Island was the first land they had seen since July 11th. "Our provisions," wrote Andrée in his diary, "must soon and richly be supplemented, if we are to have any prospect of being able to hold out for a time." By the middle of October all three men had died and thirty-three years later their remains, their logs, their journals, Strindberg's daily shorthand letters to his fiancée, and a number of rolls of film subsequently developed with great skill by Swedish experts were found by a Norwegian sealer.

In Sweden the news of the fate of Andrée and his companions assumed the proportions of a national tragedy, heightened as it was by the appearance in the printed films of the three men who had been the victims of this Arctic tragedy over thirty years before. Though courageous, this first attempt to fly to the Pole was a premature and ill-planned adventure. "Many people," Nansen had told the Royal Geographical Society in 1892, "think that the North Pole can be reached by balloons or balloon ships, and that it will be so reached one day. I do not deny the possibility of this; on the contrary I regard it as very probable. . . ." Nordenskjöld, who had been contemplating the use of captive balloons (a very different proposition) to reconnoiter above the pack ice of the Arctic, went further and declared of Andrée's project, "It has been a long time since I embraced a proposal for a polar expedition with such enthusiasm." This lavish expression of confidence by so experienced an Arctic explorer is astonishing. Andrée admittedly had been experimenting with balloon navigation ever since his first meeting with the American balloonist Wise in 1876 when he discussed the possibilities of using the trade winds for long ballooning journeys. But his earlier flights, though numerous, had been brief. His steering equipment was rudimentary; its principles falsely based. His calculations of speed and course, on the evidence of his diaries, were wildly unreliable. His lack of precautions too against a forced landing, expecially as regards clothing, contrast inexplicably with his forebodings at the start of the *Eagle*'s journey. Nevertheless in this first use of flight, in the stress moreover which Andrée laid on the future importance of air photography and mapping from the air—these ranked high among the motives of his expedition—the voyage of the *Eagle* has its place in polar history. Ill-fated though it was, it foreshadowed the birth in the twentieth century of the Air Age in polar exploration.

19. *Peary and the Arctic Obsession*

DURING THE ten-year periods on each side of the century's turn, the eyes of the public throughout the world were focused on the race for the Arctic and Antarctic poles. The scientists might continue to say that the geographical poles were no more than mathematical points in space, that their attainment could add little or nothing to human knowledge. To the public, however, the prospect of these heroic and intensely personal endeavors was most exhilarating.

During the 1890's millions had been educated to the popular magazine's concept of supermen at work in world exploration. Far from diminishing, this trend only accelerated in the succeeding decade which saw the beginning of what has often been called the Heroic Age of polar exploration—with the telegram, the wireless, and other new means of national and international publicity ready to shout about every new achievement, making the names of the participants household words.

Of the men who were to enjoy this new and widespread notoriety—Scott and Shackleton, Peary and Amundsen—none was more obsessed by his ambition to conquer, as he expressed it, "the last great geographical prize" than the American Arctic explorer Robert E. Peary. From 1886 when he made the first of many expeditions to Greenland, he had been preparing himself daily and perfecting his techniques and equipment with this single end in view. Rarely does one see a more single-minded man. In January 1897, on the eve of his *Windward* expedition of 1898–1902, he openly avowed that his plan had "for its main purpose the attainment of the North Pole." Not that Peary had

ROBERT E. PEARY

FORT CONGER

any interest in scientific work. He was an engineer, a technologist, a military planner concerned with the strategy, tactics, and logistics of a polar campaign. However illuminating Nansen's geographical discoveries and scientific data may have been, all that mattered to Peary was that Nansen had failed to reach the Pole. He was going to do better!

The main achievement of Peary's first year of work was the establishment of an advanced base at Fort Conger at the northeast corner of Ellesmere Island. Traveling according to plan through the darkness and cold of winter when

187

the ice was hardest, Peary reached Fort Conger by January 1899. By the autumn of that year fourteen tons of supplies had been deposited between Fort Conger and his ship, the *Windward*. In the spring of 1900 still more supplies were brought up until the base was fully stocked for his big attempt on the Pole.

His first and main problem was the choice of a route. Fort Conger had one great advantage, that of flexibility, for from it there was the choice of several different routes to the Pole. Of all the possibilities, however, he decided to explore the unknown coast of northern Greenland. Once he had identified it with his own name (Peary Land), he would turn northward toward the Pole.

This expedition was, even by Peary's rigorous standards, difficult going, in fog and over wavelike drifts of snow, and through impossible darkness. So he was soon forced to turn back. The attempt on the Pole had been a failure. There was, however, some compensation for Peary's supporters in the discovery of one hundred and fifty miles of new Greenland coast, and in his justifiable claim that he had "determined the northern limit of the Greenland archipelago or land group, and had practically connected the coast southward to Independence Bay."

Meanwhile, far to the east in Franz Josef Land new competitors for polar honors appeared in an Italian expedition led by Prince Luigi Amadeo of Savoy, the Duke of Abruzzi, the distinguished Himalayan explorer and mountaineer. Inspired by Nansen's attempt to reach the Pole across the ice of the Arctic Basin, the Italians arrived in Franz Josef Land in 1899 in a Norwegian sealer, the *Stella Polare*. In the following year, Abruzzi was incapacitated by frostbite and the leadership of the polar assault party fell to Lieutenant Cagni of the Italian Navy, who set off with

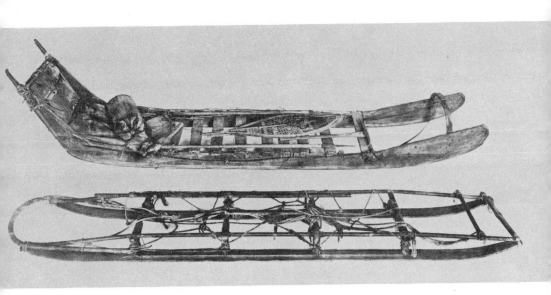

THE SLEDGES OF PEARY AND AMUNDSEN

two supporting parties. One of these parties never returned. But Cagni and his men surpassed Nansen's "farthest north" by twenty-two miles and reached within 220 miles of the Pole. It was a gallant attempt magnificiently led and the Italians were exultant. "We have conquered! We have surpassed the greatest explorer of the century." Their leader nevertheless concluded that this route to the Pole offered little prospect of success. The best hope, he thought, lay in a route northward off Kennedy Channel and Ellesmere Island.

This was the exact conclusion to which Peary himself had come. He had already discarded the Greenland route because of "the comparatively rapid motion of the ice as it swung around the northern coast into the southerly setting East Greenland current." So in the spring of 1902 Peary switched his starting point to Grant Land. In March he left Fort Conger, distant from the Pole by about 450

189

miles in a straight line, and attempted to pass from Cape Hecla by sledge on April 6th. But once again he was defeated.

In places the snow overlying the pack was so soft that "the dogs wallowed belly-deep." Peary and his men were constantly forced to double in their tracks or to make long and exhausting detours to find more tightly packed ground. In mid-April after a blizzard had set the pack ice moving, two wide channels—one he called "The Grand Canal"—opened across their path and forced them far off course. In such conditions, advancing at a rate of no more than six miles a day, Peary reached to latitude 84° 17′ N. on April 21, 1902. Here was another failure and one which Peary took to heart. He suffered intensely at the thought of it. Like the earlier Greenland venture, however, it was not wholly unprofitable, for he had been able to establish a number of advance depots along this new route ready for another attempt and he had learned one invaluable lesson. This was that even here, far to the west of the East Greenland current, the prevailing drift of the ice was from west to east.

To offset this a northwest course would have to be set. He learned another lesson too that was to be most valuable later on—that a rapid return which would leave little time for sleep or camping was vital if he hoped to follow the line of his outward tracks.

"I recognized," Peary wrote, "that the entire pack was moving slowly, and that our trail was everywhere faulted and interrupted by new pressure ridges and leads, in a way to make our return nearly, if not quite, as slow and laborious as our outward one."

There were some improvements that he saw could be made in equipment and in the logistics and tactics of the assault. Sledges must be lighter to ride easily over the soft

190

ice, and wider to bridge channels and water leads. A ship must be found that would penetrate through Smith Sound to the very edge of the polar sea, saving the long journey to the advance base. And, finally, a pioneer party was needed to push ahead and take the burden of breaking the trail. Through them the final assault party would pass. In this way the energies of men and dogs would be conserved for the last lap of the race. These were all lessons which he hoped to put to good use on his next and, as he prayed, his final expedition.

At the end of the *Windward* expedition in 1902, Peary returned to work in the naval dockyards. He had failed but nevertheless he was not too old to try again and he devoted

191

every minute he could spare to raising funds for a new expedition incorporating all those improvements in equipment, in tactics and techniques which his latest, most grueling and most bitter experience had taught him.

The pivot of his national campaign was a group of wealthy New Yorkers headed by Herbert L. Bridgman, who formed the Peary Arctic Club. By 1904, this group had raised one hundred thousand dollars for a new ship, the *Roosevelt*, specially designed and built to penetrate the ice off Smith Sound and to carry the expedition far up the coast of Ellesmere Island to save the long journey over the ice to the advance base. Outlining his plans to the Secretary of the Navy, Peary declared, "I should expect to accomplish the distance to the Pole and return in about a hundred days or a little more, an average travel of about ten miles a day. . . . This plan," he added, "is the result of some twelve years of travel in these latitudes."

Never did a man feel more confident of success.

In July 1905 Peary, now fifty, sailed from New York in the *Roosevelt* which, after some damage to her bows, reached Cape Columbia on the northeast coast of Grant Land within ninety miles of the advance base at Cape Hecla. The first party started off over the ice in February 1906 and the Peary system of Arctic tactics then took its classic form.

The backbone of his force were the Eskimos—men, women and even children—from whom Peary, like the earlier American explorers Hall and Schwatka, had learned in earlier days the basic techniques of Arctic travel and survival. They were employed to drive the dog teams, Peary having over a hundred dogs. They were employed to build igloos for use as staging camps along the route. The latter had great advantages, for they saved the erection of cumbrous tents and were warmer and much more windproof. The women, meanwhile, were employed to sew the seal and walrus clothing which Eskimos and white men both wore. There were five men in Peary's expedition and as always of recent years, his devoted servant and the most trusted of all his companions was Matthew Henson, the only Negro explorer in Arctic history.

The essence of the Peary system was the dispatch of small advance parties to blaze the trail and set up camps and depots along the route. These brought him within striking distance of the Pole, thereby saving the strength of the men and of the dogs reserved for the final dash. "To have a sufficient number of divisions, or relay parties, each under the leadership of a competent assistant; to send them at appropriate and carefully calculated stages along the outward journey . . . and to return by the same route . . . using the beaten trail and the already constructed igloos." These things, in Peary's own words, were the essentials of the explorer's system. Each of these parties would "knit together" the breaks in the trail created by any drift of the ice. Thus, if fortune favored them, they would keep it open for the assault party on its return from the Pole.

After so many years of concentrated effort, after so much careful thought and meticulous preparation, it seemed only right that this time Peary should succeed. But once again he had no luck. Not only the surface and drift of the ice but the weather was against him, and with a record low temperature his speed was reduced to half his original estimate. At this rate there was no hope whatever that his provisions would last his journey to the Pole.

Some record, however, had to be achieved not only to redeem his own name and reputation but to encourage his supporters of the Peary Arctic Club in New York. The Pole was clearly unattainable but he was only sixty miles behind Nansen's, eighty miles behind the Italian Cagni's farthest north. Discarding almost everything from his sledges and collecting together the least exhausted of his dogs, he plunged on, bending "every energy to setting a record pace." In a half gale and heavy drifts he persisted until Cagni's record of 1900 had been beaten. Now neither Nansen nor Cagni but Peary was "farthest north."

Peary returned safely, though as he admitted by the narrowest of margins, only to see that the *Roosevelt* had suffered such heavy damage from the ice in Smith Sound that she had to be reconditioned. Once again, however, the Peary Arctic Club came to the rescue and in July 1908 Peary sailed again on his last polar venture.

The party consisted of Bob Bartlett, the captain of the *Roosevelt,* Matthew Henson, Doctor Goodsell, and two young men, Borup and MacMillan. They called in at Etah in northwest Greenland (just north of the present United States Air Base at Thule) and collected fifty Eskimos and

LIEUTENANT PEARY IN COASTING OUTFIT

two hundred and fifty dogs. By the autumn the advance land base at Cape Columbia had been stocked. By February 1909 Peary was ready to move off again.

Peary never failed to learn from his previous failures and this time a course was set somewhat west of north to allow for the easterly drift. As a further precaution depots were left on the north Greenland coast so that in an emergency a return from the Pole could be made eastward, diagonally with the set of the ice. In case the drift was found to be unexpectedly reversed, depots were also left to the west of Cape Columbia. As it turned out, however, these precautions were unnecessary, for there was no strong westerly wind to reinforce the drift as there had been in 1906.

Throughout March they again had low temperatures and violent winds and were held up for days at a time waiting for the ice to close in over the broad black leads of water which they continually encountered. But they kept going, the advance parties bearing the brunt of the strain. By April 1st they had reached 87° 47′ N., the nearest that man had reached to the Pole. Four of the advance parties, each led by a white man, had already returned to the base with the weakest of the dogs harnessed to their sledges. Now, two hundred and eighty miles from the base and one hundred and thirty-three miles from the Pole, it was time for the last party to turn back. This was the party led by Bob Bartlett, the British captain of the *Roosevelt*. Peary trusted Bartlett as he trusted no one except Matthew Henson, the Negro, and he was anxious to show the gratitude he felt for Bartlett's extraordinary skill as a navigator. He chose Bartlett's party therefore as the last to leave, explaining afterward: "It seemed to me that, in view of the noble work of Great Britain in Arctic exploration, a British subject should, next to an American, be able to say that he had stood nearest to the Pole."

Peary and five men—four Eskimos and Matthew Henson, who was almost as skillful as they in the technique of swift Arctic travel— faced two great hazards as they set out on April 2nd on the last stage of the polar journey. A twenty-four-hour gale might spring up and open wide and impassable leads in the ice, dangerously delaying them. But more dangerous still was the imminent approach of the full moon and of the spring tides. These, Peary feared, might "stir the great ice fields around us into restlessness" and create a network of water leads across the path, some open, some perhaps thinly and deceptively coated with new ice whose strength would have to be gauged carefully if dogs and sledges were not to plunge into the deep, icy water below.

Nevertheless, as he climbed a great pressure ridge behind his igloo and looked toward the north he was swept by a sudden surge of excitement. "I felt," he wrote later, "the keenest exhilaration, and even exultation, as I climbed over the pressure ridge and breasted the keen air sweeping over the mighty ice, pure and straight from the Pole itself. . . . It was a fine marching morning, clear, and sunlit, with a temperature of minus 25°, and the wind of the past few days had subsided to a gentle breeze. The going was the best we had had since leaving land. The floes were large and old, hard and level, with patches of sapphire-blue ice (the pools of the preceding summer) . While the pressure ridges surrounding them were stupendous, some of them fifty feet high, they were not especially hard to negotiate, either through some gap or up the gradual slope of a huge drift of snow. The brilliant sunlight, the good going save for the pressure ridges, the consciousness that we were now well

196

started on the last lap of our journey, and the joy of again being in the lead, affected me like wine. The years seemed to drop from me, and I felt as I had felt in those fifteen years before when I headed my little party across the great icecap of Greenland. . . ."

In continuous daylight they traveled for ten hours at a stretch, racing at their fullest strength against the approach of the full moon. The ice appeared motionless. But they could hear the floes grinding and groaning on all sides as they neared the 89th parallel. It was not the bitter wind they feared, though it lashed their faces like a whip of steel, nor the pressure ridges which rose dark and massive in the distance. It was the water leads which were the greatest menace. "I was in constant dread," Peary confessed, "lest we encounter an impassable one toward the very end. With every successive march, my fear of such impassable leads had increased," and indeed at every ridge he hurried forward fearing to see from its summit a broad, black stretch of water barring their way to the Pole. Early in April clouds obscured the sun and left them to march on in a gray and colorless and melancholy light. But they were not depressed, for they were now near enough to be certain of success.

On April 6, 1909, Peary with Matthew Henson and four Eskimos reached the North Geographical Pole—"The Pole which was last the prize of three centuries. My dream and goal for twenty years." Five flags were planted the American flag, the Navy League flag, the Red Cross flag, and "World's Ensign of Liberty and Peace," and the colors of the Delta Kappa Epsilon fraternity at Bowdoin College of which Peary was an alumnus. In a crack in a nearby ice ridge Peary then placed a bottle containing a strip of his national flag and a brief record of the journey, due credit being given to Herbert L. Bridgman and the Peary Arctic

Club of New York City whose strenuous efforts had made possible the acquisition "of this geographical prize for the honor and prestige of the United States of America." In another document Peary claimed the entire region in the name of the President of the United States.

On April 7th Peary turned south toward Cape Columbia and there sixteen days later he composed his message to the world. "My lifework is accomplished. The thing which it was intended from the beginning that I should do, the thing which I believed could be done, and that I could do, I have done. I have have got the North Pole out of my system after twenty-three years of effort, hard work, disappointments, hardships, privations, more or less suffering, and some risks. I have won the last great geographical prize of the North Pole for the credit of the United States. This work is the finish, the cap and climax, of nearly four hundred years of effort, loss of life, and expenditure of fortunes by the civilized nations of the world, and it has been accomplished in a way that was thoroughly American. I am content."

Peary was indeed content and when he had sent his message from Labrador he was able at last to relax and to enjoy to the full the delicious prospect of his triumphant arrival in America. But he did not know that a few days earlier an even more dramatic message had astonished the world, this time from Copenhagen, which declared that the sender, the American explorer Dr. Frederick A. Cook, accompanied only by two Eskimo youths, had reached the Pole on April 21, 1908—a year, therefore, before Peary.

Peary was loaded with honors and medals and promoted to Admiral when he got home. But meanwhile, Dr. Cook was for a time feted in Copenhagen, where Amundsen came to see him. I, too, was there, having entered upon my journalistic career for the newspaper *Politiken* to write about the Cook expedition on the basis of my own experience in the Arctic.

198

THE NORTH POLE IS DISCOVERED BY DR. FREDERICK A. COOK, WHO CABLES TO THE HERALD AN EXCLUSIVE ACCOUNT OF HOW HE SET THE AMERICAN FLAG ON THE WORLD'S TOP

VIEW SHOWING ICE OVER WHICH DASH TO POLE WAS MADE

Fighting Famine and Ice, the Courageous Explorer Reaches the Great Goal

Finds a New Highway, an Interesting Strip of Animated Nature, Big Game Haunts and a Triangle of Land of 30,000 Square Miles.

ACCOMPANIED BY ONLY TWO ESKIMOS AND TWENTY-SIX DOGS IN LAST DASH

Obstacle After Obstacle Is Overcome Until at Last the Triumph Comes and the Stars and Stripes Are Set Waving on the Summit of the Earth.

HUNGER TORTURES ON THE HOMEWARD JOURNEY

The Explorer, in His Own Story of His Great Exploit, Tells of the Horrors Endured by Him and His Companions Until They Reached Civilization's Outposts.

DR COOK AS HE APPEARED JUST BEFORE SAILING

LERWICK, Shetland Islands, Wednesday.

AFTER a prolonged fight against famine and frost we have at last succeeded in reaching the North Pole.

A new highway, with an interesting strip of animated nature, has been explored.

Big game haunts were located which will delight the sportsman and extend the Eskimo horizon.

Land has been discovered upon which will rest the earth's northern most rocks.

A triangle of 30,000 square miles has been cut out of the terrestrial unknown.

Provisioned by the Bradley.

The expedition was the outcome of a summer cruise in Arctic waters. The yacht Bradley arrived at the limits of navigation in Smith Sound late in August, 1907. Here conditions were found favorable to launch a venture for the Pole.

Mr. John R. Bradley liberally supplied from the yacht suitable provisions for local use, and my own equipment for emergencies served well for every purpose of Arctic travel.

Many Eskimos had gathered up the Greenland shores at Annoatok for the winter bear hunt. Immense catches of meat had been gathered. About the camp were plenty of strong dogs.

The Combination Lucky.

The combination was lucky, for there was good material, an equipment expert help and an efficient motor force, and all that was required was conveniently arranged at a point only 700 miles from the boreal centre.

A house and workshop was built of packing boxes. The willing hands of this northernmost tribe of 250 people were set to the problem of devising a suitable outfit and before the end of the long winter light we were ready for the enterprise.

Plans were advanced to force a new route over Grinnell Land and northward along its west coast out on the polar sea.

Soon after the polar midnight the campaign opened. A few hunting parties were sent over to the American shores to explore and to seek game haunts.

The Start for the Pole.

Their mission was only partly successful because storms darkened the January moon.

At sunrise of 1908 (February 19) the main expedition embarked for the pole. Eleven men and 103 dogs, drawing eleven heavily laden sledges, left the Greenland shore and pushed westward over the troubled ice of Smith Sound.

The gloom of the long night was relieved by only a few hours daylight. The chill of winter was felt at its worst.

As we crossed the heights of Ellesmere Sound to the Pacific slope the temperature sank to 83 degrees below zero Fahrenheit. Several dogs were frozen and the men suffered severely, but we soon found game trails along which an easy way was forced through to Bound to the land's end.

In this march were procured 101 musk oxen, seven bears and

335 hares, and there we pushed out into the polar night from the southern point of Heiberg Island.

On March 18 six Eskimos returned from here, with four men and forty-six dogs, moving supplies for eighty days.

The crossing of the circumpolar pack was begun three days later. Two other Eskimos forming the last supporting party returned. The trains had now been reduced to the survival of the fittest. The strongest men and animals, the two best men and twenty-six dogs were picked for the final dash. There was still no ice incident, but at our camp to our goal.

The Torture of the Cold.

The first days prevented long marches, and with encouraging progress. The big load which separated the head ice from the central pack was crossed with little delay.

Low temperature and persistent winds made life a torture, but, cooped in snow houses, eating dried beef and tallow and drinking hot tea, some animal comforts were occasionally to be gained.

For several days after the flight of known land was lost the overcast skies prevented an accurate determination of our position.

On March 30 the horizon was partly cleared of its smoky agitation, and over the western mist was discovered a new land.

The observations gave our position latitude 84 deg. 47 min., longitude 86 deg. 36 min.

The urgent need of rapid advance on our main mission did not permit a detour to explore the coast. Here were seen the last signs of solid earth. Beyond there was nothing staple, and even on scaling nothing was noted to mark the terrestrial Polar solidity.

We advanced steadily over the monotony of a moving sea of ice.

Beyond Where Life Is.

We now found ourselves beyond the range of all life. Neither the footprints of bears nor the blowholes of seals were detected. Even the microscopic creatures of the deep were no longer under us.

The maddening influence of the shifting desert of

frost became almost unendurable in the daily routine. The surface of the pack offered less and less trouble. The weather improved, but still there remained a light life-napping wind, which drove despair to its lowest recess.

Under the lash of duty, however, interest was forced, while the merciless drive of extreme cold endured physical action.

Thus, day after day, the weary legs were spread over big distances.

The incidents and the positions were recorded, but the barometer was promptly forgotten in the mental blench of the next day's effort.

The night of April 7 was made notable by the swing of the sun at midnight over the northern ice. Sunheims and frost blites were now recorded on the same day, but the double days of glitter infused quite an inventive into our life of success.

Observations on April 8 placed our camp at latitude 86 deg. 36 sec., longitude 94 deg. 2 sec.

In spite of what seemed life long marches we had advanced but a little more than 100 miles in nine days.

Much of our hard work was lost in circuitous twists around troublesome pressure lines and high, irregular fields of very old ice.

The Weary Struggle.

The drift, too, was driving eastward with suf ferious force to give some anxiety, though we were still equal to about fifteen miles daily.

The extended marches and the long hours of travel with which fortune had favored us earlier

We were now about 200 miles from the Pole and the sled loads were reduced. One dog after another had gone into the stomachs of his hungry survivors until the teams were considerably reduced, but there seemed to remain a sufficient balance of man and brute to push along into the heart of the mystery to which we had set ourselves.

Beyond the eighty-sixth parallel the icefields became more extensive and heavier, the crevices fewer and less troublesome, with little or no crushed ice thrown up as barriers.

The North Pole the Most Cheerless Spot That Can Be Imagined, Says Dr. Cook

When the Discoverer Stood at Last on the One Point That Has Stirred the Ambitions of Centuries His One Feeling Was Intense Loneliness

NO NORTH, NO EAST AND NO WEST THERE; ALL SOUTH, NO MATTER WHICH DIRECTION

HOW THE NORTH POLE LOOKS

What a cheerless spot to have aroused the ambition of man for so many years!

An endless field of purple snows. No life. No land. No spot to rest upon. No monotony of frost. Heavens the only pulseless creatures in a dead world of ice, the I only.

From the eighty-seventh to the eighty-eighth, much to our surprise was the indication of land ice.

For two days we travelled over ice which resembled a glacial surface. The usual sea ice lines of demarkation were absent and there were no hummocks or deep crevices.

There was, however, no perceptible elevation and no positive sign of land or sea.

Observations on the 14th gave latitude 88 deg. 21 min. and longitude 93 deg. 92 min.

We were now less than one hundred miles from the Pole. The pack was here more active, but the temperature remained below all, cementing together quickly the new crevices.

Young ice spread on the narrow spaces of open water so rapidly that little delay was caused in crossing from one field to another. The time had now arrived to muster energy for the last burst of efforts.

In the enforced effort every human strand was strained, and at camping time there was no longer sufficient energy to erect a snow shelter, though the temperature was still very low.

Nearing the Great Goal.

The silk tent was pressed into service and the change proved agreeable. It encouraged a more careful scrutiny of the strange world into which fate had pressed us.

Signs of land were still seen every day, but they were deceptive illusions of a mere flight of fancy.

It seemed that something must cross the horizon to mark the important area into which we were pushing.

When the sun was low the eye ran over the moving plains of color to dancing horizons. The mirages turned things topsy turvy. Inverted mountains and queer objects ever rose and fell in shrouds of mystery, but all of this was due to the atmospheric magic of the midnight sun.

Slowly but surely we neared the turning point. Good astronomical observations were daily procured to fix the advancing stages.

The ice steadily improved, but still there was a depressing monotony of scene and life had no pleasures, no spiritual recreation, nothing to relieve the steady physical drag of chronic fatigue.

But there came an end to this as to all things. On April 21 the first corrected altitude of the sun gave 80 deg. 59 min. 44 sec.

The pole, therefore, was in sight.

We advanced the fourteen seconds, made supplementary obser

20. *A Case Against Dr. Cook*

ONE EVENING in the fall of 1909 I received a letter from
the newspaper *Politiken,* asking me to call on the city
editor immediately. I hurriedly answered the summons
and was told the sensational news about a cable which had
just arrived from Scotland and which stated that Dr. Frederick Cook had discovered the North Pole. Cook, the cable
went on, was now on his way to Denmark on board the
Danish steamer *Hans Egede,* which had made a special
stop to pick him up in Greenland.

This was a tremendous story, but as there was nobody
in *Politiken*—then the largest newspaper in Denmark—who
had the faintest knowledge of the Arctic, the editor asked
me to help him out. Could I write something for them
about this great event, in which all their readers were
interested?

I was flattered and pleased to enter into journalism this
way and I assured the editor I could whip off an article
for him in no time. I wrote about the North Pole, mentioned the many unsuccessful attempts to reach it, and
made careful speculations on the basis of scanty information
in the cable. I was very satisfied with my story when I was
interrupted by a visit from the editor in chief.

"This North Pole affair seems to be quite a sensation,"
he declared. "Cables are pouring in asking for details. We
need a few more columns. Make up something about nature
up there, traveling conditions, the people in the place and
stuff like that. I'll kill some book reviews to make space."

I was bursting with pride as I continued writing about
my own experiences for two and a half years in the Arctic.

"More copy," I was told when that was delivered, and I went on writing.

Around midnight the paper went to press and I thought I was through. But at the last moment the editor announced that he needed still more material.

But I was dried up. I could write nothing more about the Arctic regions. Suddenly however I noticed the date. Cook claimed that he had been at the Pole on the twenty-first of April. In my confusion and weariness I thought this date was that of the vernal equinox, and I wrote another piece in a highly poetical vein about the dramatic coincidence of Dr. Cook's arriving at the Pole on the very day when the sun for the first time in six months sent its golden rays over the icy wastes.

Imagine my humiliation when I discovered the following morning what I had done. The afternoon papers were already making fun of the young explorer who had postponed the vernal equinox from March to April. I felt very small, almost despairing, when I went to see the editor.

"Congratulations, my young friend! You did a great job and I am well pleased with you," he said.

"That's very kind of you," I answered, "and I want to assure you that I am truly sorry about what has happened."

"Why, what has happened?"

"It was all my fault, please don't blame anyone on the paper." And I told him of the mistake I had made and that the whole town was laughing at his newspaper.

"Is that all? What is a month one way or the other?" he said. "We all make mistakes sometimes, and in your case you have shown yourself to be a man with imagination. Would you like to join the staff of *Politiken?*"

After this surprising start I was put on the payroll.

The steamer carrying Dr. Cook was now approaching

Denmark, and a great many foreign journalists came to Copenhagen to interview him. I was very flattered when I was approached by Philip Gibbs of the London *News Chronicle* about the discovery. Among other things I told him that Knud Rasmussen, who was then in Greenland establishing a missionary station in the North Star Bay, had sent a letter to his wife in Denmark on Cook's steamer. And if, I told him, we could get hold of that letter we might find out what Rasmussen had to say about Cook and make a scoop. We persuaded Mrs. Rasmussen to go with us to Elsinore where the ship would dock, and she promised to show us the letter if it contained any news about Cook.

We made the trip by car, which was quite a stunt in those days, and arrived at the dock ahead of the other journalists who were coming by train. We asked the harbor master to let Mrs. Rasmussen board the ship with Gibbs and myself. Unfortunately a man with him when we made the request turned out to be Captain Bang, whose fireman I had been on my first trip to Greenland. The result was that permission was granted to Mrs. Rasmussen and to Gibbs but not to the former fireman.

I had no intention of being left behind and managed to get into the coast-guard cutter going out to the steamer and sneak on board the *Hans Egede* even before Mrs. Rasmussen and Mr. Gibbs.

Dr. Cook received the press in the dining room. I don't know exactly how it came about, but after the first few minutes I was convinced that something was seriously wrong with his story. At first I could not believe he was simply making it all up, but as the press conference proceeded I was certain he did not know what he was talking about. I did not dare say anything since I was not supposed to be there, but I listened carefully to Cook's every word, and when we were on deck again I asked Gibbs for his opinion.

Philip Gibbs began a series of articles in the *News Chronicle*. His newspaper, it should be pointed out, had certain traditions to live up to. Its editor had been the first man to see through a famous hoax a few years before—a best seller called *Thirty Years Among the Savages* by Louis de Rougemont. The *News Chronicle* had proved that this man's dangerous journeys in uncivilized regions were wholly imaginary. So Gibbs at once set out to expose Dr. Cook. Lacking any knowledge of the Arctic, he pumped me dry. We wrote a daily article charting the travels of Cook, who had already begun publishing his diaries. We found in these half a dozen claims obviously contrary to facts as well as numerous dubious statements. So we decided there was no reason to believe the rest of it.

Like Gibbs, I did not hesitate to state my conviction publicly. I gave several lectures, and I wrote an article presenting all the evidence against Dr. Cook. But my editor refused to print it. "We cannot wine and dine a man one day and call him a fraud the next," he declared.

So I took my article to another paper and was received with open arms by the editor, who nevertheless did not use the article either.

During the height of the strife Roald Amundsen arrived in Copenhagen. I went to his hotel at one o'clock in the morning and talked to him for five hours. There had been mention of sending an expedition up to Etah, in northern Greenland, to search for the two diaries Cook claimed to have left there. I felt that I must join this expedition and asked Amundsen to help me. He promised to do what he could for me, but he expressed his faith in Dr. Cook. Amundsen liked Cook and, consequently, believed in him. In any case the expedition never materialized.

203

The Cook case went on and on. The university finally ordered an investigation, with Knud Rasmussen as a member of the commission. The investigations were shrouded in secrecy, and the results were awaited anxiously. Then one morning all the newspapers had extras in the street: The University of Denmark had found no evidence supporting the claims of Dr. Cook that he had been at the North Pole!

A few days after our arrival in North Star Bay a steamer put into port. It was the *Beautic,* commanded by the famous Captain Bob Bartlett and chartered by Harry Whitney and Paul Rainey.

Whitney was no stranger in these waters, as he had once wintered at Etah. He was the man who had rescued Dr. Cook, when that curious person came home from his "North Pole" trip. Cook and his two fellows had no dogs and had walked all the way from Cape Sparbo at Jones Sound, and they were completely done in. Harry Whitney was, at the time, at Anoritoq. He saw three miscroscopic dots far out on the ice and went to investigate. Whitney took Dr. Cook on his sled and brought him to shore.

Cook was very weak, and if it had not been for Harry Whitney, who nursed him back to health, and a gale which broke up the ice immediately, the doctor would never have been able to foist his trickery upon the world. While Whitney never believed in Dr. Cook, he did not take the trouble to go for the instruments which Cook said he left at Etah. Neither did he question the two Eskimo boys, Itukusuk and Apilak, who had accompanied Dr. Cook. He merely took it for granted that nobody would believe Cook's story—he did not take into consideration the gullibility of the civilized world concerning events in out-of-the-way places.

Later on I got hold of the "instruments"—a common sextant, from which a man could tell nothing. Itukusuk

DR. FREDERICK A. COOK

sold it to me, glad to be rid of it, because Cook had paid him only a few boxes of matches for a year and a half's work. Besides, during his absence with Cook, Itukusuk had lost his wife to a stronger man.

He told me that he had been happily married when Cook took him on his expedition and that he had to leave his wife alone in Etah when he went away. Shortly afterward Admiral Peary was looking for Eskimos to accompany him to the North Pole, and he took Itukusuk's wife with him as a seamstress. When the expedition was stationed at Cape Columbia on Ellesmere Land, Peary gave the girl away to a young hunter in need of a wife.

Itukusuk returned from his trip more than a year later to find his wife was still at Cape Columbia with Peary's expedition. Peary had traded all the belongings Cook had left in Etah for furs. There was, therefore, nothing left except a few matchboxes. These Cook gave to Itukusuk as his whole reward for the trip and hurried south to avoid meeting Peary.

Shortly afterward Peary returned from his victorious trip to the North Pole. This was his last expedition, and he was saying good-by to the Eskimos whom he had known for many years. Peary never failed to pay well for everything he got, and on this occasion his rewards were more generous than ever. He allowed all the Eskimos whose marriages he had arranged to keep their women forever. And so Itukusuk was left with three matchboxes and no wife.

Before he departed Peary told the Eskimos that Cook was "no good." This was a further humiliation for Itukusuk, who had been Cook's guide, and he kept quietly in the background and did not even ask for the return of his wife.

I gave him an alarm clock for the sextant, which he immediately took apart and divided among his many friends and relatives.

206

People still argue about Cook and Peary, even today, and therefore I should like to put forth my private theory about the man and his reputed exploits.

I don't want to defend Cook in any way, and really can't see how I could, but I think he was to some extent what people call a "victim of circumstances."

As I mentioned, I am the man who got hold of Dr. Cook's sextant, and some other property he left in Ellesmere Land before he and his two Eskimos, Itukusuk and Apilak, ventured out over the ice from Pimps Island to Greenland.

It was late in the winter and the ice was breaking up. Had it not been, as I said, for the American sportsman and Arctic traveler, Henry Whitney, who spotted three black dots out on the ice, and went out on his sledge to rescue them in spite of the Eskimos' warning, they would have never reached Greenland.

Mr. Whitney was a friend of the late Admiral Peary. He had gone up north and returned home with one of Peary's boats. And though, like Peary, he did not like Cook, there was nevertheless no question about helping Dr. Cook in such a situation. He brought him into Anoritoq, northeast of Etah, and he helped him and gave him new clothes and an entirely new outfit.

Dr. Cook had a house in which a German named Rudolf Francke stayed during Dr. Cook's absence. They had quite a lot of goods stored there and when Cook had left with his friend Bradley, Francke occupied himself in selling the goods for foxskins. So there was very little left, not even enough to eat .

When Dr. Cook heard that Admiral Peary was on his way back from up north and was expected the same summer he decided to leave immediately.

Peary and Cook were not on friendly terms, though Dr. Cook had been on one of Peary's earlier expeditions and was known as a rather pleasant man and an exceptionally good traveler. After a few days' rest, then, and after Mr. Whitney had fed him and paid the natives to make him new clothes, Dr. Cook took leave. He hired four Eskimos to drive him south across Melville Bay to the Danish Colonies. The ice was pretty bad, as the year was advanced, and the spring setting in. But they hurried across Melville Bay in record time. They reached the northernmost Danish settlement where the Americans were required to change sledges. The law, at that time, forbade dogs from the Smith Sound Eskimos to come in contact with the dogs from the colonies, because they were regarded as infected with disease.

So the old hunter, Simon from Eetooasadik, took Dr. Cook to the northernmost trading post, Tasiussaq. There he was received by the trader Mr. Dahl.

Dr. Cook stuck to his sense of economy and sent back to each of his followers from the Melville Bay a piece of thin white linen, to be used for shooting seals. It cost 44 öre, that is, ten cents. So he didn't quite ruin himself financially on that.

Mr. Dahl could speak some English but he didn't know what a prominent man he had as a guest, because Dr. Cook didn't tell anything about the North Pole. And Cook had never in fact, during the entire trip with his two Eskimo men, mentioned that he had been at the North Pole, so no one could have known of it. They went up north from Etah past Grant Land, and reached two small islands, northwest of Grant Land. But as the rough ice started up there, they turned around and went the long way, along the west coast of Ellesmere Land, and spent the winter at Cape Sparbo, Jones Sound.

Here they were hunting for provisions, depending most on bears and musk oxen.

The picture Dr. Cook has in his book, which he claimed is taken at the North Pole, is probably from that camp at Cape Sparbo. This can be argued from the fact that one of the natives stands with his big boots made out of musk-ox hide with the hair on; it would be impossible to prove that they could have killed musk oxen at the North Pole—called in Eskimo "the navel of the earth."

Neither did Dr. Cook tell his story to Mr. Whitney. So Mr. Dahl at Tasiussaq had no clue to ask him about his explorations—something which he should have immediately mentioned since the Pole had made sensational news for years all over the world.

Dr. Cook's only object was apparently to come south, so he could get a boat and go home as soon as possible—not to announce any big discoveries. Mr. Dahl provided him with a couple of sledges that brought Dr. Cook safe to Upernavik, which is the main trading post in that district, then the northernmost one in Greenland.

Dr. Cook arrived there at two o'clock in the morning. At that time it was bright all day there and in regions of the same latitude.

In Upernavik, there was at that time a strange old gentleman named Mr. Kraul, who acted as manager. He was a bachelor and consequently a man of certain restricted rules of living. One of those was that he didn't like to be disturbed while he was sleeping.

Nevertheless, because an unexpected visitor from the north had arrived, some of the natives dared to knock at his door to announce the sensation. And as nothing is locked up there, they went inside and woke the gentleman up from his bed. They told Mr. Kraul that an American had come.

Meanwhile Dr. Cook walked back and forth outside the house and Kraul went out of his bed and looked at him through the window.

When a man comes from a long trip, he is not, of course, very dressed up and nobody can see from his appearance what kind of man he is.

Mr. Kraul judged Cook to be a sailor, one (he thought) who had run away from a whaling boat, and he no doubt felt regret about having been troubled with such a guy. So he was not very enthusiastic about the visitor—or at least not enough to have his sleep disturbed.

He chased the Eskimos out and then went back to bed again.

Meanwhile Dr. Cook killed the time by pacing back and forth between the flagstone and the stairs up to the house, looking hopefully at the door the whole time.

This lasted until a quarter of eight in the morning when Mr. Kraul emerged at his usual time.

He looked at Dr. Cook and said, "How do you do!"

Dr. Cook answered with the same words and then Mr. Kraul asked him, "Where do you come from?"

To this Dr. Cook answered, "Oh, I just came from the North Pole!"

It is my honest belief that this was just one of those casual remarks that very often are said without any meaning. I know that I myself—who have certainly never been at the North Pole—am quite often referred to (because I'm an Arctic explorer) as "the guy from the North Pole." This is nothing but a saying, and I firmly believe that it was just "the saying" that fell from Dr. Cook's mouth.

But Mr. Kraul might have been in his morning moods,

ARCTIC OCEAN

90° E

10° E

GREENLAND

85

80°

180° W

SEA

0°

Cook Land Ice

140° W

10° W

C. Morris Jesup
Cape Neumyer

Peary Land

Independence Bay

85°

Peary's route to the Pole

130° W

Bradley Land

Cape Columbia
Cape Hecla
Cape Sheridan

Peary Channel

20° W

Crocker Land

120° W

Cook's route to the Pole

Cape Colgate

Grant Land
Fort Conger

Robeson Channel

GREENLAND

30° W

Svartevoeg

Nansen Sound

Ellesmere

Kennedy Channel

Crown Prince

Eureka Sound

80°

Axel Heiberg

Grinnell Land
Cape D'Urville

Kane Basin

Annoatok

Flagler Bay
Cape Sabine

Etah
Nuerke

McCormick Bay
Inglefield Gulf

110° W

Ellef Ringnes Land

Amund Ringnes Land

Cape York

40° W

Melville Bay

Land

Upernivik

Jones Sound

Cape Sparbo
Devon I.

75

Umanak

Lancaster Sound

Baffin

Bay

Somerset Island

Bylot I.

Prince of Wales I.

Brodeur Pen.

B

DAVIS STRAIT

50° W

Holsteinborg

Boothia Pen.

70°

100° W

Melville

Pen.

Foxe Basin

60° W

HUDSON STRAIT

90° W

80° W

70° W

or he may not have known that expression. Anyway, he became Frederick A. Cook's first believer.

He stood for a moment, solemn and silent. Just then Reverend Knud Balla came out from his house and Mr. Kraul eyed him and shouted, "Pastor Balle, the North Pole has been found, and here is the man who reached the North Pole!"

And before Balle crossed over to the two of them, Mr. Kraul had already opened the door to his house and cried to his Danish housekeeper, Miss Gudrun Larsen, "Miss Larsen, Miss Larsen, get us some coffee, the North Pole has been found! Make us some breakfast, Miss Larsen! The conqueror of the North Pole is our guest!"

There was a young Danish assistant, Mr. Fencker, and also a Danish cooper, Klintrup-Jensen, at the colony. They were easily summoned, and the little party showed their respect for the visiting American who was so great.

In Danish colonies people usually have an amount of wine, bottled with labels for the months in which they are to be used. The uncurable bachelor, Mr. Kraul, broke all the rules. Wine of every month came to the table and the party was rather gay in the early morning.

During the festival, Mr. Kraul took time to step into his office, write a letter to the state's official representative down at Godhavn, announcing that there was the conqueror of the North Pole having breakfast with him. He advised that the first possible ship from Denmark should be sent up to fetch him and bring him back.

Mr. Kraul, of course, in making such a request, had certain personal advantages in mind: getting his mail, papers and everything, at least a month and a half before the usual schedule. So he cannot be considered absolutely disinterested.

212

Dr. Cook was now honored as the first man to reach the North Pole and he probably realized that it was too late to back out. He did not remain in Upernavik waiting for the Danish ship to fetch him but made his way farther south by boat and sledges. Everywhere he went he was recognized as the man who had conquered what thousands of people had tried before him.

I am absolutely convinced that Dr. Cook never conceived of himself as the discoverer of the North Pole until the morning of his breakfast with Mr. Kraul. After that, he built up his whole story; he invented the idea of being "the first man" to the top of the world.

Cook nevertheless expected Peary to come home as soon as the ice opened up, perhaps making some announcements of his own, so he was anxious to arrive first. He thus went immediately toward Denmark.

But on the way, the ship stopped at the Shetland Islands from where Cook sent messages out over the whole world.

There were quite a few passengers on board that boat, also some Danish scientists who knew nothing of observations or travelings. All of them recognized Cook as the passenger of honor and since Cook had always been a rather poor guy, he saw the situation as his Big Chance.

So Cook came to Denmark and was received with "that open mind" my countrymen always like to show, to all men who claim some achievement of this sort.

There was a short examination given Cook by the Danish professor Elis Stroemgren—a teacher in astronomy at the University of Copenhagen. His pronouncement, after having talked with Dr. Cook, was the following:

"This man knows so little about astronomy that it would be impossible for him to make some fake observation, which is far more difficult than taking the real sights."

Unfortunately, the learned professor didn't get a chance to see any evidence of observations of any "real sights," but he couldn't apparently let himself think that a man would come home to civilization and tell something that wasn't true.

It is almost forty years since Dr. Cook came to Denmark but still people talk about those days—the exciting time when two men claimed to have conquered the North Pole. I can never forget how strange it was to stand before him and realize that he was deceiving the whole world, perhaps even himself, except for me and Gibbs and a few others. It takes a man a whole lifetime to understand how this can happen. But even now, I am not sure that I really understand it, though I am sure of the case against Dr. Cook.

21. *Ahdolo, Ahdolo: The Eskimo Idea of Matt Henson*

I NEVER SAW Matthew Henson, Robert Peary's faithful servant, in the Arctic, but for years I heard story after story about him—more than about any other man.

I came to visit the Smith Sound Eskimos in 1910, the year after Peary had been at the North Pole. His four Eskimo followers lived there and became my best friends, and they all spoke about *Marripaluk*. Everybody, in fact, in that tribe liked to talk about him and liked to relate how close they were to him, because Marripaluk was the hero and the mystic man of the expedition.

His manner was different, they all told me, his way of living different, and he was the outstanding man in all Eskimo travel and work, far better than any American, even better than the Eskimos.

Marripaluk was the name the native had given to Henson.

Odark—the oldest of the four Eskimos to go with Peary to the Pole—told me that Peary had had all of the Eskimos with him from the time they were young boys:

He had trained us, like a man trains his pupils to grow to be like he wants them. We therefore knew Peary and we liked him and we looked at him as if he had been a father to us.

But if it had not been for Marripaluk, Peary might have been quite another man. Both of them came from the far-away White Man's country and there were so many things they did not understand. But they learned everything—far more than the rest of us put together.

215

Courtesy of the American Museum of Natural History

MATTHEW HENSON

Marripaluk was the only man from Peary's land who could learn to talk our language without using his tongue like a baby.

If a stranger walks during the winter when everything is dark and someone meets him and asks who is there, the Americans will always answer in a funny way. One was glad it was dark, because it is difficult not to laugh at the way they speak our language. But Marripaluk could talk like a full-grown and intelligent person.

Besides, Marripaluk always showed that he did not look down at people from up here. He wanted to learn our ways, and he surely did. Nobody has ever driven dogs better than he. And not only could he swing the whip; whenever a sledge broke down, he could fix it like any of us. He could repair the harnesses or make new ones. And no one has ever made a snowhouse faster and better and bigger than he could.

Indeed Marripaluk is the greatest man after Peary, and he showed how intelligent he was by always taking advice from "Peeulee." Whenever Peeulee said something, Marripaluk would do it, and do it much better than the boss could do it. Peeulee never learned to drive dogs himself, nor build a snowhouse nor catch a seal. He had too much in his head to bother with such unimportant things as we people up here work at.

But Marripaluk could also sing like us, dance like us, and his mouth was always full of stories no one had ever heard before.

Therefore we liked him, and we all felt sorry when we understood that we would never see him again.

But we will always tell our children about him and we will sing songs about him.

Every morning when we travel, Marripaluk was the first

one to wake up. Peeulee had to take his watch out from his breast and look at it. Marripaluk had the time in his mind, even if he was asleep.

He knew when the dogs had had enough rest. Then he would get up and start to cook.

We all dreamed so nice, when the smell of the food reached our nostrils, even if we slept. The morning dreams were always the best ones. One always was tired in the body when one traveled with Peeulee, because he wanted us to go far and fast. We could sleep only when snowstorms kept us down.

But not Marripaluk. He could never be tired. When he had the food ready in the mornings, his cry woke us up.

"Ahdolo! Ahdolo!" He yelled and we had to get up. Often it ached to move, because we were tired from the day before. But his voice made it easy, nobody could help laughing because the sound was as good as the food he made. So we all laughed. And if one begins the day with laughter one can run faster and longer and keep awake much longer, than if one starts the morning without a smile.

Ahdolo ahdolo is now a word used by all of us. He learned to say this when he was newborn in this country, and he was quick to catch up with the way we are talking. Later on he could have used the right words for getting people up but he kept on saying the same thing every morning, because he thereby remembered the first years he was here. He felt so happy that he had come to our country and many times he told us that he would like to stay here all his lifetime. But he said that he had promised to help Peeulee as long as this great man wanted him. And nobody has ever seen either of those two men forget what they had once promised.

And now we all are used to saying these words in the

218

morning; because when we do so, we all think of this man whom we liked better than any other man from the far-away great country. We like him and we love to tell about him, because he could do everything as good as the very best man up here.

What a great hunter he could have been if he had stayed here! Marripaluk will never be forgotten, because we tell and tell about him. And we always finish the story with his morning greetings:

Ahdolo Ahdolo!

IV. World War I and After

22. The Air Age Begins

INTEREST IN Arctic exploration has taken a new and much different line of development in our time. People don't go to the Arctic nowadays to find out where there is land, where there is ice, etc. All these things have been done, and the map can be reversed and corrected only to a slight, insignificant extent.

Nowadays much bigger matters are at stake. It is almost impossible to talk about the Arctic without talking politics, air bases, uranium, oil fields, and such things—matters that were never known to even the most avid explorers at the turn of the century, and are now discussed by every schoolboy.

In the technical field, the most important new development after World War I, even more important than the introduction of steam-powered ships in the nineteenth century, was the entry of the polar regions into the Air Age. This came about not only in the sense of the use of air power for reconnaissance in exploration, for transport

220

and supply, for communication, but in providing motives for research—especially in meteorology—which would directly benefit polar aviation. There were, too, important developments in the political field leading in the years between the two World Wars to the partitioning among the interested powers of almost all the discovered polar areas. Governments claiming sovereignty over polar territories became enthusiastic patrons of polar exploration, seeking to consolidate their claims by establishing land bases or by fostering research and development projects.

Occupation, administration, plans for research leading to the development of natural resources, mapping—these were all evidence of state activity supporting claims to sovereignty. These new incentives to exploration were valuable—even if they were not particularly attractive—to the explorers and scientists concerned because they aided the advancement of exploration and research.

Parallel with these technical and political developments were important happenings in the scientific field—ones brought about by the demand for a greater co-ordination and exchange of information about polar exploration, scientific discovery, and techniques. In the national field this led to the establishment of polar centers or institutes, such as the Scott Polar Research Institute founded in 1920 out of the proceeds of the Scott Memorial Fund; or, among government organizations, the "Chief Administration of the Northern Sea Route" set up by the Soviet Government in 1932. In the international field this same need for great integration of effort, the more urgent as exploring expeditions multiplied and specialization increased, led to the launching of the Second International Polar Year of 1932–33. The First International Polar Year, of 1882–83, too often remembered only by the calamity which befell the

Greely expedition, had added substantially to knowledge of geomagnetism and meteorology. The Second International Year, which was concentrated like its predecessor in the Arctic, made further advances in these branches of geophysics and in addition embarked upon studies of the ionosphere—the ionized region of the upper atmosphere responsible for the reflection of radio waves. This was research for which the polar regions are particularly important because of the long alternating period of daylight and darkness. It became increasingly important as radio communication developed rapidly after the First World War. The most important advances during the Second International Polar Year were made, however, in meteorology. This was a field vitally important to the progress of polar aviation in peace and war.

During the Second International Polar Year, ninety-four meteorological stations were manned in the Arctic. For the first time reliable information was provided about Arctic weather and the relation between ice drift and movement and the behavior of the winds.

The realization that commercial aircraft, if they could be safely navigated across the Arctic by Great Circle routes, could appreciably shorten the flying time between the great centers of population in the eastern and western hemispheres led many exploring expeditions between the wars to study the meteorology of the Greenland ice sheet. This sheet lay, scientists realized, in the track of future air routes. Its great mass of ice had a profound influence on weather. Studies of Arctic weather and Arctic ice were no less important to sea navigation, particularly for the new Soviet Government of Russia whose northern coast is especially vulnerable to the circular and branching ice movements of the Arctic Ocean. Thus the beginnings of

222

an organized effort by Russia to promote and expand Arctic research was a development of prime importance between the wars.

The impact of air power did not greatly affect the pattern of polar travel until after the Second World War. This remained, in the classic tradition established by the North American and Scandinavian travelers, as firmly based as ever on the dog and sledge. Even the British, opposed as their leading explorers had for so long been to the use of dogs in exploration, had learned their lesson. They not only adopted but now tried hard to improve upon the sledging techniques which had won the Pole for Peary and for America.

KNUD RASMUSSEN

23. *Portraits in Endurance*

ONE OF the earliest Arctic expeditions after the First World War was the Fifth Thule Expedition led by my close friend and colleague Knud Rasmussen, the Danish explorer. It took the pattern of prewar exploration. This traversed for the first time by dog sledge the Northwest Passage. Accompanied only by an Eskimo woman and an Eskimo youth, Rasmussen started in March 1923 from Repulse Bay (in the northern waters of Hudson Bay, near Southhampton Island) and traveling by way of Rae Isthmus, Boothia Peninsula, King William Island and the Arctic coast of Canada, reached in August 1924 the eastern shores of Bering Strait.

As a fact of endurance and an exposition of sledging technique this was a remarkable performance. By this single continuous journey Rasmussen linked together many of the discoveries arduously won by Canadian trappers and traders and British naval officers during the nineteenth century.

There was, however, little scope left in the Arctic in the second quarter of the twentieth century for record-breaking journeys of such magnitude. Indeed only within the great ice sheet covering Greenland was there scope for exploration on anything like the grand scale.

For this reason and because of its great significance in ice and weather research, a succession of expeditions—German, British and American—took place between the wars. In each case, a central weather station was the core of the scientific program.

Between 1926 and 1931 three expeditions established

224

WEGENER EXPEDITION

stations of this kind: the University of Michigan Expedition led by a vigorous controversialist in Antarctic history, Professor William H. Hobbs; the German Greenland Expedition led by the fifty-one-year-old Professor Alfred Wegener who had been with Mylius-Erichsen in Greenland; and the British Arctic Air Route Expedition, led by an adventurous and volatile young Cambridge Arctic traveler, H. G. (Gino) Watkins. Of these Wegener's was scientifically the most productive. In the use of motor sledges, new instruments for measuring the thickness of the ice cover by echo-sounding methods, it was technologically the most advanced.

A central weather station was built on the 71st parallel, some 250 miles from the west coast. But in November 1930 the expedition ended in tragedy. On a journey, Wegener and a companion, Willemsen, died of exhaustion and exposure.

The British Arctic Air Route Expedition, led by Gino Watkins, was the most ambitious Arctic expedition sent out from Britain since the Scott and Shackleton days. Its motive was meteorological research and survey against the day when commercial aircraft flying over Greenland would accomplish a Northwest Passage by air. The most promising air route from England to Canada and the Pacific coast, which lay across Greenland, Baffin Island and Hudson Bay, crossed the least-known part of Greenland. The coast, moreover, for two hundred miles north of Angmagssalik was unsurveyed and the interior was unknown. To survey this coast, to explore the interior—looking especially for high mountains—and to make observations of weather conditions from a central station: these were the aims of the expedition.

Its members were for the most part young men from

226

Cambridge which had since the war become Britain's chief center of polar activity and the breeding ground for her polar leaders of the future. This was no accident. Living there were no less than three polar veterans—men who had personally shared in the adventures, the dramas, the tragedies and disappointments of British polar exploration in the prewar Heroic Age. All of them were in excellent position to stimulate, advise and instruct the younger generation. Two, Raymond Priestley and Frank Debenham, had been largely responsible for the foundation in Cambridge of the Scott Polar Institute. A third, J. M. Wordie, chief of scientific staff to Shackleton on the Trans-Antarctic Expedition, organized and led a number of summer expeditions of young men from Cambridge and elsewhere during the thirties. The value of such training was clear from those who gained distinction later in the nineteenthirties and became the leaders after the Second World War when Britain once again took a foremost part in polar exploration. The release from the long isolation and restrictions of war has always been a spur to travel and adventure. Of the young men who thus emerged after the First World War none seemed to his elders to personify more completely the spirit of youthful adventure, none seemed to show greater promise of being the leader of the future, than the twenty-three-year-old Gino Watkins.

The British Arctic Air Route Expedition sailed in July 1930 in Shackleton's old ship, the *Quest*. Watkins had become a passionate advocate of Eskimo methods of travel, which had indeed been the secret of American and Scandinavian success. So dogs and sledges were to be the chief means of transport as well as kayaks, in the handling of which Watkins had learned to display extraordinary skill. Two motorboats were also carried in the *Quest* and two

DeHavilland aircraft for reconnaissance and air photography to aid the land surveyors.

All this was a sign of the times. But it was not the first use of aircraft by a British Arctic expedition. Six years earlier a party of young men led by George Binney had been pioneers in this respect and had made a number of successful flights in a seaplane over Spitsbergen and Nordaustland.

The expedition's most important contribution was probably their very careful survey of the eastern coastal strip. Two long sledging trips were also made westward across the ice sheet, one carrying kayaks for use in the fjords and streams between the ice edge and the coast. But the most adventurous journey was one in open boats made by Watkins, Augustin Courtauld, and Captain Lemon of the Signals along the ice-infested east coast from Angmagssalik southward to Prins Christians Sund—a distance of seven hundred miles. One episode at the inland station was reminiscent of the feats of endurance and fortitude of the Scott and Shackleton days.

Watkins' plan had been to relieve the central weather station on the ice sheet every month. But the blizzards, blandly prophesied as infrequent by the weather experts, blew weekly during October at over a hundred miles an hour. In such conditions repeated journeys to the heart of the ice sheet were impracticable and Courtauld volunteered to remain at the station alone, to maintain observations throughout the winter.

On December 6th he began his solitary watch. On May 5th the following year he was relieved. Snowed in toward the end of his lonely sojourn, his submerged hut swept by blizzards which roared across the ice and snow above his head, without fuel for either heating or cooking for weeks before relief arrived, Courtauld survived and returned in perfect health after a physical and psychological experience unique in polar history.

Allied to the meteorological studies which had been the central purpose of all these Greenland expeditions was the study of ice, its thickness, its composition, its movement and drift in relation to climatic factors. The study of ice drift and ice movement over the sea was an urgent matter for Russia's Administration for the Northern Sea Route and in May 1937 Soviet scientists led by Ivan Papanin embarked on an exciting expedition. In its use of an ice floe as a scientific base—one that would drift with the Arctic currents—it was no doubt conceived in relation to Stefansson's pioneer drift over the Beaufort Sea. But it must also be viewed as a forerunner of the air-supported Russian and American ice-drifting stations after the Second World War.

In May 1937 Papanin's expedition was landed by aircraft on an ice floe near the Pole and on this Papanin and three companions began a drift of nine months, southward with the cold currents flowing down past the northeast coast of Greenland. More than once, as when their floe collided with some grounded ice and was split apart, they were in great jeopardy. But their slowly diminishing base lasted long enough to bring them to 70° 54′ S., midway between Scoresby Sound on the Greenland coast and Jan Mayen Island. There they were picked up by Soviet ice breakers on February 19, 1938. Soundings near the Pole revealed an ocean depth of 14,000 feet and, throughout the drift, ice and weather observations were made. The latter enabled Russian pilots in 1937 to fly nonstop across the Pole to the North American Pacific coast.

Courtauld's five months of self-imposed imprisonment in the ice and this adventurous Russian enterprise greatly

229

stimulated public excitement about polar exploration. But it was in the air rather than at sea or on land that the most spectacular, the most ambitious, and the most costly Arctic undertakings took place, though many of them contributed more to the progress of aviation than to geography. The Scandinavians—Salomon Andrée, the Swedish balloonist, and none more than the great Norwegian Nansen—had all along been enthusiastic about the possibilities of trans-arctic aviation. So it was fitting that the first pioneer after the war was Nansen's protégé Roald Amundsen, the conqueror by sea of the Northwest Passage and the first man to reach the South Pole overland. In May 1925 Amundsen and the American aviator Lincoln Ellsworth, who was later to gain distinction in Antarctic flying, left Kongsfjorden, Spitsbergen, in two Dornier flying boats and landed 120 miles from the North Pole. They managed to get only one of their aircraft airborne again and in this returned to Spitsbergen, having made soundings of the Arctic Ocean near the Pole and accomplished a reconnaissance of over 12,000 square miles of the polar basin.

The following year Commander R. E. Byrd of the United States Navy, who was to be the first since Wilkes to lead an American Antarctic expedition, joined in these Arctic flights. He had already gained experience of Arctic aviation with MacMillan's 1925 expedition to Parry's mythical "Croker Land," and on May 9, 1926, he flew from Spitsbergen to the North Pole.

24. *Heroes Over the Arctic*

THE NEXT flight, the same year and again by Amundsen and Ellsworth, was indirectly to lead to one of the earliest disasters in Arctic aviation. The aircraft was an airship, the *Norge,* designed by an Italian designer, Colonel Umberto Nobile, and in this, the first flight by airship over the Arctic, Amundsen, Ellsworth, and Nobile tried to fly from Spitsbergen to Alaska. The first stage of the flight was remarkably successful and three flags, American, Norwegian and Italian, were thrown down on the tumbled sea ice around the Pole. But during the flight onward toward Alaska they were constantly in imminent danger. Ice thickly encrusting the sides of the ship was torn loose by the whirling propellers and flung against the gasbags. Ice heavily encrusted the bows of the *Norge.* Their radio equipment had long ceased to function, and even their sun compass was heavily coated in ice. Nevertheless, navigating almost blind and without contact with the ground, they made an exceedingly fortunate landfall in Alaska on May 14th. They had flown nonstop from Europe to America, a distance of over 3,400 miles.

The year 1928 was a notable year in the history of Arctic aviation, both for the flights of the Australian airman Hubert Wilkins and for the disaster which befell the airship *Italia* launched by the Italian North Polar Expedition. Wilkins had learned to fly in the early experimental days of 1910–12 when aircraft seemed little more than a batch of fragile wires and struts. He was also an experienced Arctic traveler, having been second-in-command to Stefansson on his Canadian Arctic Expedition during the First

THE NORGE

World War. He had all along been convinced of the value of aircraft in polar reconnaissance but more important from the point of view of his backers, a group of Detroit businessman, was his conviction that the day was not far off when commercial airways would fly on schedule across the Pole. Wilkins' transarctic flight of 1928 was the climax to numerous earlier efforts, as costly as they were discouraging. On one of these, in 1927, he and his co-pilot Carl Ben Eielson crashed five hundred miles from Point Barrow, their starting point, and marched for fourteen days over the ice—an experience they would never have survived had

234

it not been for the lessons Wilkins had learned from Stefansson on their long journeys over the sea ice of the Beaufort Sea.

The flight in 1928, in a Lockheed Vega, began on April 16th from Point Barrow. Wilkins, nearing Spitsbergen, was almost within sight of victory when he was forced, after a continuous flight of 20 hours 20 minutes, to land on Likholmen—"Dead Man's Island"—off the west coast of the archipelago. It took both men a week to become airborne again, with Eielson in the cockpit and Wilkins pushing with one foot on the ice. But they succeeded and within half an hour landed at Grønfjorden, Spitsbergen.

The Arctic flight of the Italian airship, the *Italia,* was in many ways a senseless affair which had arisen out of a quarrel between Umberto Nobile and Roald Amundsen about the technical qualities of Amundsen's transarctic airship *Norge,* built to Nobile's design.

Determined to prove his point, Nobile persuaded the Italian Government to launch an Italian North Polar Expedition. In order to give some semblance of serious purpose to the flight, he declared that he would not only land and moor three weeks at the Pole but would also survey from the air those islands off the north Russian coast and in the Canadian archipelago. The Russian part of the program was completed successfully. Then Nobile set out across the Arctic Ocean for the Pole. The *Italia* was forced down one hundred and eighty miles northeast of Spitsbergen and the subsequent search for Nobile and his men lying with their wrecked airship, no one knew where, in the heart of the Arctic Ocean was the sensation of the year. At first there seemed no hope that they would ever be found.

Then a Russian wireless amateur near Archangel, on the

basis of a garbled and puzzling message, tracked them down and the search started. Norwegian sealers, Swedish sealers, Italian, Norwegian and Swedish aircraft all joined in. At Amundsen's personal request a French seaplane was put at his disposal to search for the man whose quarrel with him had been at the root of this unfortunate enterprise. After many attempts failed, Nobile at length was rescued by one of the Swedish pilots and the remainder of the party was picked up by the Russian icebreaker *Krassin* after they had been sighted by the ship's light aircraft. But of Amundsen no trace was ever found.

The fate of Roald Amundsen and his crew was sealed long before most of the rescuers even started to look for him, and an indication was eventually found of what that fate must have been. Quite some time after Amundsen's airplane disappeared, one of its gasoline tanks drifted ashore on the northern coast of Norway. It was battered and split, as such a tank naturally would be after exposure to waves and rocks, but it had been emptied of its gasoline through the outlet valve which was soldered to it. The fact that it had been emptied through the outlet valve showed that the men themselves had done it.

At the time the tank was found it was felt that it would be cruel to let the families of the lost men know of it and its implications. They might have suffered deeply from thinking about the agonizing fight for life which must have been made by Amundsen and his men—the long hours in the cold sea while their waterlogged plane gradually sank from under them.

For a while the story was not given out publicly. But that is not the way to think about it. I feel certain from personal friendship with him that Amundsen experienced no fear, then or under any circumstances.

So died Roald Amundsen, in an attempt to rescue other men in distress. He could not have had a finer end to his magnificent life.

One more but quite different attempt at a transpolar crossing must be mentioned because it is the antecedent of a remarkable achievement still fresh in the memory. This was the attempt by Sir Hubert Wilkins in 1931 to cross the Arctic Ocean, as far as the Pole, by submarine. Wilkins' vessel, the submarine *O-12* renamed the *Nautilus,* was lent to him by the United States Navy and he crossed the Atlantic in her to his starting base at Longyearbyen, Spitsbergen. In August Wilkins set out. He had no luck. He encountered violent storms, his driving gear was damaged, and after a voyage of three weeks he returned to Spitsbergen. Nevertheless, he managed to reach 82° 15′ N. during this first voyage; a voyage which contributed more to Arctic science than his aeronautical expeditions, for his chief scientist was a distinguished Norwegian oceanographer, Professor Harold Sverdrup, whose observations of ice movements and currents were to prove of lasting value. Despite this failure Wilkins remained optimistic about the prospects for under-ice navigation and about the commercial possibilities of a northern passage route for cargo-carrying submarines. Almost thirty years were to pass before Commander W. R. Anderson of the United States Navy in another *Nautilus* would make the trip successfully.

25. *Radar Fences and Floating Airfields*

THE AIRPLANE and the helicopter are the symbols and
the instruments of Arctic progress today. Commercial airways navigating along or near Great Circle routes fly
regularly across the Arctic, spanning in hours the stark
mountains, the tumbled sea ice, the vast and empty surface
of the Greenland ice sheet over which Nansen and Peary
and so many others painfully trudged.

Air power, too, is the key to the economic and industrial
expansion upon which Canada is now embarking in her
Arctic territory. It is the key, moreover, to the strategic
significance of a region where potentially hostile powers, in
North America and the Soviet Union, confront each other
across an Arctic "Mediterranean" and prepare elaborate
and costly defenses against the possibility of air attack. Defenses in Canada's case are more than anything else responsible for the widespread opening up of her Arctic
regions since the last war. Greenland also has been brought
into closer contact with the outer world and has moved
—in the west and south at least—out of a hunting into a
fishing and monetary economy in which her mineral resources, of cryolite especially, play an important part. No
doubt comparable developments have also taken place in
the Soviet Arctic. The secrecy which surrounds Russia's
Arctic possessions, however, allows little information to
escape.

It is impossible to give more than a rapid sketch of the
broad trends and developments which have led to this
Arctic transformation. The period opens with an exploit
in the old style, the traversing of the Northwest Passage

by one of the outstanding pioneers in Arctic Canada today, Sergeant (now Inspector) Henry Larsen, R.C.M.P. In a little ship, the *St. Roch,* one hundred and four feet long, he made the Northwest Passage twice, passing on his voyage in 1940–42 through the swirling ice of Bellot Strait, then on his second voyage in the summer of 1944 along Prince of Wales Strait, and along Melville and Lancaster Sounds. Stopping at Winter Harbour in Melville Sound, he saw, carved on a high rock, the names of Parry's seamen and Her Majesty's ships *Hecla* and *Griper* which had wintered there in 1819. Larsen's was a truly audacious achievement —one which Parry himself would have been the first to admire.

Larsen's voyages in the *St. Roch* stand out in romantic contrast to the network of air, land and sea operations, economic and strategic, which since the war have covered Canada's Arctic sector. Those directed to the exploitation of the Canadian North have been based mainly on an extensive program of air survey, supplemented by ground parties working mostly, not with dogs and sledges but with aircraft, especially helicopters. The aim has been to exploit the rich mineral resources of the Canadian Arctic— petroleum, graphite, coal, iron, nickel, copper and gold as well as, just south of the Arctic Circle, radium and uranium at Great Bear Lake. Geological prospecting in Canada's Northwest Territory, greatly speeded by the use of devices such as the airborne magnetometer, has been so widespread that a Canadian geographer has lately remarked, "It is probably true that no single part of the Canadian Arctic even including remote islands not visited since they first were placed on the map long ago, has escaped the recent attention of the geologist, geographer or other scientist. . . ."

An even more important factor in this transformation

of the Canadian Arctic and in the opening up of many territories explored but unvisited for generations has been the Air Defense Program focused on the so-called D.E.W. Line (Distant Early Warning Line), once known under the Orwellian name, "Project 572." This radar fence, with more than forty manned stations stretching from east Greenland to Alaska, has spurred the making of innumerable airfields, the building of small townships of scientists and technicians, the bulldozing of Arctic highways, and the employment of around twenty thousand men. The names of some of these prefabricated, air-conditioned, electronic stations recall the debt which those responsible for this spectacular if gloomy project owe to the early explorers. There is, for instance, Frobisher, in Frobisher Bay on Baffin Island.

All this rapid development of course has inevitably brought in its train sociological problems concerning the Eskimos who have been brought into contact with the diseases and the temptations as well as the benefits of civilization. They are at the same time fast losing the native skills which have enabled them for so long to survive.

Greenland, too, has been brought into the stream of world affairs. This is largely because of its importance as a landing stage and weather observatory along a polar air route. Greenland's key role in the future of polar aviation had been forseen as far back as the early thirties by the British Arctic Air Route Expedition sent out to test possibilities by the Royal Geographical Society.

But the British were not the first to anticipate such developments. In the nineteen-twenties, the Norwegian Arctic explorer Bernt Balchen, who flew with Amundsen and Wilkins in the Arctic and piloted Admiral Byrd to the South Pole, forecast the role of Greenland as "the great aircraft carrier of the Arctic." The urgent needs of war saw

240

this forecast realized. In 1941 an agreement was signed between the United States and Denmark. This, while reaffirming Danish sovereignty over Greenland, granted the United States the temporary use of certain bases in west and southwest Greenland for defensive purposes, and in particular as staging points for the ferrying of aircraft to Britain. The first airports, planned by Balchen himself as Arctic adviser to the U. S. Air Force, were at Julianehaab, in southern Greenland, and at Søndre Strømfjord in the southwest.

After the war, the greatest of these Arctic airports was established at Thule, far up the west coast near the entrance to Smith South, the "Sir Thomas Smith's Sound" discovered in 1616 by the Englishman William Baffin. Thule, with its airfields, its aluminum buildings, its radio and radar tower lower only than the television mast on the Empire State Building in New York, is now a pulsating modern Arctic town.

The pioneer days of transarctic flying belong to the period between the wars when the flights of Amundsen, Byrd and Wilkins were succeeded by the survey flights of Van Gronau of Germany and of the U. S. aviator Lindbergh. But it was not until the airfields in southwest Greenland had been built that the first commercial air service between Europe and the West Coast of North America could begin.

This took place in November 1954 when the Scandinavian Airlines System made the first commercial flight from Copenhagen to Los Angeles by way of the airfields at Søndre Strømfjord.

While west Greenland was thus fast developing under the impact of war and air power and the energetic measures of the Danish Government to develop the settlements north and south of the capital, Godthaab, Greenland's ice sheet

241

and its northern and eastern coasts (where the musk ox and the kayak could still be seen) continued to attract exploring expeditions.

First among these after the Second World War were the expeditions known as the *Missions Polaires Françaises,* launched by the French ex-parachutist and anthropologist Paul-Emile Victor who, more than anyone else, has been responsible for the remarkable revival of French polar exploration since the last war. These French expeditions, working between 1948 and 1957 and supplied in large degree direct from France by air, have been concerned chiefly with the seismic investigation of the central and southern parts of the ice sheet. Seismic and other glaciological investigations also preoccupied the British North Greenland Expedition of 1952–54, working in Dronning Louise Land.

This, led by a naval officer, Commander C. J. D. Simpson, has a special place in the history of recent British exploration. Like the French expeditions, it relied greatly on supply by air, using aircraft of the Royal Air Force, but one of its aims was to bring about the re-entry of the Navy into polar exploration. This was a reminder that in Britain belief in the traditional role of the Navy in polar enterprise, so staunchly held by Clements Markham in the nineties, still survived.

Another large expedition working in Greenland since the Second World War was the Danish Peary Land Expedition, led by Count Eigil Knuth. This too, working in the extreme northwest of Greenland, relied considerably upon air support and was involved in survey and in investigations of the ice sheet. The latest of these large Greenland expeditions to study the conditions and history of the ice sheet is the International Expedition to Greenland of 1959, organized and led by M. Paul-Emile Victor.

Before turning to different forms of Arctic exploration since the Second World War one other aspect of Arctic activity must be mentioned. This is the annual flow of undergraduate expeditions to the Arctic, which have greatly increased in number. Easily and cheaply accessible, with a climate at its best during the months of the summer vacation, Iceland, Spitsbergen and Nordaustland, Greenland, Jan Mayen Island, have all been targets of such undergraduate parties combining adventurous travel with scientific work. The Svalbard archipelago has been especially popular and a more or less continuous series of small expeditions from Cambridge have, in proportion to their size and resources, added considerably to the detailed geological mapping of these islands.

Since the war, however, not land expeditions but those traveling on or even under the ice, particularly the floating ice which covers almost throughout the year the central polar basin, have made the most important and exciting geographical discoveries in the Arctic. Until the year 1937–38, the year of Papanin's Russian drift expedition, knowledge of this region was still based upon the work of Nansen in the *Fram* and upon evidence from the drifting *Jeannette* (both of the late nineteenth century) as well as upon Amundsen's drift in the *Maud* in 1922–24. Following Papanin's drift, however, there were other Russian drift expeditions on the eve and during the first two years of the war, and then from 1948 a whole series of expeditions, Russian and American, drifting on ice floes and ice islands over most of the central polar basin. Aircraft combined with these drifting stations not only in manning and supplying them but also in supplementary ice reconaissance and observation.

In this curious world of floating ice laboratories and floating airfields, circulating around and about the Pole regardless of any political sector boundaries radiating from it, the Russians have been most active. Geographically, the most dramatic discovery by the Russian ice-floe parties since 1948 has been that of the great submarine Lomonosov Ridge (so called after the famous Russian inventor of the eighteenth century). This was found to range below the sea ice from Canada's Ellesmere Island to the New Siberian Islands. It divides the central polar basin into an Atlantic and a Pacific sector; a division which must powerfully affect the movement of surface currents and the drift of ice.

Much else has been discovered by these postwar expeditions about the relations between wind and ice drift and about the history, the growth, and the decay of sea ice. It was for instance learned that in the Atlantic sector the ice drifts much faster than in Nansen's time, whereas it is slower in the Pacific sector; that ice floes in the course of a three-year period, while retaining the same over-all thickness, diminish on top but increase below. The Russians obtained clear proof of this steady process of growth and decay in 1954 when they rediscovered a campsite on their drifting station S.P. - 2, abandoned three years earlier. Their old tents were still standing but they were standing isolated on pillars of ice 1.6 meters high, pillars which the presence of the tents had prevented from melting.

BOOK TWO

Some Not So Famous
Explorations in the Arctic

Exploration for a Woman in the Arctic

The Explorers Who Found the Doll of Gold

The Explorer Who Killed a Ghost

How European Traders Helped a Poor Eskimo

A Motorboat Expedition and Its Strange Consequences

The Big Strike

I. Exploration for a Woman in the Arctic

WE WERE pushing to Sixty Mile. We'd left Nome a couple of days before and we were pretty tired, all three of us. So were the dogs. We weren't tenderfeet, certainly; but on the other hand we weren't any spring chickens either.

Every man on that crazy trip had thrown a big chunk of his life to exploration in the Arctic—ten years at least—and paid extra besides with a piece of himself. Carl, the Swede, who was leading, had lost his right eye in a barroom fight and had to get along with the one that was left over and a thirty-five-cent marble from Sears Roebuck. Wasserfall, the German geologist, used to have so much hell with his teeth when he couldn't get within three days' hike of a dentist, that he had them all yanked at one sitting and sported a double set of porcelain ones. He had a way of taking 'em out and snapping them at people with his fingers. He wasn't a bad guy, at least for a scientist. Myself, I'd had a leg amputated after it was frostbitten, frozen almost to the bone, and to add to the difficulty, accidentally harpooned. But people wouldn't have known it if I didn't tell them, even if I say so myself. These newfangled artificial limbs are good, almost as good as the original; and sometimes they are better, as I intend to show.

So it was a slightly secondhand gang which made that trip and none of us was too keen on wearing ourselves out any further. Or at least Wasserfall and I weren't. But Carl the Swede seemed to be in a hurry, and was always for "pushing on." This was funny because he had the least reason to do so. He had simply heard there'd be a wild time in Sixty Mile around Christmas. He'd persuaded the Dutchman and me to come along by telling us that a new mine was opening near there. We were both broke and didn't have anything better to do, though I for one hadn't much faith in the big Scandinavian. He had a reputation all through Alaska for being a drunk and a troublemaker and for not paying his bar debts. There were a lot of towns where he couldn't even buy a drink without paying in advance.

We were on the third day out and tired. Around evening we came to a roadhouse, and Wasserfall and I were delighted because we could rest there for the night. In Alaska a roadhouse is anybody's house. The visitor must only wash the dishes and leave as much chopped kindling as was found when he entered.

"*Na*," said Wasserfall, "in my whole life there never such a welcome house was."

"Yep," I agreed, "I could do with a bit of shut-eye and some java and bacon beforehand."

You should have seen Carl turn on the two of us. He stood as high as a pair of skis and as wide as a tree.

"We're gonna make town tonight, you bozos," he said, trying to sound mean.

"Oh yeah," I said, "General." I'm not much for fighting

248

but I've got self-respect. Besides, big guys like Carl are mostly noise, and you can always back down if they call your bluff.

"There's three of us here," I said, "and I propose a vote." Wasserfall backed me up.

"Sixty Mile will tomorrow also yet be there," he said.

Carl saw that rough stuff wouldn't do him any good.

"Listen fellows," he said in his Swedish accent, "it's only five hours to Sixty Mile. Only five little hours. What's that to strong fellows like you? When we get there I shall show you a helluva good time, you bet."

"Oh yeah," I said.

"You bet."

"Whiskey?"

"You bet."

"Women?"

"One damn fine big woman!"

"Baloney," I said, "where is all the dough coming from?"

What then happened made me sorry I had come on that trip. It made me sure that Carl, the Swede, had gone balmy.

"Dough? Carl don't need dough," he bawled, laughing so hard that some of his straw blond hair shook loose from under his parka hood. "This here is money." And he dug a square box out of his pocket and opened it, shoving it under my nose. It was chock-full of glass eyes.

For a minute I couldn't say anything. I just stood and looked. Those eyes stared at me from the box, shimmering and glinting in the dim light. Carl was still roaring with laughter when his hands shook and the glass eyes seemed to move, becoming more frightening than ever.

"You're nuts," I said.

"*Verruckt,*" whispered Wasserfall. He'd been looking over my shoulder. He sounded sort of worried.

249

"So I ban crazy, eh?" Carl asked, quieting down. "You come see, and if there not plenty whiskey and one damn fine woman, you can call me one damn big liar." Then he put the lid back on the box and returned it to his pocket. "You come along . . ."

There wasn't much else we could do. They were his dogs and his sled and anyway the idea of spending the night in a shack with 250-pound lug who had gone crazy didn't appeal to either Wasserfall or myself.

We were tired then, but when we got to Sixty Mile, we were wrecked. By that time we didn't care if Carl was a liar or not. All we wanted to do was sleep. But when I say "we" I mean Wasserfall and myself, for Carl seemed to get peppier by the hour.

But he wasn't as crazy as he seemed; he was just smart, shrewd as a trader, which we never would have expected out of such an innocent and dumb-looking guy.

He dragged us into a saloon.

"Whiskey," he said, "I promised you." And his eyes twinkled.

We didn't feel like going in with him and wanted only to flop somewhere quickly and go to sleep. And we didn't want to have to foot the bill with the little money we had.

But Swedes can be stubborn. He tied up his dogs at the first saloon, and pointed to the second saloon which was, he said, where we'd go next.

"Are you going to buy out all the saloons in Sixty Mile?" I asked.

"You bet," he said, "we get drunk tonight."

"On glass eyes?"

"Shut up," he said, and pushed me in the door by the scruff of the neck.

Well—they did get drunk that night, and *on glass eyes.*

There are eight houses in Sixty Mile and twelve saloons. We went to seven of each, bought a bottle everywhere we went. Carl paid for all of them, and he did so *in glass eyes*.

This is how we did it. Sixty Mile, it turned out, was one of those towns where Carl couldn't buy a drink without putting down the cash first. He knew that and he figured on it. He'd go up to the bartender, trying to look all worn out, and say hello. And the bartender, seeing who it was, would just grunt and pretend not to see him.

"Bottle of whiskey," Carl would say. The bartender would ask him for his money and Carl would tell a long hard-luck story how he was just in town and sick, and how tomorrow he would get a big payment from the mining company and come across sure. Then he'd say that he was willing to give bond, and take out his glass eye. He'd give it to the bartender and say, "Keep that for me. You know I can't go without my eye." He managed to look so pitiful that the bartender always gave him the whiskey. After all a man can't go around without his eye.

"You must have the eye in a whiskey glass full of whiskey," Carl would say next. "I'm gonna get drunk tonight and I want my eye to be happy too." That convinced the bartender that he was nuts but at least on the level.

In fifteen minutes he worked the same trick in seven bars. As soon as he was out of one saloon he would take an eye out of the box, squeeze it into his socket, and pull the whole show over again.

"You think Carl is crazy," he said to us standing there afterward with bottles sticking out all over us. "Now I show you one damn fine big woman."

He led us across the street to a house. He hammered on the door. Nobody came and he knocked again. Then a man came out in his underwear.

"One damn fine big woman," I said.

"Shut up," Carl growled, then asked the man where Blondie was.

"Blondie?" The man rubbed his eyes and yawned. We had aparently awakened him up out of a sound sleep.

"Yeah, said Carl, "Blondie."

"Oh," said the man, "she has moved out. She ain't in the business any more, she's got married and gone respectable."

"Respectable? Blondie?" Carl was profoundly hurt.

"One damn fine big woman," I said.

"To a shoemaker," said the man. "And now she's got religion and nerves."

"What do you mean nerves?"

"I mean she jitters when you say boo to her."

I repeated what I'd said before. This seemed to make Carl mad.

"Religion! Nerves! She can't do that to me! Where does she live?"

The man pointed to the last house down the street.

"Be careful," he yelled after us, "she has awful nerves...."

Carl walked so fast we had a hard time following without dropping some of the bottles. When he came to the house he knocked hard.

"Who is it?" piped a voice from the inside—a voice that sounded so greasy we could tell it was a fat woman.

"Carl."

"Carl who?"

"The nerve of her pretending not to remember me!" he muttered and rattled the door.

"Go away," a voice shrilled from the inside.

"Open up or I'll break down the door," Carl yelled. He could boom like a foghorn. We could hear somebody rummaging around in the bouse.

252

"Go away," the woman yelled. "What do you mean by bothering a lady at this hour of the night?"

Carl put down the three bottles he was carrying, stepped back a couple of paces, and then threw himself with his whole weight against the door. The whole house shook.

"Go home, you good-for-nothing drunk, or I'll shoot you," she screamed.

Carl pushed us away from the door. "She's still got her old double loader," he whispered; then, standing well to the left he kicked the door on the far side with his heavy boot.

Crack! A bullet came through just a few inches above the place where he kicked. "You shoot too far to the right," Carl yelled. Then, nimble as a weasel, he scurried across and kicked from the the other side. *Crack!* came another bullet.

"Now," said Carl, "before she can load again."

"The poor helpless woman," I remarked as we threw ourselves all together on the door, breaking the hinges. By the time people got out on the street to see what all the shooting was about, we were inside.

"Blondie!" exclaimed Carl with open arms. "I'm glad to see you."

"I beg your pardon," said Wasserfall and brought in the bottles. I didn't say anything. I just looked.

There was plenty to look at. For a former lady of joy Blondie sure had proportions. When we had blown in with the door she had squeaked and retreated to the farthest part of the bed, dropping the double loader on the way. I thought at the time it was only characteristic of her that she should look at a bed for a place of safety. And when I say at the farthest corner of the bed, I am inaccurate, because she was all over it, every part of her blubbering.

Now that he was in, Carl seemed stumped. I guess he had not had too much acquaintance with hysterical women.

"Blondie," he said sort of dumbly, "what's the matter, Blondie?"

What she said didn't make any sense. It was all garbled, mixed up with laughing and crying and sniffling screams and whining. She had peroxide hair, a pink face with creases like a suckling pig, and red flannel pajamas which impressed me.

"Blondie!" Carl kept on pleading, still perplexed. Then he seemed to have an inspiration. "Your husband—he don't treat you right, I bet. Where is the son of a gun?"

"Go away," she yelled again. It seemed the only thing she could say so you could understand her. "When he come back he murder you all."

"I like to see him try it." Carl sat down on the edge of the bed. There wasn't any more than an edge left over. "We gonna stay here the night." He turned to me. "Gimme a bottle."

I looked around the room. It was small. I couldn't imagine where she had room to put her husband.

"Where we all gonna sleep?" I asked.

"Get out," said Blondie, "you make me nervous. I'm a nervous woman."

This remark must have struck Wasserfall funny. Germans are strange people. You never know what they're going to do next. They have their own idea of a sense of humor.

While I was busy pulling the cork out of a bottle and Carl stood there like a bump on a log not knowing what to do, Wasserfall crept up from behind. He'd taken his teeth out of his mouth and was clapping them together with his hands. He sneaked around the two of us and stretched the teeth at Blondie.

"Grrrr, Grrrr," he went, "bite, bite."

She stopped yammering as if she'd been shot, staring at those fingers with the teeth on them. Her eyes seemed to be swelling out of her head.

Her sudden silence must have fooled Carl; he must have thought she was amused.

"That's nothing," he said, and took out his eye. He moved it all around her saying, "looka, lookee, look what I see."

She still didn't make a sound. Just quivered like jelly. Her lips moved, then just hung open, and then she tried to shrink into the wall.

Well—I wasn't going to be outdone. I saw some spikes and a hammer. I went over and got them.

"I like it here," I said, "I'm gonna stay." I hammered a couple of spikes into my leg and hung my cap and gloves on them.

I guess this was too much for Blondie.

"Wah!" she screamed and jumped up. She ran out into the street, flannel pajamas and all. We didn't see her again that night. But we drank the seven bottles of whiskey, laughed during most of the night, and the next morning we pulled out.

All this just went to prove that Carl the Swede is not a liar, after all. If you explore hard enough, you can even find a woman in the Arctic.

II. The Explorers Who Found the Doll of Gold

WHITE MEN are like women, fussing over all sorts of trifling matters that have nothing to do with food. Thus do the children of the Arctic conclude whenever, during the long winters, they rehash the tale of what happened that time the expedition of the white men came to explore for worthless things and shed blood to get what they were after. . . .

Natoo was the luckiest child in the Eskimo village of Nekre:

Mayak, the master hunter, finding that he had more skins than he needed or could trade in the village, had been the first man from the north country to get through to Koogak after the long winter night. He had returned bursting with news, proud to be the first to tell about white men he had seen down there. His fabulous tales had sent the villagers home to get their traps and begin setting them all over the thawing hills, intent on getting down to Koogak with fox pelts to see for themselves. But only Agpalerk, mighty huntsman and father of little Natoo, was ready to start out the very next morning; for he had furs to barter.

The little girl had lain awake the whole night thinking about the white men and their big house. And once she had awakened her mother to ask what she ought to do if the white men should aim their talk at her. She had heard it whispered that their tongues were uneven, that their words were rough and could not penetrate the ears to enter into people's heads.

Her mother, Alluk, had told her not to bother. But the troubled little one had persisted in her question. So Alluk, who was gentle as well as wise, had said:

"Bring Pipaluk along with you, and talk to her."

Smiling happily, Natoo had fallen asleep. Yes! She would take her doll along, so that she too would have someone to talk to about the wonders she would see in the big house of the white men.

Traveling at good speed, Agpalerk and his family spent their first night on the trail in a cave. The next night he built a snowhouse for them; but even in this warmer shelter, their eyes did not stay shut very long. Natoo whispered to her doll Pipaluk that soon they were to see lots of strange and wonderful things.

When they swept into Koogak, Agpalerk did not show any hurry or curiosity.

"Hello," he said almost indifferently. "We happened to take a little trip." This he said to show them that he didn't care if they withheld the big news of the season for a while. . . .

The next day was the greatest day in the life of little Natoo; her parents too could hardly contain themselves. Agpalerk, as soon as he stepped outside, called loudly to his neighbor, Kreelerneq:

257

"It seems to me somebody once told about white men being seen hereabouts."

And Kreelerneq, delighted that the Nekre headman's curiosity was aroused, replied evasively:

"Oh, now you remind me, this is where the white men put up a little igloo." This was said as if the speaker were part owner of that igloo, and therefore had to speak of it modestly.

The Agpalerks sauntered up to the big lodge of the white men and glanced inside. It was so high that a man could stand upright anywhere under the roof. Lamps were as numerous as stars, and as bright as suns. And so much wood had been wasted on the inside that Agpalerk's head ached just to think of it. But Natoo crept up the step of the doorway like a young seal climbing out of the water, cautious and curious.

The white men proved to be friendly. All the stories told about them lost importance in face of the truth.

Natoo looked and looked. Her bright slitlike eyes weren't big enough to see everything at once. When anyone spoke to her, she did not listen. She kept turning around and swallowing the strange and unbelievable sights, her eyes bigger than ever. Her fingers were crazy to touch and to feel, but she obeyed Alluk and behaved, went and squatted quietly in a corner, from where she could see everything by moving her eyes about.

A man in a white apron and a funny white hat, who did all the cooking, carried her in his arms to the big board. The soup was given to each of them in a cup with a handle white and hard as stone. Sweet stuff was added that tasted as flowers smell in summer. Huge heaps of funny kinds of food from which smoke curled covered the table—enough to serve the belly-needs of thrifty people for a whole winter.

259

As last they stopped eating, stuffed with strange food. Then along came the man who was said to make all the decisions for the whites, who did the deep thinking for them. Agpalerk was privately informed that to become the friend of this headman, one had to help him carry stuff around, because that was a sign that one was willing to be of help to them. So Agpalerk offered to lend the headman a hand.

He stood before the maker of decisions and two other white men and gave his name. The whites did not get it; whereupon one of the villagers, who had learned how to let the words of the white men slip into his ears, spoke up for Agpalerk. As if afraid of forgetting, one white man wrote down what the villager said in tiny lines and pictures on a white sheet of skin, then asked questions about Agpalerk's country, which Agpalerk answered in his own simple tongue and the villager translated—until before long, the skin was covered front and back with lines that resembled tiny lice.

After dark the white men said they had heard enough and sent Agpalerk home. But Alluk and Natoo remained, the cook saying that the white men's hospitality toward them included a warm bed till tomorrow. At that, the headman and the one with the poor memory laughed boisterously.

Thinking that in his ignorance of their ways he had somehow offended them, Agpalerk feared that Alluk would suffer for it. Therefore he hastened to his igloo, gathered up three fine fox pelts, and returned to the house of the white men.

He entered, and found the cook beside Alluk, and felt easier in his mind. His wife had won favor with the mighty man who fed all the whites. Leaving the pelts, he strode home to bed.

The Explorers Who Found the Doll of Gold

On the last day of their stay, Natoo brought her doll up to the white men's lodge. How nice it would be if Pipaluk could see all the wonderful things there, and they could talk about it all long afterward! Of course Pipaluk did not talk, but she could remember. She was a lovely doll, made out of the beautiful soft stone that was to be found in such abundance up in the moraine near Nekre. Her father had found a good-sized chunk and carved it into Pipaluk with a sharp stone, hammering the face into a smiling friendly one so dear to Natoo. Never did Pipaluk lose her color, not even when she was kept in water for a whole summer and frozen solid through an entire winter— that was when Natoo had mislaid her and thought her doll had run away. For Pipaluk was made out of sunstone, so called—old people said—because it came from a mountain where the sun always shone, having once hidden from a bear inside that mountain, and gave it its color.

Natoo showed her doll everything of interest, speaking in a whisper so as not to disturb the big white man sitting in front of the fireplace, and raised her high to show her the glass in which to look was to see one's self as in the water of a lake.

Pipaluk slipped out of Natoo's upraised hands and fell to the floor, causing the white man to turn around. His eyes flashed as he quickly reached down and picked up the doll. Natoo was afraid she had angered the white man by disturbing him, and that he would throw Pipaluk out of the window. But the man rubbed his hand over the doll, examined it closely—as if, Natoo tremblingly thought, he wondered if he could break it in two—then jumped to his feet and shouted for his friends.

Now he will tell them all that I have done, Natoo

261

thought, ready to cry. She couldn't understand why he made such a fuss. Maybe they will kill me! She ran to the door, but the big man grabbed her and held on to her. The other white men stamped in; they all talked at once in high voices, and then addressed her in seeming anger. The poor frightened little girl failed to understand; their words melted like snow under a warm sun. By now, however, their faces were friendly; so she considered: "Perhaps the white men smile when they are ready to kill. They are so different."

Not a word did they get out of her. One ran out and soon came back with her father, and Natoo felt her fright oozing out. There was hard and fast talking, a little laughing. The headman told everyone to keep quiet, and so mighty a man was he, that none disobeyed, although words hung on every lip.

So the white men came and crowded into Agpalerk's house, while he made them welcome with an indifference he felt sure the men of Koogak had noticed.

Well, the end was that Natoo did not get her doll back. But her sorrow was lightened, because the white men gave her everything her eye fell upon—as many needles as she had fingers, a little cup, and other gifts she had never known the existence of.

During the easy four-day journey home, Natoo played with her new belongings and forgot about Pipaluk, except one night, when she suddenly burst into tears. Alluk, her gentle mother, soothed her that night, and hushed her lest the white man, who had decided to go with them in order to find the mountain of the sunstone, wake up.

"Pipaluk will be taken to the white man's country and will see places," her mother said to comfort her. "And your

262

mighty father has promised to find another big piece of sunstone and make a nice new Pipaluk for you."

All Nekre was there at the edge of the ice to greet them on their homecoming. A man from Koogak, up for the summer hunting, had already told how Agpalerk had made the trip in two sleeps. Even Mayak, trekking the way alone, had slept three nights on the trail! And so, when Agpalerk didn't seem to notice how warm their welcome was, they resented his boastful manner, and outdid him at his own game:

"What a man! He travels without sleep!"

"Oh, the great Agpalerk comes back to us!"

"He has the best dogs alive! And a wife and child as tireless as he!"

"See the important visitor he brings!"

The white man really impressed them, but he paid them scant attention. He seemed to have gone crazy about dolls. Every one he could lay hands on he fondled and kept. He also ran around and collected every scrap of sunstone he could find, bits which the children had thrown out in the garbage heaps. Without shame he gave the children sweet things to eat in exchange for their little carved dogs and other play toys. And when the sweets were eaten up, and the children bawled for their toys, he refused to give them up.

Angrily the parents hinted that it was better if this childish white man went somewhere else. The women chattered and fidgeted like penguins, for fear they might otherwise please the foolish man and be disgraced by his admiration. Somebody told him that in the next village the children had lots of those yellow stones. But being full of pity, they did not try to explain to him that these stones were worthless, useless, just like the sun—nice to look at, but of no

263

use, because she came in the summertime when it was warm anyway, and stayed hidden in the winter when warmth was wanted.

So badly did the white man want to go to the next village, that Mayak went up with him. Next day two more white visitors came up to Nekre. They had had a hard time making the trip, that was plain; their clothes were thin for cold weather, and the delicate food they kept in cups couldn't have kept children at home warm. They arrived weary, worn out. Yet even before demanding food and rest, they asked about sunstone. Somebody told them about the other white man who had gone up to seek for more sunstone, and the new visitors growled with rage.

In the evening they asked for all the dolls that could be found, but the white man who was two sleeps ahead had not left much behind. Now the white men explained that in their country sunstone was used to pay for everything— for food or wood or clothes. He who had a big supply of it was a headman, he never worked or hunted.

At dawn the whites pushed on and overtook the first white at the next settlement. The three exchanged loud words, made grim faces and raised their fists high. But after a while they must have come to an understanding, because when they emerged from the first man's igloo which Mayak had built for him, they were wearing smiles.

Everybody from Agpalerk's village had dashed up to the next settlement, unable to talk or think of anything but the white men and their funny antics. Now one of the whites approached Agpalerk and asked where it was all the nice shiny sunstone came from.

Said Agpalerk:

"Not along the cliff will you find the stones, but in the moraine at the left side of the glacier, among the rock and gravel. But not till the snow is gone. Anyway, they're good for nothing—except for the kids to play with. We have tried to make things out of them, but hammering doesn't change them much, and fire will not melt them down. For they are made by the sun which forever remains."

His wise words fell on deaf ears. The whites legged it out to the moraine, but found it still buried under layers of ice and snow. There was no chance to get at the stones unto well into summer.

Sometime later all the other members of the white man's expedition arrived and made camp. When they favored little Natoo with smiles of recognition, her playmates looked at her with open-eyed envy. It was jolly to have them around, the whites; they supplied the villagers with food for endless gossip, and had wonderful things to sell and exchange.

But gradually they changed. Natoo, who still nursed her grievance against them for keeping Pipaluk prisoner, was quick to notice this. They forgot their old interests—or rather, they did not begin to behave as Agpalerk told they had down below. One, who used to search for flowers, no longer looked for them although they were beginning to blossom in abundance. The medicine man had no eyes for the heavens. All the whites were busy watching each other, never allowing anyone to leave camp alone. To pass the time, they invited the women to come and stay with them, to mend and make boots for them, to patch up worn-out clothing.

When it was discovered that Alluk had gone off with a large piece of sunstone for Agpalerk to make into a doll for Natoo, the white men decided not to let the women leave the camp, either. And so fiercely did they threaten Alluk that she went and fetched the sunstone, which she returned to the foolish white men. Natoo languished, grew thin and sad with longing for her doll.

At last the sun began to shine steadily, warming the soil. The snow melted away in brisk rivulets, and the white men began working, working without stopping, digging away until they found some of what they were after.

But if the women were to be believed, this did not make the whites any happier. They hollered at each other and the cook would not feed the rest, and they were all anxious to dig for the sunstones.

The time had come, too, for the people to go north and hunt walrus on the ice. They all had to go, as the winter's supply was gone, and dogs and humans had to be fed.

"We must have our women back," said Agpalerk to the white men, who were like babies and did not realize anything.

When the whites did not offer their women back, the men talked it over and decided to smuggle their women out while the whites were away digging like mice for that which was valueless.

Said and done! But the whites espied them and dashed back to their camp. Agpalerk tried to explain matters. The cook, who had evidently gone mad, struck him in the face. Forgetting that his assailant had a white skin, Agpalerk struck the cook with his stick.

A fight began. It was long since the villagers had fought about anything, for they knew how fruitless was battle, except occasionally for a woman. But once at it, they found a fierce lust to do battle rising within their peaceful souls.

A loud voice, the voice of the former headman of the whites, checked the affray. They had found, he said, that there was no more sunstone to be had here, and so they

266

would be leaving right away, dragging their sleds and their goods with them. They would go south to their ship, and sail as soon as the ice permitted. No women should cause trouble between his men and the men of the north country.

Clearly enough, the whites were afraid to fight. Contemptuously the natives let them begin packing their stuff.

Just then Natoo, whose little heart pained her because Pipaluk was to go away with the whites, begged her father to get her doll back. She knew her mighty father could do what other men could not do—even talk sternly to whiteskins.

"My little daughter wants her doll," he courteously addressed the white headman.

But none of the whites seemed to get the meaning of his request. At that, Natoo began sobbing, something Agpalerk could not stand. Going over the loaded sleds, he began to rummage in the heavy sacks full of sunstones, little thinking the whites would mind, as the sunstones were after all of no use to anybody but children.

At this, a madness seemed to possess the whites. They rushed toward their sleds, while one of them lifted little Natoo in his two hands, just as she had got hold of Pipaluk, and flung her aside into an adjacent field. She fell, little Natoo, and never moved again, her neck broken.

For a moment there was a stunned, horrified silence. Then the whites moved to their sleds without another word, anxious to be gone. When they did so, Agpalerk forgot his awe of them, brandished his harpoon and crashed it through the breast of the one who had killed his little daughter. The man staggered back as if under a heavy load on his chest, sagged down, quivered and was dead.

At once the guns of the whites spurted flame, roared loudly; and Mayak, two more men and three women fell to

267

the ground, convulsed or shrieking. That did not stop the rest of the villagers from going for the whites; and before the white men broke and ran, two more lay dead.

Out over the infirm ice they scattered, and at a distance were seen to come together, stop and talk things over. Anybody could see how scared they were. They did not dare come back.

Next day the ice broke up, and the white men, rooted to the ice floe, were carried away on the drift. But to this the villagers gave no thought. They sat in their homes and mourned their dead.

Deepest was the sorrow of Agpalerk and Alluk. The big hunter said in deep tones: "Why did they not kill me instead? I have had my full share of days."

At the end of the customary five-day period of mourning, the dead were laid away in graves, and all talk of them ceased, was forbidden. Only when some women suggested that the whole load of sunstones which the white men had dug up should be packed into little Natoo's grave, was there any discussion. Some thought it should be done, because she had always had such fun out of sunstones. But an old man said that it was far better to dump the sunstones out in the sea—the children could play with other toys, and the adults had no use for the shiny worthless things.

And this sage advice was followed. The sacks full of sunstones were dragged from the white men's sleds and sunk far from shore, the heavy sacks rapidly disappearing in the clear blue water. And as the whites had done a thorough job digging, no more sunstones were ever found in the moraine. . . .

That's the story. People have never ceased wondering

at the white men who will not fight for a woman, although she is necessary, but will kill and be killed for useless little stones that shine like the sun and are only good for dolls and toys for children to play with.

III. The Explorer Who Killed a Ghost

I SHOULD NEVER have taken him along, of course. I can
see it now, but that's only because one knows so much afterwards. I can see it now as I sit here in the . . . the police
court, I guess you call it. I'll try and tell you all about it now,
sir, because I want you . . . I want somebody to understand
what really happened. You may still not understand, Sheriff,
but perhaps it doesn't matter so much. . . .

The whole thing began, you see, the evening he came
up to see me here in town. I was just considering my next
trip to east Greenland, getting ready for another lonely
year of exploration up there in the snow and the darkness.
I was trying to figure out whom I should take along with
me. When you spend a whole year in the Arctic with only
one companion, it is quite a serious matter. . . . But you
know all about that, Sheriff, you know I've been going up
there every fall now for a good many years.

Anyway, I was thinking about these things when the
doorbell rang and I let him in. He told me right away that
he would like to go with me to Greenland. He said that

270

he had no experience since he had never been out of the country, but he was a strong man and he was used to hard work. He didn't ask for anything and he would bring his own guns and ammunition. He even wanted to put up some money for equipment, fox traps and other things. Half of the food supplies he would pay and he would let me do all the buying. We talked about the details for a while just as if I had already decided to take him along. Then he got up to say good night. He'd be back the next afternoon, he told me.

As soon as he left, I got angry with myself. I saw that he had talked all the time as if the matter had been settled. The decision seemed to be up to him and not to me from the way he had talked. No, I told myself. Why should I drop Thomas who had been going with me for several years? We could always settle our quarrel about the furs which had rotted on our way down from Greenland last spring. We could let bygones be bygones. There is still no doubt that Thomas was to blame for the furs that got ruined, but we could always get along. Thomas was easy to get along with if you left him alone. It was that crazy wife of his who made the trouble. That darn old hag. . . . Beg your pardon, Sheriff, but Thomas told me all about her himself. Still, I thought I could fix it.

But the next evening Gustav turned up again, acting like my partner already. I had made up my mind to tell him that Thomas was going with me, but I never got a chance to say it. He pulled out price lists and told me about the things he had bought already. He could get the oil cheaply through a friend, he was bringing his tool chest which was very well stocked—he had even figured out the cubic feet and the freight for all his gear.

I never had a chance, you can see that, Sheriff! It wasn't

271

that he talked so much or so fast, but he had everything figured out on paper. It was hard for me to say that all his troubles had been for nothing since he would not go with me. Just as I was going to explain it to him, Gustav said he thought it right that he should have one third of the profit while I got two thirds since I had all the experience, but that we should split the expenses half and half.

"We might as well put our names to it," he told me and darn if he didn't have it all on paper already. He pulled it out of his pocket and before I knew it I had signed my name to it. I told myself that Thomas had gone too far, after all, suing a fellow trapper just like landlubbers sharing a shoe-maker's store! This would teach him a lesson, I thought, as I signed the contract with a firm hand. Gustav signed his full name, Gustav Krakau it read. He told me he would give the contract to his lawyer and have it notarized. That showed he was on the up-and-up, wanted it all legal and solemn—just a man to your taste, Mr. Sheriff!

He was going away for a while, he told me as he left. He had some private affairs to settle before we went north, but we were in no great hurry. He didn't say where he was going or when he would be back. All the time he talked as if he was the leader of the expedition. I mostly said yes and agreed. He knew what he was talking about, of course, and what he didn't know he left to me.

And still I hesitated. I didn't care about the paper I had signed. I could still have a talk with Thomas and forget about the other man. As the days went by I got more and more convinced that Gustav Krakau was not the man for me and I was ready to go to Thomas when the letter from the lawyer arrived. I had to sign for it, so you can see that it was no ordinary letter. And there was a lot of money in it. Good, solid, Danish kroner. The letter said that this was

272

Krakau's share of the expenses and the contract was very legal and notarized. The lawyer called Gustav his client and wrote a lot of other things which made little sense to me.

That settled it. The next day I went down to the ship chandler and made all the arrangements. I told him I was taking a new man with me this time and I knew that the whole town would know about it the next day. Next I went to the Consul's office to order our passage and get space for all the freight. I told them I wanted to be put on shore at the same old place and that I had a new partner this year. "And here is my deposit!" I told them and showed all my money. That brought the Consul out from his office. Until he heard about my money he let Danielsen take care of everything, but now I was invited in and offered one of the cigars he kept in the bottom drawer. I told the Consul about Gustav Krakau too. As I walked home, I met Thomas and his crazy wife strutting around as if she owned the whole harbor and the shipyard too. "Hell," I said and put a finger to my cap. That was all I said and that took care of Thomas.

Gustav was seasick on the way up north on board the *Blue Whale*. He had never been to sea before and he was pretty sick the first few days, unable to eat a thing. The crew was joking about it day and night. I knew them all from previous years, of course, but I didn't like them to make fun of my "tough new partner."

"What the devil!" I told them at last when I got angry. "What's so strange about a body not eating the foul stuff you serve as food on this wreck of a ship?" Pardon me, Sheriff, but that's what I said and since there are witnesses, I had better tell the truth.

As soon as we were in the ice and the sea got calm, Gustav

was all right again. He came on deck with me and as soon as I got talking with him it turned out that he was a man who knew a little about everything. He could remember what he had learned at school—and he had even continued reading! He even told me that he had brought along quite a few books he was going to work his way through during the winter. If I had known that I would certainly not have taken him along—a trapper who reads books is a man to watch carefully.

At last we arrived and the *Blue Whale* left us behind. As soon as the ship disappeared out the fjord with its load of other trappers going farther north, Gustav turned to me, grabbed my hand and began saying a lot of serious, high-falutin stuff. We were going to stay together there for a whole year all alone, he said. Then he talked like he was in church, about friendship and confidence and what not. I don't go for stuff like that and I told him it was all nonsense, turned my back to him and asked him to carry our gear up to the blockhouse as fast as he could. Then I left him and began fixing the roof which the bears seemed to have been playing with during the summer.

We began making our preparations and I must admit I have never met a better man for a companion. And clever—you never saw the likes of it, Mr. Sheriff! He had never seen a walrus before, of course, but as soon as I showed him how to hit the animal right behind the ear, he got the knack of it in no time. He had no idea about skinning and flensing the animals, but he stood watching me just like a little boy. Then he asked permission to do the next walrus himself in order to learn it. And believe me, he worked all night long before he was satisfied.

And what a cook he was! Greenland has never seen anyone like him before. Besides the usual supplies, Gustav

274

Courtesy of the New York Public Library

had brought along all sorts of nonsense—curry and spicy sauces and other useless things. But it sure tasted good! It made you feel like staying on at table after the food was finished, just to keep the good taste in your mouth.

And Gustav always had plenty to talk about. He never got tired asking questions and you knew he always listened to the answers. He told me he was writing down everything I told him. When I explained to him how to do things he had never done before, he would go outside, try it out and teach himself how to do it.

From the time he was a small boy Gustav had done a good deal of hunting in the woods at home. Once he told me that he had always dreamed of being a trapper one day, but his mother had kept him from it. She wanted him to study, that was why he had plowed through so many books. It got to be a habit with him and he went on reading. Can you beat it—reading books after he was grown up and didn't have to!

But he was a good man with a gun and we had quite a bit of meat during the late summer. When fall came with the first frost, we got our first bear. I remember Gustav got all excited then and asked if he might have the first shot. Sure, go ahead, I told him. I would just as soon not shoot when I don't have to. He was like a child when he felled the bear and I must say he made a good job of it. Later on we saw bears every day, of course, sometimes several big ones in one day. Gustav skinned them all and he studied their insides to see what they had been eating. He did the same thing with all the animals, he even wrote down what he saw. Yes, he was a deep one!

Soon it was getting darker every day and the sun would be gone for a good many months. It was time to set our traps and that was something new to Gustav. He worked at it at home and he got to be pretty good. He caught onto it in no time like with most things you told him. I showed him how to set the traps, how to cover them with a thin layer of snow and make them look natural to the fox. In a couple of days he was as good as I and we set out. I went with him at first, showing him where to put the traps and how to find them when he came back. In a few days he could do it all alone.

After that we split up the territory between us. Everything to the north was his field while I kept to the south. We made a regular routine out of it. Every Monday morning we set out with two dogs each. They pulled the little sleigh with sleeping bag and food. We could move faster that way, and the dogs would always warn you about bears at night. I have had the same four dogs for years and it was funny the way they made friends with Gustav right away. Thomas always had a hard time getting along with them, but they took to Gustav from the first day and he had a good way with them.

He went north and I went south and we kept walking all day Monday and Tuesday. At night we slept in some small huts I built many years ago. Half of Wednesday we kept on walking, checking up on the traps, but in the afternoon we turned around. Wednesday night we slept in the Tuesday hut and Thursday night we spent in the Monday hut. Friday we were back again. If we met a snowstorm we had to stay over in one of the small huts, of course, and wouldn't get back until Saturday. Some times we did not meet until Sunday and once in a long while we did not see each other until the end of the next week again. But I had stored plenty of food in all the huts. We were both careful and there was never anything to worry about.

Soon I noticed that I was really looking forward to Friday. I began missing Gustav when I was all alone with the dogs and I was eager to sit listening to his talk again. Nothing much happens up in that wild, icy country, you know. Everything is the same year after year. Animals and nature always behave in the same old way and you don't think much about the job unless something unusual happens. Coming across a rare animal, a snow owl or something like that, is enough of an event to make a man happy to live up there in the Arctic darkness. It doesn't happen often though.

Life with Gustav was quite different from all the winters I had spent with Thomas. We never spoke a word to each other, Thomas and I. What did we have to talk about? We knew our work and both did it well enough. That was all. Gustav was another story! He had always lots to tell when we met again. During the week he had seen so many things he had to talk about—things we all knew but never talked about because they did not seem worth wasting a word on.

What a talker Gustav was! Mr. Sheriff! I could not help thinking about all the things he had said when I was walking alone during the week with my two dogs behind me. In the end I got so used to all this talk that I began saying things on my own. Sometimes Gustav discussed politics. Did you ever hear of such a man, Mr. Sheriff? A trapper talking politics—as if that was the concern of a man making his living by trapping fox in East Greenland.

But Gustav said that politics was necessary to make people happy. I should think he was the only man with such a crazy idea in his head. And I didn't think there was anything to his words. Oh yes, said Gustav. It was the truth. And he even talked about religion. That was the first time I knew for sure he was wrong. He never went to church, he said. He didn't believe in ministers—they did not know

278

the people, he said. That was all nonsense, of course, but I would never dream of contradicting him. He could always remember something he had read and use it against me. And he knew the Bible by heart, it seemed.

After a while it got to be with Gustav just like with the heat in the house—you can do without it, but you get mighty cold. I missed him more and more during the week and he made the winter quite different for me.

Christmas came and we had something extra to eat. We even washed and shaved ourselves and lit candles. I put on a clean white shirt. After all, it's Christmas only once a year. But Gustav didn't seem to be very moved by the Holy Day. He went out to check his traps just like any other day. I didn't like it, but there was nothing I could do since we were partners and he was as good a trapper as I.

It was shortly after New Year when Gustav complained that he didn't feel so well. His legs were like lead if he walked any distance. I could see that he moved very slowly and he went early to bed. But he would always read in bed and tell me about all the things in his books. Never any stories, only facts about the world and sometimes deep thoughts which I could make nothing of. I understood that his folks must be educated people, but he never told me where he came from. I never asked—if he wanted me to know he would have told me.

Next Monday we got ready as usual. Gustav still moved slowly but he seemed all right as we parted. I said good-by and told him I would think about all the things we had talked about. "I'll tell you what I think about it all when I see you on Friday," I told him.

"Consider it well," he said and laughed as I left. The week was like any other. I looked after the traps and had a pretty good load with me when I returned on Friday. Gustav's dogs were by the blockhouse already and I could see lights in the house. It's the first time he got there ahead of me, I thought, but when I entered I found Gustav in bed looking poorly. He told me he had had some fever but was all right again. He had felt pretty bad and had returned the day after I left him. He had only wanted to wait for me, he said. Now he wanted to set out right away to get the animals in his traps before the wolves got them.

He was right, of course. We had to think of our catch before anything else, that's what we were there for. I didn't say anything, although I had been looking forward to his company over the weekend. I felt very lonely as he left. I had never thought of it before, but now I knew Gustav had spoiled me with all his talk.

Monday I set out again and I had extra good luck that week. The load was heavy and it was late in the evening before I was back at the blockhouse the next Friday. There was no light to be seen in the house as I approached it. I had really expected Gustav to be there, since he had started out earlier than I had.

But something was wrong. I could soon hear that his dogs were inside the house, howling and barking when I came close. My dogs began barking too, but still no light in the house. It was strange and I felt a little scared. I took my time unreining the dogs so he would wake up, the dogs making enough noise to rouse anybody. He would soon make a light and come outside, I thought. I noticed there was no smoke coming up the chimney and that he could not have been outside for a couple of days since quite a lot of snow had settled in front of the door.

At last I went in. It was pretty dark and I got out my matches. It was just as cold in the house as outside. The dogs jumped on me, howling. Strange! I took off my clothes and lit a candle. Gustav was in bed with his back to me.

"Gustav," I called. No movement. It didn't take me long to understand that Gustav was dead.

At first I could not believe it was true. I made a fire in the stove and cut some ice for the pot. The whole water barrel outside was a solid block of ice and it had always been the duty of the first man home to thaw some ice. I even began scolding Gustav for neglecting his duties. If you have made an agreement, you have to stick to it. Right, Mr. Sheriff?

I didn't want to look at Gustav. As long as I didn't I could pretend that he was asleep, that he would wake up soon. I fed the hungry dogs and told them that Gustav was drunk, that that was the reason they never got their food. I knew it was a lie, of course. It was just something I said.

I kept up the pretense that Gustav was asleep. I knew how miserable I would be once I admitted that he was dead. Suddenly I was much, much too tired, I could only go to bed and settle down for the night.

People who don't know loneliness, especially in that total darkness, don't understand how you can make yourself believe something you know is not true, something which is obviously a lie. When I got up in the morning I told myself that I had to keep Gustav from getting up to tell me that he was dead. I made hot cereal for both of us.

"Do you want some?" I called to him. He didn't answer of course. But I didn't want to let him know that I knew it.

This was Saturday morning and I decided to keep him in the house until Sunday night. I wanted some company over the weekend at least. Then I could bury him Monday morn-

ing and set out on my usual round right afterwards so I wouldn't have to sit alone at home feeling miserable. I decided to look at his traps too. There must be plenty of foxes and I would bring them back home to him.

Nonsense! I thought. Gustav was dead. What would he do with foxes?

Suddenly I wanted to have a look at him. He was lying hunched over in bed with his legs pulled up. It looked just like he was sitting in a chair. I lifted him up and put him down on a chair by the table. He was frozen stiff, of course, but the face looked as if Gustav were laughing. I think I talked to him as I ate my food. I had to give him my answers to all the things we had been talking about the weekend before—about the soul and immortality and such things. He did not believe he would go to heaven, he had told me straight out. He didn't know where heaven was or what it looked like, he had said. It's hard to answer a man like that, Sheriff. I'm only a sailor and a trapper. We didn't take school very seriously when I was a boy and since that time I have just about forgotten how to read.

Gustav just sat there laughing. That was the way he looked, anyway. I went on talking to him; it would have been too lonely otherwise. And I answered too—answered all the things he would have said, or what I thought he would have said. Then I could talk back again and that way I forgot that he was dead. It was hard to keep up, of course. What can you say when there isn't much to talk about? I didn't feel up to saying the same things over and over again.

In the evening I took Gustav outside. I put him on a small sleigh and pulled him over to a cliff behind the house. First I put him down in the snow and then I covered him with stones, lots of stones piled neatly on top of him. I didn't want wolves and bears to eat my good friend Gustav.

283

It was a strange week. I looked after my own traps first, then his. And I took all four dogs along. I didn't want his dogs to stay home and howl when I approached the house again, coming back for a lonely weekend. It would have been sort of spooky, you see, Sheriff.

But I didn't go back to the house that week after all. When I had finished my own round I went straight on to his traps without any rest. I got a better catch those days than we had ever had before and I was glad to have all the dogs with me. I got home late the following Sunday, I was tired and I decided to stay in the house for a whole week. I had to soften up all the skins and put them up for drying. There was a lot to do and I was alone with the job.

As I sat there all alone I began thinking that it had been better, after all, when I had Gustav at the table with me, even though he was dead. Now he was outside, freezing in the terrible cold. That was all nonsense, of course, but when you are so utterly alone you . . . well, you lose your grip sometimes, I guess. And Gustav wasn't really buried, only covered with stones. I had to sit alone and eat all by myself. I had to go out by myself, look after the traps by myself. I had to feed the dogs myself—and now one of them was having puppies on top of it all. Gustav had been looking forward to that.

It was nobody's business, I thought. Since I was all alone, it didn't really concern anybody and it was my intention all the time—I swear to it, Sheriff—it was really my intention to pull him out again, to bury him decently. But just while it was so terribly dark . . . you can understand it, can't you?

In short, I took Gustav in again. I regretted it once he was inside, but then I had done it and had to stick to it for the sake of my self-respect. You can't go on thinking and planning all sorts of things and then never do them. Once

284

I had him sitting there on the other side of the table things seemed a little brighter. I talked to him and went on answering for him. I knew him pretty well by then, of course, so it was sort of liking playing with dolls, you see. I know Gustav would never have objected to it, I can assure you of that, Mr. Sheriff!

We had quite a good time together. I prepared our food and set a plate for Gustav. I even served him, I think. Yes I did, I know, because I got angry when he didn't eat his food and I gave it to the puppies. I only pretended to be angry with him because he was so finicky. That was part of the game, you see.

When I went to bed that night, I left Gustav sitting by the table. That was a mistake, because I woke up in the middle of the night. And Gustav was moving! I swear to it that he was moving! I was wide awake in a second— and here is the strange part of it· I wanted to be afraid that Gustav was waking up. I knew all the time that he was only thawing, but I would not admit it. If I did, I would have to give up the game of make-believe, of pretending that he was alive.

I guess I can't expect you to understand it, Sheriff. But that's the way it was. When Gustav died he was all hunched up and one arm was bent forward a little so I could put it on the table edge for support. He looked quite natural that way. It was that arm that began thawing. I had to have some heat in the house to thaw the stiffly frozen foxes, but I should not have let Gustav thaw with them. I understand it all now, but that night I was so scared I hardly dared move. I even said the Lord's Prayer but I knew at the same time that the body was only softening, that the whole thing was quite natural. And toward morning I calmed down again.

"Come along, my fine friend," I said to Gustav as I got up. "You are going out in the snow again—you are through scaring decent people!"

And once more I covered Gustav with stones before I set out on my round. I worked out a new system with my rounds. First I looked after half of my own traps to the south and half of his to the north. That way I came back to the blockhouse twice a week. And never, not for one second, did I dream of doing Gustav out of his share. He was going to get one third just as we had agreed.

Every time I got back to the lonely house, I felt drawn to that stony grave again. The urge got too strong and after a couple of weeks I gave in again. I brought Gustav into the house and put him at the table once again. I served him his food, like before, and the puppies got what he left on his plate. If anybody sees me, they'll think I'm crazy, I thought. But I didn't care, I just kept talking all the time, for him and myself. If I stopped for a moment, the cold silence would come between us again and I would have to admit that he was dead. Of course, he really was, all the time, but . . .

When the light came back to Greenland, a little more of it every day, I thought I would get over it. Once I could really see him it would be too crazy to carry a dead man back and forth. I have seen too many friends and fellow trappers die to be impressed by death, but everything was different with Gustav. Little by little I began hating him. Every time I returned to the house, I was determined not to take him back again, but I always found some excuse.

There was hardly a weekend when I did not have him in the house with me. Of course, he got a little worn from all this handling. The sun was getting warm and sometimes it would shine right in his face. I noticed for the first time that his skin was dark yellow. I was furious with him, telling him that he was dead and should stay dead. I didn't want to see him again, I shouted at him. This is the last time you'll be in a room with me, I told him. Gustav just sat there grinning at me. He had been a little too close to the fire and his mouth had sunk a little, making his grin even more gruesome. I knew that I was sure to go out of my head all together if I kept it up until the warm weather set in. Gustav would thaw completely and his body would get too repulsive.

But how could I stop it, Mr. Sheriff? One day I noticed a snow sparrow outside and I knew I had to do something. The sparrow was a sure sign of spring, the fox trapping was over for the winter, soon the ice would break up and the *Blue Whale* would return to take us home to Denmark.

I was afraid, I was really scared when I returned to the house with the last traps. Scared of Gustav, scared of his ghost—for he was really a ghost, the only difference was that he did not walk around of his own accord but because I carried him. It was just like when he was alive—he could make me do things I would never have done by myself.

The idea came to me all of a sudden. I knew what I had to do; and I knew it was the only right thing to do. I took Gustave inside and went on talking to him as if I had nothing up my sleeve. I smiled at myself when I told him about all the things we would do the next day . . . just to reassure him, you see, Sheriff. After a while I told him that I had to go out and get some coal for the fire. I had my gun outside of course. I didn't close the door all the way as I left him. I left it open just a tiny crack. He couldn't call to me and complain of the draft, poor Gustav. But I was going to fool him.

I sneaked back to the house with the gun in my hand, ready loaded. I think it took me at least an hour to get the barrel of the gun through the crack and get it in the right position. Gustav sat there just the way I had put him. He had his back to me, but he was turned a little to the side, just enough to let me see his smile—a disgusting grin which wasn't really like him at all. This time he was alive, but I had had enough of him now and I cocked the gun. Taking good aim was a slow business. Even if he was a dead man it was, after all, a friend I was going to shoot. Then it happened! Just as I was trying to make myself pull the trigger, Gustav moved again. The arm was getting soft again, I could see it clearly, but still . . . Don't you see? He was only a dead man, but still it was hard to shoot him while he was moving.

But I had to rid myself of Gustav. He had become a ghost—this is the case when you are absolutely alone, hundreds of miles from the nearest trapper! Suddenly I got furious with him for trying to scare me at the last moment. And then I shot him, Mr. Sheriff!

A deafening roar shook the small blockhouse. His whole head was blown to pieces. At last he was really dead and he was through visiting me in my loneliness. Carrying a man without a head into the house . . . that I knew I would never do.

I buried Gustav the real way this time and I made a wooden cross for his grave. *Gustav Krakau* it said on the cross—and the skipper on the *Blue Whale* will bear me out, for he took the cross home with him.

It was good to be alone. Nobody to pay any attention to. The dogs had a good time with nothing much for them to do any more. They did not miss Gustav—and I didn't either.

He was dead, true enough, and it was a great pity, but now there was nothing I could do about it. Quietly and peacefully I made everything ready for the trip home. I knew that the *Blue Whale* would come any day.

The others can tell the rest of it, Sheriff. The skipper was the first one to ask about Gustav. "He died, poor man," I told him and even mentioned the date. Gustav had been sick for a while, I told him, and I had found him dead in bed one day when I returned to the house. That was true enough. I didn't say about taking him into the house and all that. That was nobody's business and I did not want such things written down in the logbook.

It was Godtfred Mortensen who started the trouble. The busybody said that they had to have a look at Gustav. So many strange things happened in the Arctic, he said. Godtfred used many fancy words but I understood they had to dig up the body to make it all according to the law.

They went down to the grave and started digging just when I had made it so nice with the cross and all. I had even put some red paint on the letters. And, of course, they saw that the head had been shot to pieces.

They all began staring strangely at me. That was the worst they could do, for I knew what they were thinking. But they never said anything. I tried to tell them what had happened, but trappers . . . well, you know what trappers are like, Mr. Sheriff. They can't understand the thoughts of other people, they can only eat and sleep and look after their traps. They are no good for deeper things.

The skipper said they would make a coffin and take Gustav along. During the whole trip home I wanted to throw myself overboard. The only thing which kept me from it was the fact that then they would only think worse of me.

They never spoke to me, nobody, on that trip home. They gave me a cabin alone and I had to eat all alone, nobody would sit at table with me.

When we finally got back here, the skipper said he would deliver my whole catch to the Consul just like he always did.

"Yes, you do that," I told him and went on shore. But I knew what would happen, and I was right. This morning the whole police force came to get me. We only got back yesterday, Sheriff. I walked alone to my house then. Today you needed four policemen to bring me here.

I am no murderer, Sheriff! I only used my gun to make Gustav leave me in peace once he was dead. There is no law against that! Or is there? You tell me. . . .

This strange and shocking story is true in every detail, as those people know who were living in the Arctic wilds of Greenland just a decade ago. The life of the trapper is dangerous, for he gambles with his own life and the sanity of his mind as the stakes, facing months of darkness and possible starvation, sometimes all in vain when there is nothing to catch and nothing to bring home for his trouble. One of them is locked up now and must spend the rest of his life behind bars, suffering for what happened up there in the loneliness. Nobody knows what goes on in the soul of such a man.

He is a lonely old man, brooding on the events of the past. If he is spoken to, he always answers in the same words. He does not want to see Gustav any more, he says. He asks only for a gun to defend himself against the fear and the loneliness.

IV. How European Traders Helped a Poor Eskimo

IT IS FUNNY that people always think of the Arctic as a place of snow and frost and terrible winters. They forget, or perhaps they have never heard, about the summers when the sun is in the sky both night and day, when your eyes get tired even when you wake up in the morning because the tent is so bright and when it is too hot to cover your head with caribou skins to get some darkness. In such a smiling summer there is dead-calm weather for weeks at a time. There is not wind enough to blow out a match, and not a cloud is in the sky. Such things are hardly known in other places of the world. I have spent days and days in the Arctic at such a season sitting out in a kayak waiting for seals to pop up to the surface of the water so that I might either hurl my harpoon into them or shoot them with a gun. In the latter case I always hope that I can get close enough to them to get my harpoon into their bodies before they sink, because a seal is lean at that time of the year. It has been sleeping on the ice throughout the spring instead of eating, and does not have enough blubber to

buoy it up, so it sinks to the bottom—to the great delight of the sharks, but not the hunter.

When you are sitting in a kayak on a seal hunt you must not move a finger at all. Any little motion will be noticed by the seal and he will keep away. For he hears extremely well while submerged. It is only when his ears are above the water that you can fool him.

If, then, you are on a seal hunt, sitting in your kayak motionless under the warm sun while the light on the water is reflected right back into your eyes, you are literally in great danger. I don't know anything about crystal balls—I understand it is possible to hypnotize people by having them look into one and concentrate their minds on certain subjects—but I do know that if you sit in a kayak while the sun burns in the sky and its rays are reflected from the water right into the retinas of your eyes, you can be put to sleep in no time. This is extremely dangerous, so if the hunters see a fellow falling asleep in his kayak, they have to hurry up to him and wake him up lest he tip over and drown. Many kayak men who have disappeared from villages have undoubtedly died in this way.

I myself have got dizzy many times in just such a situation, had to shake my head, take a stroke or two at the oars and possibly turn the kayak away from the sun. Funny as it may seem, as soon as you are sitting immobile again, waiting for the seal, the kayak always turns around ever so slowly until the reflection from the sun cuts into the corner of your eye again. Then you have to turn around again or else you are done for.

My friend Joseph was one of the very great Eskimo hunters who got kayak sickness when he was looking for seals in this way. He lived in the Danish part of Greenland. Whenever I came to his house, he fed my dogs without asking; in fact he overfed them just as he did myself and my friends. We used to come from the north, from way up in Smith Sound across Melville Bay. Occasionally we had our sledges loaded with bear meat or something else, because we had struck it lucky on the way down. But at other times our dogs were starving—it would have hurt our pride to bring dogfood along because we were young and did not want people to think we could not furnish enough for ourselves and our dogs during the voyage.

Joseph always had enough for dogs and men, whether we brought something or not. He had walrus meat and walrus hide cut up into lumps for the dogs. He threw whole carcasses of seals to them, and his wife, Benigne, took our clothes, picked the lice from them, and dried them while we slept. The sleeping place was covered with bearskins and soft tanned caribou skins were the covers. The children were playing inside and outside the house. Whenever they felt hungry they ate. And when they were sleepy, they might sleep outside on the sledges, or else go inside to their mother who stripped them and put them up on the skins where they played until they fell asleep.

Somebody was always cooking at Joseph's house, even when we were eating dried meats and frozen meats and rotten meats and eggs—all these delicacies that Joseph had in great store for guests at any time during the year.

But one winter I came rather late in the season to Joseph's home. It was funny to see that only a few dogs were lying around outside the house. Even these looked thin and shabby, so I understood at once that Joseph was ill or out hunting or had gone down to the trading post to get some of the goods that all his skins and his blubber used to bring him. But Joseph was at home—not the same smiling and shouting and joking Joseph I had known for many years but a sad, despondent Joseph. He looked like a completely different man. His clothes were poor, ragged and badly kept. He did not come running down welcoming us by shouts and laughter. He even looked smaller, he walked in a funny way and he was thin and his face was sort of withered out.

We saw at once that something was wrong, but we went into his house. Fortunately we had just killed a bear, so we could feed our own dogs, ourselves and our host. From the way he ate it was evident that he had not eaten much for a long time.

Nobody is as tactful as the Eskimo. My friends who came with me from the north acted as though nothing was any different from before. Nobody mentioned anything. We just brought in some bear meat, chopped it up and ate some of it raw, frozen, and put the rest of it in a pot. Then I noticed that one of my fellows had brought in blubber from his sledge load. He had seen at once how little there was in store in the house.

After a while I went outside to look at my dogs and there I met some of the fellow travelers who had gone into other houses.

"Joseph got the kayak disease," they told me. "Poor Joseph!"

When the evening came and while the children slept heavily from overeating, all of us just sat and talked. Nobody mentioned anything extraordinary until I clumsily asked for some caribou sinew to mend my mittens. Benigne began to cry. "We have no sinew, nobody has brought game to this house in the fall!" We sat for some time and nobody

296

said a word; I was afraid of hurting anybody's feelings, but finally Joseph himself talked and explained what had happened.

"It began last year, but I didn't realize it. I was used to mastering everything and I wouldn't tell about it. I caught many seals, as you know, last winter; I went caribou hunting and I forgot about everything. But then in the spring, when the ice had gone, my disease became really bad. The first days I felt it only as if my head had become heavy. I did not know that the curse was on me. Then it grew worse. Sometimes the head would swell up and it was impossible for me to move my neck. The sun crept into my eyes and grew and grew inside my skull. It burned my brain out—it was impossible for me to move and I felt the water coming up over me, and over me, and over me as my kayak sank.

"Sometimes Gaba was rather close to me but I couldn't even shout to him. It happened that a seal came up right in front of me and stared at me with his big round eyes, and I could not take my harpoon and throw it at him. I could see the seal laughing at me but I could do nothing to him! This happened over and over again. One day I sat paralyzed in my kayak and a little wind came up. Oh, a beautiful little wind ran across the water. I saw it coming up toward me, and I felt as happy as I used to do when I spotted a narwhale that was easy to catch. The little wind brought a small movement on the surface of the water, and right away it was over. I could move again, I could row, and I joined the other hunters. We caught three seals that day. But when I came home I was so scared that I could not sleep during the night because I knew I had to go out again the next day. I carried my kayak across the island to put to sea where the current runs between here and the mainland. That always causes some movement in the water,

297

and I knew I could do some hunting there. I hunted there for a few days, but it hurt my pride to come home without anything. Everybody knows that the seals are not there in the summertime. I had to go out with the other men, though I felt a fear just as if I were up against a bear without any weapon. If only I could have cried, it might have helped me, but I couldn't.

"Finally the other men found out. They could see my fear and sometimes they looked after me during the hunt. And if they saw that I was sitting petrified, they just rowed up to me, put their hands on the stern of my kayak and right away it was over. I could move again, I could row to shore. But I could not keep this going for a long time. I was so scared. I lay down on the beach crying like a baby. I didn't care that the other men or the women or even my own children saw it, I only was frightened to go out in a kayak. I was not a kayak hunter any more. That is how it is to have kayak disease."

We sat quietly for some time. And as men do not like to be pitied, the only thing I could say was that misery comes unexpectedly and it was good that the winter now gave him an opportunity to go bear hunting and also that in the spring, when the seals were basking on the ice, he would no longer feel any of the weakness. That, I said, would make up for the kayak season. But Joseph told me that everything had gone wrong for him. A hunter can have abundance one day and a week later he might be destitute.

This was the case with Joseph. He was destitute as was his whole village. As soon as he stopped going out in his kayak his neighbors did the same.

No Eskimo is the chief or boss of the others. None of them has command at his settlement, but it's always the case that poor hunters gather around a big one and he encourages them. He tells them in the morning to get out. He is the first man to propose excursions, and even if the hunters themselves are mostly inclined to stay home, their wives will tease them, and so-to-speak chase them out, because the rest of the men are going to sea.

But now Joseph stayed home. Nobody was there to call out in the morning, so why should the other men take the trouble? It was so much nicer to sleep a little longer, and they did. The result was that pretty soon there was no more meat to cook. There was no blubber to sell in the store, and they were not yet so used to poverty that their craving for coffee had faded out. They manned their umiak or skin boat and rowed to the trading post, which took them a day.

Arriving there without any blubber to sell, they had to bring some sealskins originally supposed to have been for new clothes or even heavy skins from the bearded seals meant for new covers on the skin boat. They returned with coffee and some hardtack and they ate it in a hurry because there was nothing else to have. Then the disaster struck.

No more money for coffee or bread. Meat they could only have in the beginning, as long as they had powder and lead enough to shoot some birds. Eventually even this source of food was gone.

After this it did not take a long time to bring them down to extreme poverty. Joseph could do nothing, and soon the other five or six hunters at the place had no more ammunition; their kayaks fell to pieces; their clothing could not be mended because the women had no sinew to sew with. They could not go caribou hunting which everybody looks forward to in the fall, which meant no warm clothing for the winter. Their food was now scolpins and grayfish and oovak which the women caught at the beach. At low tide they also collected some clams, but how could a man keep warm by this? Once in a while they found a piece of drift-wood, so they could start a fire, and to get some meat they killed their dogs. First the bad ones were eaten, then more and more of the good ones. Finally some of the hunters needed skins for coats, and that took care of the rest of the dogs. As their soles wore out in their kamiks, the kayak skins were cut off for that purpose.

Eskimos are Eskimos; when they have no more dogs, what is the use of sledges? Why not use the sledges for fuel? As their kayaks were now without skins the wood could also be burned.

The ice began to form and they put out two hooks for sharks. But shark meat is terrible. It is poisonous, so it has to be boiled three times before people can eat it. What nourishment can there be in thrice-boiled fish meat? Of course the sharks provided them with liver, more than they could use themselves for their lamps, so Joseph was able to go to the trading post with a little load of liver. It gave him a few kroner and he was sensible enough to buy two more lines for shark hooks before he procured a little tobacco and coffee.

The traders looked at Joseph, the man who used to be their best customer and who always brought in bearskins and blubber and sealskins! But they were not philanthro-pists. They put the liver on the scales, paid the value of it, and sold Joseph what little he wanted from the store.

It certainly was a different Joseph who now returned home in a dogskin coat, walking behind his four dogs to save them what little strength they had left. He had not been invited for coffee by the trader this time, nor by the teacher: everybody knew about him. Now he was just an-other of the poor Eskimos at the trading post. As he returned home there were hardly a few cups of coffee for each man at the settlement. It was roasted with a double amount of peas to make it stretch.

Such was Joseph's condition when we came from the north, three Eskimos and myself, all of us with big teams, twelve to fifteen well-fed dogs, bear meat on our sledges, and ammunition and whatever else a traveler needs in the Arctic.

I told Joseph that if he thought his disease was going to be permanent, he had better join us and come up north to stay up in our part of the country where sledges could be driven eleven months out of the year, where kayak hunting was not essential to a big hunter, and where men always have enough food.

But Joseph understood at once how foolish my proposal was. "How could I come up?" he said. "I have four dogs in all. Benigne has no coat, the children have no clothing. No, I was born here and we are not used to travel like you people from up north. I can't get away, I will have to stay here and take what is coming."

I agreed. To move a whole family in the wintertime across Melville Bay takes some outfitting and they did not have anything. Nothing, moreover, could be bought in the district. None of the people had caribou skins to spare, and even if we had divided the family on our sledges, they could not have resisted the cold and the snowstorms. They had no sleeping gear, no warm clothing. Furthermore, my own Eskimos were not too keen on having a new man along. They knew that he would be a nuisance until he learned to hunt like polar Eskimos and settle down among them.

In short, we left Joseph behind. I helped him out with a few things he needed most and he assured me that he would try the best he could on the ice-hunting in the spring because now he had ammunition enough. He also could go after eiderdown in his skin boat, as I managed to get some repair skin for him.

Joseph had been the leader of his settlement, and maybe his worst suffering came from the fact that now he had nothing to impress the others with. He was a defeated man and everybody knew it.

But suddenly he got a kind of new start. We bought twine with which he made nets for the seals. In the part of the world in which he lived there are numerous rocks and small islands, and high tide and low tide make a terrific current around the points and in the small straits between the islands. Ice therefore could never form there. This gave the seals places where they could go to breathe—better places than just blowholes in the ice. Joseph put his nets down into these currents, or close by, and caught quite a few seals this way. And when the spring came, when seals were basking in the sun, he had his big chance with a new gun and sufficient ammunition.

Joseph caught many seals. He even got hold of some dogs again, and generally did very well. And what a difference it made in his mind, his manners and his attitude toward the other people at the settlement. Again he was the top man in his place and his good spirits encouraged his neighbors as well. Again Sarfak became a place the trader could count on when Joseph came to the post with blubber and skins. Once more Joseph was invited for coffee at the trader's house, which of course was no great expense for the white man since Joseph always brought meat and seal liver as gifts for the kitchen.

When summer came, however, and the ice was gone, Joseph stayed on shore. He had been with his umiak after eiderdown at the outermost islands and he came back fully

loaded. There any anorak, any pillowcase and bedcover was stuffed with down. He had bags piled up in the boat and when they came to the trader, he got good money, so he could stock up on coffee for the whole summer, the whole family got new anoraks, shirts, and the man who returned home again was the Joseph of former days.

Just the same, the idea of sitting up on the hill with his spyglasses and looking out to sea was annoying. He resented the fact that the other hunters were such poor guys at the harpoon. He knew for sure, when he sat and watched them missing the seals, that here he would have hit the seal, here he would have done otherwise, if only—if only—but it was of no use thinking about that. The mere idea of going out in a kayak frightened him; he knew that the same spell would come over him, no matter how much he regretted it. No kayak hunting for Joseph any more!

The fall was setting in. Joseph walked along the coastline. He was a man who did not want to let any opportunity pass by. A polar bear might come on shore—a dead whale might be sighted. He didn't miss anything by walking, and he walked. And then it was that he spotted something green at the beach. At first he could not make out what it was. It looked like a pile of seaweed, but it was too green for that. Then he thought it was some lumber from a shipwreck, but finally he saw that it was a dory—a real nice wooden dory, the kind the Portuguese fishermen use far out to sea. Joseph had seen one once, and he had heard much about it, so he knew what it was.

The first thing, of course, was to drag the boat high up on shore so that the high tide could not reach it. Joseph examined the craft. There were no oars, no mast nor sails on it, but all the same it was a beautifully shaped dory. Joseph could not help admiring its lines. He could see that it was most seaworthy. He was a good kayak builder himself, so he could value every part of the boat highly. Here he got his chance. On the bow of the dory were painted some letters that Joseph did not understand. But he could understand what the cross and the anchor signified. He knew that all Portuguese fishermen sought alliance with heaven and with God by painting divine symbols on their boats. Maybe it was not a nice thing to do to paint that over, but Joseph thought that God would not be angry about it, because the teachers had taught him that Portuguese were Catholics, that they did not worship Jesus and the Holy Spirit in the right way. They were even worse than the unbaptized pagans up north where Peter Freuchen was living.

So Joseph hurried back to his house. How fortunate it was that he had some paint left which he had intended to use before Christmas to brighten up the room in his house! Now it came in handy because he had to cover all the Portuguese letters and pictures as soon as possible. Should the inspector come—and one never could be sure—he would spot the Portuguese signs at once, and the dory would be taken away and given back to the Portuguese. White people don't have the same ideas as Eskimo people who say that when something is lost and the owner ceases to look after it, it belongs to the finder.

Now Joseph had a dory! He had his old kayak paddle and took it along with him when he went out the next day. Benigne looked at him, but she didn't say a word. She knew how it hurt him to think about his misfortune, but his face did not seem sad now. He was joking and said merry words to the children as he left.

Nothing can happen at Sarfak without anybody knowing it, so all the women got together and talked about the mysterious attitude of Joseph. Their husbands were, for once, all of them out in kayaks, excepting of course old Simon who was too weak in the knees to walk far. But Simon said that it did not look good to see a kayak-sick man walk out with his paddle—maybe he would never come back!

Hours went by. The day passed. The hunters came home empty-handed, which was not unusual, but they heard about Joseph's mysterious doings and they joined Simon and the women and talked about what might happen. None of them dared to go out and look for Joseph—if he had killed himself in despair it would have been dangerous to meet his ghost; if he had gone insane he might attack them, or he could even have sold his soul to the Devil and been changed into a *Tupilak*.

It was already so far into the season that darkness came at night—not absolute blackness, but a twilight in which things are even more frightening to people. So when Joseph finally came paddling in his dory around the point and calling happily to his people as if he had brought some game, everybody got frightened. Benigne was already crying. But when she heard the other women screaming, she was absolutely bewildered, yet she didn't run away like the rest of them. She went down to the beach and soon she could distinguish Joseph. She could also make out that he sat aft in a boat paddling while he was smiling and laughing with joy.

Joseph had a dory! He had made two small oars for rowing, and he had gone out hunting. He had rowed out and pulled in his oars; he had sat and waited and it was as though the seals were attracted by him as before, when he was a great kayak hunter and always brought in more game than the rest of the men combined.

Still, he liked it better when there was a little wind so

the surface of the sea was not absolutely still. Fortunately his son Kale was big enough to go along. Joseph took him out with him, taught him to sit absolutely motionless, told him about the habits and the nature of the seal, when to shoot, and how to use the harpoon. Oh, Joseph was doing well and he looked forward to the coming winter when we would again come from the north on our way down to the trading post after mail. Now again he would serve us dog feed and boiled meat of all kinds. And before it turned completely dark, just before the ice would form, he intended to go up to the head of the fjord after caribou. Joseph was going to show us!

One day the little Kale asked Joseph who had really built that boat and how he got it. Joseph told his son that he didn't know; the boat had been sent to him from the sea, and the man who had lost it was probably dead.

"Did you find him and bury him?"

Joseph said no.

"But if he is not buried and got a cross about his head, won't he come as a ghost and demand the boat back from you?" the little boy asked his father. He knew very well that once a year the minister from the colony went around to all the settlements and threw three spadefuls of earth on all the buried ones who had died since the holy man was there last. Only after these three spadefuls of earth were thrown at the graves could people be sure that they would not come back and look for their property and frighten the life out of the survivors.

Joseph did not answer the boy. These were funny words the boy had spoken. It was true that he had done nothing to prevent the unknown fisherman from returning for his boat. Of course, it was no use for Joseph just to sit there and talk about it. So the next day he tore a leaf from the

hymnbook and put it into the stern of the boat and nailed a piece of skin over it so that it would not blow away. But this was not enough either. He felt that the dead Portuguese might turn up some day from the sea and crave his dory back. Or maybe the dory was such that it would kill any man who used it! The Portuguese had painted all the holy marks on it and those Joseph had taken out. Perhaps this would never be forgiven!

Still, Joseph got plenty of seals with it and his dory braved the waves nicely. But when he returned home at night he could not forget his worries. Now it grew colder. The time arrived for caribou hunting. So Joseph decided to start out with his whole family in a few days and everybody at the place was anxious to be allowed to go along. They were to have women to row the umiak and carry the meat for the hunters down to the camp. This meant that half the settlement was preparing to leave.

Yet it would take two more days, and Joseph could not remain idle, so out he went alone in his dory to try to catch a seal. He waited for some time close to an iceberg. Some harp seals came along, those playful animals which come in small flocks, jumping up and down in the water, sometimes popping right up into the air to fall down with a splash. They were not close enough to shoot, so Joseph rowed farther out, and again and again they were teasing him, but he did not come within range. So excited did he become that he quite forgot to notice the southeastern clouds in the sky. Not until the wind caught him!

By that time he was way out in the open and drifting wildly. The waves grew around him and his boat was being carried away. He saw Kitisut, the outermost island where they all had spent happy summer days gathering eiderdown, but now it looked dark and menacing in the growing dusk.

Joseph realized that it was impossible to make Sarfak. If only he could manage to reach Kitisut he could consider himself lucky. It was his only chance. So he rowed with all his might. People who have not worked with an oar for dear life in a boat cannot conceive how it is. Your back is aching. Your arms feel twice their usual length and are filled with pain. Your hands get sore with open boils, but worst of all is the taste in your mouth. Your tongue grows large and parched and your nostrils are not big enough to permit enough air to pass for your lungs' needs.

But Joseph kept on. He had to, because he could see that he was making only slight progress. The wind soon became a real gale. The oars went steadily down and up, down and up.

Then suddenly he saw the Portuguese. He sat in the stern of the dory. The dead man in his sailor's oilskin and his "southwestern." The eyes were not in their sockets, but their hollows turned toward him accusingly. The dead man's lips were moving, and he lifted his hands as if he wanted to seize Joseph bodily. Joseph could see that there was no flesh on the hands, just the bones, and then he did not see any more. He did not remember anything after that, he only knew that somehow or another his boat reached Kitisut and he felt it running up on the sandy beach, and there the ghost could not follow him further.

Joseph fainted. For how long he did not know. He first realized that people were around him, and it was not the ghost or other drowned sailors. It was the inspector and his crew. The Danish official was on his yearly trip to the north. He had intended to make the northernmost settle-

311

ment before Melville Bay, but his boatsman had seen the clouds in time, and they knew that the snug little harbor at Kitisut was just what they needed. There they landed, and of course his men went up on the hills to take a look. It was from there that they spotted the dory out at sea.

Joseph was received as never before. The inspector took him down to his own cabin. He was given coffee and food. He sat in the warm place and when he felt sleepy, he was offered a bunk. The next day the sea was calm, and the inspector told him that he was afraid Benigne and the rest of the settlement might be anxious about him.

"So I will go straight for Sarfak to bring you home. The crew has bailed out your dory, and we can take it along. By the way, I am happy to see that you built such a beautiful-looking boat now. It is much safer than the kayaks, and it lasts longer. If everybody would follow your example, there would be more sealskins for sale and both Eskimos and Danes would profit by it.

"I didn't know that you were able to build them so well, but I know your reputation as a great and clever man. I wish you would teach our people to use their tools and make that kind of boat. It was surely a happy coincidence that we saw you here and I think I will give you a premium, because you are the first one to abandon the kayak. Twenty-five kroner is for your ingenuity, and my best congratulations!"

Now Joseph had the greatest authority to confirm his ownership of the boat; everybody knew that the inspector was much higher than even the minister at church, so Joseph could never again see the ghost in his dory.

V. A Motorboat Expedition and Its Strange Consequences

THERE WAS at one time an expedition by motorboat out to the Kitisut Islands never before reached by Eskimo people. In wintertime the islands were surrounded by circles of firm ice and impassable open water and in summer, though the trip was possible by kayak, it was not wise, for even if something should be captured out there, how could it be brought home? So the motorboat expedition caused a lot of excitement—not only because the boat could run without oars to paddle or sails to catch the wind but only with the noise of a bumblebee, but also because people could bring home what was caught. The white man at the little wheel can turn it from side to side, and if he makes it hum little the boat goes slow and if he makes it buzz in a high voice the boat runs fast with all the pieces of ice brushed aside like little lice on the body of a great hunter.

Polo stood and philosophized over this ingenious manner of sailing by which the noise of a thing brings it forward. He was standing on board the craft, for the white men had told Polo to come along and show them where to put in

313

during the first night in a cove they did not know themselves. White men are like little children. If they come to a place once they forget about it rather soon. They never pay attention to the hill to find out whether the wind sweeps down with drifting sand, so one can know if it is a good place to put up an igloo or anchor safely for a night.

All this of course was only for the better, because it gave Polo an opportunity to follow them out on this trip that would give him respect and also recompense in different ways. Polo had just got a woman in his house, and he needed a lot of things for her.

And being a married man fills a fellow up with a feeling of being important, for he can talk to his wife when they are alone and she has to believe him. That's what she is there for.

But Polo had just got his wife through a stroke of luck. He was in fact not good enough at hunting to have a wife right now, since other men farther up the coast who brought in more game than he usually did were craving for women to take care of their skins and sew their clothes and so on.

But the father of Polo's wife was Ehre, and Ehre was a good-minded man. It happens sometimes that young men give up the dignity of the sex and show openly what great interest they put into special girls. Is not a woman a woman, and ought not an old and experienced girl be taken at first —not if she is too old of course, but a reasonably old woman who can sew for a man and who knows all the ways of preparing good food and is used to running a household? With Polo it was the opposite: he cared for Kadara and nobody else but Kadara. He had several times made himself ridiculous by bringing good pieces of meat home for her in his mitten. He had carved out a handle for her

314

woman's-knife and put the head of a bear on it. He had refused to trade the skin of the big bear he shot last winter for ammunition for his newly bought gun, but pretended to want the skin for pants for himself—though everybody knew that he wanted the long hair on the backside of the forelegs for Kadara, so she could boast the longest bear hair on top of her boots of any of the women in the settlement.

This did not make people any more friendly toward the two of them.

And then came the big scandal in the year that showed a new attitude of youngsters who did not respect the old way of behaving. It was told time after time to the girls, that when the time came that a man arrived and claimed them of their father, they had to cry and yell and scratch him in the face and show how unwilling they were to follow him. It was a custom from days of old and each of the old women liked to tell how they had fought their husbands-to-be for a long time. The sun moved from one side of the tent to the other before Airuna gave up her fight, Amemee was not brought out from her father's house before the dogs of the man who tried to marry her had eaten the harnesses to pieces. As a result of the way she fought her husband, he could not take her but had to wait until he prepared new harnesses. The entire settlement had laughed at him and everyone was happy!

But Polo and Kadara had evidently talked everything over ahead of time. He had shown interest in her when playing and also when they were hunting for birds together. Now he asked for her from Ehre while she was listening to it. Ehre had told him that he had to stay in the Ehre house and that meant he had to deliver all his catch to the father-in-law, to do all the unpleasant work, and to have his wife-to-be acting as she had done for years, just a daughter of the house. Polo could have no rights, no property of his own. Still Polo had agreed. In presence of the father and the mother he had made promises and showed himself so devoted to Kadara particularly, that people all over the tribe said that Polo had shown that he cared less for being laughed at than he did for that girl. Polo had, moreover, lowered himself below his dignity, as Ehre was known as a bad hunter.

But Polo was happy and he became more of a man. He liked to see his little wife feel proud when he brought home game on days when no other man had anything. Then she was the hostess at the fire outside where everybody ate together. Of course the catch belonged to her father because they stayed with him, but she couldn't help shouting out to the people that they had to help themselves:

"Oh take some more, Kale! Let me help you to a piece. Oh don't I feel sorry that it isn't just as good as it ought to be. There wasn't quite that much blubber under the skin last time when you made the meat. Hey, you children! You certainly are not to sit without a piece too, take what you want! I can go and cut more and cook it rather fast; there is plenty of blubber to feed the fire with!"

She couldn't keep away from bragging a little, especially about the blubber, and Polo sat among the older men, who actually talked to him. He also noticed how often Kadara ran into the other houses and brought meat, fearing that they did not have enough inside but would allow her to hand them a little piece.

Before marriage Kadara had the experience of living in a house where the meat too often was sent in, and where they never had anything to give away. Now she saw the world from the other side, and she heard even the big man Mayark thank her, and she saw how Anarwree smiled to get an opportunity to have real good bear meat from the ribs at a time when no man was at home to prevent her from taking the best parts. Kadara also was talked to by the elderly women.

Happiness spread over the two young people.

Now came this motorboat expedition and Polo was asked to go along! Not the men Odark or Avatak who used to follow the white men but only Polo. And they went straight to him and asked him to come on. Everyone in the place saw it and heard it, as the whole settlement had gathered down at the beach to salute the boat coming in.

The white men were in a hurry as they always are. Polo called out for his wife and told her to get two pairs of boots ready and also she had to go for his gun and his knife. She jumped over the rocks and ran quickly to carry out his orders. But Polo just stood there and waited for her to come. Then he took his things and went on board.

He was careful not to look at her but to show the most indifferent face he could as they hummed away. He acted as if it was an everyday job to leave with white men, and she on her side only got interested in driving away a couple of pups that played close to where she had spread some skins out to dry. It was of no special interest to her, whether her husband sailed off with strange people or not!

The boat speeded on and the settlement disappeared behind some icebergs. They were on their way to the Kitisut, the islands way out to sea.

The three small islands did not offer any very interesting sight to Polo. Some rabbits were seen on the hills and some birds on the cliffs—not anything to talk about. He

317

saw signs of foxes too, and in the water outside quite a few bearded seals poked their heads above the surface. But the white men, crazy as ever, seemed to enjoy their stay here very much. Polo did not pay much attention to their talk, knowing them to be like children. He couldn't help smiling over their pleasure, finding flowers of different kinds around. Everybody knew flowers were to be found, but only women and children could feel any joy for that. There is no value in such things—who could eat them but rabbits? So why show any interest in them? It wasn't dignified for a man, but the whites are shameless, as everybody knows.

A storm was coming and the sky showed it beforehand as usual. But the white men never understood how the world acts. When small spots are to be seen in the southeast, it is time to look out, but white men don't seem to care.

Polo was not the man to tell them. If they thought nothing was to be feared, why should he expose himself as a frightened man? Maybe they had their ways of conquering the strength of nature. Old Ajorsalik in the settlement could, it was said, do magic things to avoid rain and southwest wind. So white men too might be able to master all kinds of gales. Polo said nothing. And as he saw the others go to sleep and keep talking and taking interest only in flowers and small pieces of rocks, he had no reason to worry. He went to sleep too.

But Polo was the first man to jump up, when the storm came over them. He got in his clothes and peeked out of the boat. A heavy cloud was right over them, he could feel what was coming, and he wondered how the white men's spirits allowed them to stay asleep—those who were supposed to know so much. But he dared not call them, for a man who is asleep has lost his soul, and if he is waked up before the soul has come home again and moves, the soul can't find him again, and he must die.

Polo was scared and he realized that unless the noise of the boat had power to stop the gale, there would be a terrible mess out here in the open and no shelter at all from the waves.

The white men came to and showed a face that did not correspond to the calmness they had before. Polo did not understand how white men could change like that. The anchor was broken when the first attack of the storm hit them, and they were washed out to sea, unable to know which was up and which was down because water was all over from above and below. The storm roared and roared —so much so that Polo knew it was unwise to speak, for no one could hear him. They all had no thought but to hang on to what they could grab. Polo knew this was all caused by white men running around and putting their noses in everything that was meant to be hidden away and forbidden, since this made the spirits and the ghosts very angry.

They drifted way out to sea. Once in a while they saw a huge iceberg looming up, towering high above them, and they felt the snow and water it sent down on top of them. But the boat was always kept away from the immense ice masses and tossed around like a piece of wood in a river.

What Polo and the white men experienced they could never tell, as their memories were blotted out in fear. But they lived, they survived the gale, though they did not have any way to tell how or why they did so. But they were very far from land, away out to sea, and they were tired—

dead tired since they had had no chance to eat or relax for a long time, and everything was ruined inside the boat. For two days they had done nothing but pump, and patch the three holes made in the body of the boat from hitting against the ice in the uproared sea.

Calm and nice weather set in, and after some time the sea became smooth and the men in the boat acted like dogs coming out from a battle with a bear. They felt surprised over being alive at all, and they forgot that they were not yet rescued. They did not know where they were and how far from home and if it would ever be possible to get back. This was a situation none of them had planned, but this was where Polo came in handy. He realized that the food on board was spoiled by getting mixed with gasoline and would not be too pleasant to eat, so why not try and get something else? So he started in hunting as soon as they came to an ice pan and he managed to locate a big seal and shoot it by acting as a fellow seal and crawling close to it. After this he showed his ability to find fresh water on the ice pan, he put the boat to order and he became the big man in the boat even if he never acted as commander. Only he did what had to be done and the white men looked at him as the only one to give advice.

They got the different wheels down in the interior to hum again and the noise soon brought them into the coast. Polo at once recognized where they were and told them how far they had been out of their way. The white men now were confident again and even if they hurried home, they stopped several times, and again began their foolish search for flowers and stones and pieces of rocks which they hammered out of the cliffs, not fearing anything, even though they had been warned by the spirits.

Polo, who could see how close they were to his home,

looked forward to seeing Kadara again and other human beings. It was not good to have to spend so much time with white men. And if Polo had known what was going on at his place he might have given more attention to his thoughts.

Most of the people at Polo's home were asleep when the gale started. They had seen the signs of the storm in the sky and stones were put on top of the kayaks, all the men were called in from the hunt, and they got otherwise prepared.

But this wind was worse than usual. The tents shivered and trembled. Ehre had to go out and support the tent by something heavy. It was no miracle of a tent and he had very little wood to keep it up. The women inside heard him complaining that he was alone and Polo was not there when he was needed. Old Inaluk the mother said that yes it was too bad, but Kadara could not help but feel some pride in the fact that her husband had already made himself wanted. He was a big helper of the house.

The wind kept on. It was as if the water had forgotten that its place was in the sea—it wanted to run up on the land. Small stones and gravel were lifted like grass and drifted like snow. It certainly hurt the face if one went out. After some time it grew worse, and the tent could not stand it. It bent over and the lamp blew out. Only three poles were left upright. There was no space at all in the tent to move around in, and they all had to sit and hold their arms around the poles still upstanding to keep them from falling in. If everything was tipped over, their possessions would fly all over the place and be lost.

Suddenly they heard a voice outside. It was Odark that came fighting the gale and shouting to them that Ehre had to come out! All of them had to come out! Old Asivak was

missing. Ehre crawled out and heard that the old hag had
gone up on the hill close to the tents and tried to calm down
the wind or in any way turn it around so the mountain
would provide a shelter for the settlement. She had said that
she felt strength in her soul to persuade nature and conquer
the wind. But unfortunately she had in her excitement forgotten to say words strong enough to resist the effect of the
tempest against her own weak body. She thought of everybody in the settlement, so now everybody had to think of
her. They had seen her fighting her way up the hill, but
she tumbled over as she raised herself to start singing and
away she was carried over the rock and down into the water
on the other side. Odark proposed that they should run
for her, she might be rescued if they could manage to get
the skin boat hauled across the hill and down on the other
side; if not, no one in the world could do her any good.

Ehre came out, the women and children in the tent had
ventured to crawl out too. But it was impossible for them
to stand straight upright. People gathered down in a crevasse in the cliff where the men used to protect their kayaks
from the wind. This was quite a shelter, at least enough to
allow them to talk to each other and listen. Odark once
more proposed to help old Asivak. But the only answer he
got was silence.

Then someone said he thought it already was too late.
Silence again—if only a little time would go, they could be
sure that her fight for life, wherever it was to be fought out,
would be ended. Finally Ehre took the word. He was a
poor hunter, but now he got an idea:

"I think we very often have to pity old Asivak. She is
old and without any relatives to support her. This is very
bad. So if we only pity her very much now and not move out

to help her, we will be free from having to pity her any more in the future!"

They did, and old Asivak was gone. None of them could have done a thing for her. She had tumbled down over the steep cliff into the roaring sea, and people ceased to mention her name.

They also decided that she had died away from their settlement, which meant they did not have to mourn and keep at home five days for her sake. So all of them hurried home to protect their tents against the gale.

The sun came back and men went to repair their dwellings. New skins were put in, poles were lashed together where they had broken. The tent stones were out of position and it took quite some time but everything was finally put in the old shape.

They avoided mentioning that somebody was missing, and the next day the men went out hunting as usual. Seals are always easy to get after a gale, and the walruses too came close. A big walrus was killed early in the morning, so happiness returned to the place again. There was a feast around the fire and boiled meat in abundance. But Kadara thought about her husband. If he had been at home maybe he would have killed the walrus, and she would have been the one that invited the rest of them to eat and fill up. Now she had to listen to Sauneq, a woman with no courtesy at all. She screamed and shouted as if nobody had ever caught a walrus before in the history of the world:

"Oh eat, do eat and let me put some more in the pot. Oh my teeth are so happy to work at tough meat once again. Oh I am such a sweet tooth, am I to take big pieces myself?"

So Kadara could not help it and said: "Yes, we certainly are happy to have a hunter here at the place that can get a walrus, which I guess was never heard of before."

Sauneq quieted down a little at this but then she went high again. Lying in bed in the night Kadara thought it all over; her husband should have been home by now! But if he just stayed over at other places where the girls enjoyed his catch, it was not any fun for her here.

Next morning was bright and calm, the sun tried to make up for the bad days and the men were out. The women sat together and chewed skins in the sunshine, the fire burned and made nice cooked meat for them, the children played around on the cliffs.

They chatted and talked woman-talk. And Kadara said that she expected her husband home today and maybe Polo had something good from the white men he was required to follow and help.

Laughter greeted her. Even her own mother laughed. "Oh listen to a woman who is dying to get her husband home! Listen to her craving for him! Why don't you mention his name time after time and enjoy hearing the word? There is a devoted wife. Oh I wish many women were that admiring. Why don't you run uphill and look out for him? He might come more quickly if you see him a long time ahead."

Kadara felt ashamed for having shown her yearning. She arose and went home. Later her mother told her not to make herself ridiculous by mentioning her husband. She had to show decency and behave. People were going to talk about it too often if they saw how she and Polo were attached to each other.

Next day she never mentioned her longing to anybody.

But next day some of the men said it was funny the boat was not back yet.

But who can tell about white men, they go and you can never figure out where they go and how far.

Several sleeps went by. Kadara looked at the faces of the older men and said nothing, but she had seen that they turned back when she stared at them. She had a few nights without sleep and she was thinking quite some thoughts too. But then a boat was announced from the hill by some children playing up there. Kadara heard the news and her heart started beating and hammering.

She busied herself with thoughts of different things. Polo's boots and other things were dried a long time ago, everything was in order. She pretended to care for some pups that were there and was so strongly occupied with this that she didn't pay the slightest interest to the boat coming nearer and nearer. What was that to her?

But it turned out to be different than she expected. She saw at once that something bad must have happened.

She couldn't help it, she went down. Everybody was there and their faces showed seriousness.

The boat was the second one belonging to the white men, and in it were some whites but also Itukusuk and two more men. They came down to inquire about the party that went to the Kitisut Islands.

Then everything stopped in the mind of Kadara. She knew that people said to each other that the gale had been too strong for the little boat, and even white men could not command nature. And her mother told her, she better take these pants and put them on top of her head as a sign of sorrow.

She did. It couldn't hurt anybody and she sat there on

325

the ledge in the tent, sobbing and not eating for days. Her mother told the small sisters that this was done because the missing man might return. It is only possible for him to find his way back to his wife, if she sits with his pants over her head for five days. She felt pain, terrible pain in her back and thighs by sitting upright, but every time she fell over and went to sleep, the mother hauled her up again and told her to fight for her husband. She also mentioned that it would not be easy to find such a nice son-in-law for herself next time.

Kadara nevertheless heard that the men did not go hunting; she also heard one of the little sisters punished terribly because she mentioned Polo's name. The mother told her that chances were that Polo was dead, and therefore it would be dangerous to mention his name just now, especially as long as poor Kadara was mourning for him.

Finally she got almost unconscious and only kept her place on the ledge sitting up because they piled so many skins up around her that she could not fall over.

Nine sleeps had gone, when a boat come from the north. A skin boat with several people and Itukusuk among them. He went and talked with Ehre.

And Ehre called Odark and Mayark, and they talked together. After that they went into the tent and took all the belongings Polo had gathered. What Polo had given Kadara was also taken, and everything was divided between the fellows at the settlement. They told her that she was now to be taken away by Itukusuk and that everybody would quickly leave the place. It was time to go caribou hunting, and this had shown itself to be an unlucky place. Two people disappeared this summer. The mother said that it might have been due to the way Kadara and Polo had behaved and if she had not talked and mentioned his name at the time when he might have been struggling for his life . . . That might very well have upset his helping ghosts and disturbed them just when they were taking care of him.

But now finally the world had showed itself reasonable and sent Itukusuk who had lost his wife some time ago. He had volunteered in taking the Ehre family along too, and happiness was once more at the place.

Tears and fight did not help little Kadara in any way. The rules of the tribe were to be obeyed. Sullen and sobbing she went down to the boat, and away they all went.

She was a widow now and deprived of everything that could remind her of the first man. She could never again mention his name. The belongings he had were distributed to the men who departed to different places or who had gone along caribou hunting!

If Polo had died at home, his things of course would have been placed on his grave. When things are put there everyone can swop with the spirits by making a model in wood of anything he wants and then just taking it.

Poor Itukusuk had no gay life with a smiling wife and song and laughter in his camp as Polo had. Kadara went with him when he walked out from the main camp to go after caribou. And she carried loads of meat home when he killed animals. But she never forgot Polo, and she was found sobbing and crying many times, when Itukusuk returned from the hunt.

It was a very tired party that finally returned to Polo's place. The last day a little breeze had allowed them to stop the humming and they made a sort of sail and reached Polo's settlement, or rather where the settlement had been.

They found only the places where the tents had been taken down. No people were to be seen nor any sign of them going away in their boats.

Polo felt a disappointment that acted on him like hunger. He had been the rescuer of the party; he had heard the white men in their childish language stammer to him, tell him how they were grateful to him, and they would repay him highly. Now he was here, and his triumph could have been shown to the folks—but they were gone. He understood at once that he himself must have been thought lost. No other reason could explain their leaving the place. He had been the real provider in Ehre's tent. Dark forebodings rose in his mind.

The white men wanted to take him along. They would like to keep him up at their headquarters for the rest of their expedition. But Polo refused; he wanted to get out of there right away and go and hunt for his wife.

The leader of the men told him that they had nothing with them to pay him with. He realized that of course, for everything on the boat was eaten or broken or used to repair the craft with. But now at least they had meat enough to reach home. They got the humming noise up again and off they went.

Polo stood alone at the place he had been dreaming of for so long. He was alone and missed Kadara terribly. Gone were his things! But who had taken them, and where could he ever get them again? He had his kayak and his harpoon, but in his pocket he had two spoons nice and shining, given to him by the white man as a gift to his wife until they could send something down from their headquarters in payment for his services.

He looked at the spoons and polished them with his

sleeve. Then he went over the place and tried to find out what happened.

He found two of his dogs killed but still not rotted. That indicated that it had not been too long a time since they left. Polo assured himself that if he was a man that could save white men, he also was the man to protect and defend his wife. He had grown up in these few sleeps he had been away more than in years before it, and he was going to find her and fight for her.

Polo paddled down along the cliffs. A kayak doesn't make much impression in a Greenland fjord. The high steep mountains tower up and the huge masses of floating ice in the sea dominate everything.

A little skin boat with one man paddling along disappears in the picture. He followed every little bay in and out and, as Eskimos do, he kept as close to the coast as possible.

Polo had just put his feet on shore at one of the fjords and relaxed by stretching up his back and bending his knees. Suddenly he saw a woman emerging from one of the houses. It was Gaga! She was not a nice girl but she looked beautiful to Polo since the rest might be here!

Gaga had been awakened by the dogs' howl and saw a strong broad-shouldered man stand on the beach beside his kayak.

She did not try to hide her joy. A man! Not only company in her lonesomeness but even a man and a nice, good-looking one. She saw that it was Polo, the boy she knew so well. On her way down to the sea she thought of why he left his wife and came here. Newly married he was; she already made up in a hurry that the wife might have died and he went out to forget his sorrow. He came to the right place.

"It happened that somebody came to your place," said Polo.

"Oh joy, happiness and luck came along with you!"

"It is not impossible that one should like to stop and have a hole in the poor kayak mended."

"This is the place for mending kayaks. There might be some little threads left, only there is no one that can sew here, since I am left alone and all the good sewers away."

"Are you the only one in the place?"

"Until you came and became the one I have been looking for."

Polo felt a little uneasy. It was nice to have a woman, since his clothes needed care. He had been out with the white men and his skins had been wet the whole time. At home he had found nothing; his dried boots and whatever else he had was now in use on different feet and bodies somewhere. Here was a woman capable of doing what was necessary.

And Gaga showed eagerness to do it. She took him up to the hut. She did not even have a tent during the summer, but she slept in one of the winter houses of stone and peat. It was not comfortable but good enough.

She got hold of his boots. The kamiks were thoroughly wet and were open at several places along the soles. She did a little too much talking when she took the stockings out and removed the grass between the soles. She made many remarks about how this was to be done proper—words that were absolutely useless as Polo knew.

But he realized that she had been alone for such a long time and she needed talking, so he let her explain and entertain while he dozed away on her ledge feeling fine lying in a place that was not wet and not rolling in the waves.

330

She never observed that he went to sleep. She was happy and she showed it. Taking care of a man and his things had been in her thoughts for a long time, when the dogs left her time to think.

Here he was. She brought his things out on the cliffs and spread them in the sun to dry.

When she found him sleeping she stood and looked at him for a while. Polo was so beautiful and strong. Just the right young man to make a girl happy! And especially Gaga, who had seen years go by and had only bad experiences along the road of love.

She knew all about men. Therefore she went for a fresh codfish she just caught the same morning and boiled it while he was asleep.

She waked him by her singing her joy out in the air. And he jumped to his feet. Was he sleeping here on a strange and dirty woman's ledge, even though he had set out for his wife?

He ate the fish silently. The sleep not quite out of his body. Then he asked for his kamiks. Only one of his two pairs had dried, Gaga said, but it was not yet put together. Oh she was going to get everything in fine shape. No hurry! She would fix it!

And she began asking him about what had happened. She already understood that something serious had taken place.

They helped each other by mending his kayak. He had patched the hole with blubber but water still came in. Now he had her using her needles while he stretched the skin out for her. They came close to each other while doing this but he only smelled that she did not have the scent like Kadara, and that kept him even more distant in his mind.

She looked at him and sighed. She on her side also did some smelling. But what she smelled only attracted her!

331

After this was over, she invited him to come inside and rest. She told him about the dried meat she could provide for a meal even taken in bed. She was sorry only that she did not have fresh meat to serve, but rest she could offer, for her little ledge in the hut was big enough for both of them.

Polo took the hint about the seal meat. At the same time he realized that he was hungry himself. The food with the white men had not been too substantial at the end.

"It happens that somebody gets inclined to try and kill a seal." And he took his newly fixed kayak and took off.

She was told to use the time to finish the work with his clothes.

Sarfak is situated as a peninsula running out in a sound between some islands. Seals are abundant there and Polo saw several but he missed the first ones. Then he sat in his kayak looking out for some others. The sun was shining and there was not wind enough to blow up the slightest curdling of the water. A fellow gets awful sleepy in such a situation. The light in his eyes reflected from the surface of the water, the silence, everything seems to make him go to sleep, so Polo got the overwhelming temptation to rest a little bit. But there was the woman on shore. He thought it over for a moment, a very short moment—and then he paddled over to the other side and went on shore.

Gaga had for hours kept an eye on him. He sat in his kayak outside her living place. It was like having one's real husband hunting for one, and she knew that she was the one he did it for. She worked at his clothes. Skins need such care. She had to run both sides out and turn it in such a way as not to dry it too much.

And each time she slipped out she saw Polo sitting watching for seal. Once she happened to be there when he tried to harpoon a seal. She felt she could not breathe with all the excitement, but when he missed she felt sorry, because that would keep him away still some time. She realized that she ought not to have said what she did about having no fresh meat. That of course made him feel he had to get some for her.

Suddenly she saw him going on shore on the other side. Maybe the kayak had drawn some water and was to be drained. But she saw him walk around over there and finally lie down in the grass and sleep.

She told or at least tried to tell herself several times that he liked to sleep in the sun that was shining on the other side of the cliff. But why didn't he come over to her and sleep in her skins? She told herself that he was ashamed for not having got anything to eat for her so far, and with this consolement she went in and fell asleep. Yet she cried a little. Gaga was such a lonesome girl—living all by herself here in the summer when everything grows inside you and there is so much sunshine and life everywhere.

When she waked up she heard the dogs howl again. Polo was back. He had two seals in tow behind his kayak. She helped him getting them on shore.

Poor girl, she was not handsome but she could work. And this was like having her own husband coming home. She skinned the seals for him, and she cut the meat. Together they ate the warm liver and took some fresh, still-shivering blubber.

Polo crushed one of the skulls and took out the brain. He chopped it up with his knife and chopped blubber into it. Here was a paste like the sunshine itself, like a dream about the heaven. They ate it silently and after that she told him she would boil some meat.

"Oh no! Keep it for yourself for when I am gone!" He

333

had already heard that she knew nothing about his wife.
The party had not been this way. That told him that he had
to search in the other direction; they had gone to the south,
and he knew where to go now.

Bring me my kamiks and you can have the skins and the
meat here." She looked at him and went for the things.
Meanwhile he occupied himself by taking the intestines and
pouring out the contents and hanging them upon stones
to dry and become delicious.

She came with his clothes. They were mended nicely
and ready to wear now. She looked at him but said nothing.
More than ever, she felt herself a lone woman in the Arctic
without means of getting anybody else to come to her!

But he told her that he was in a hurry and went his way.
Just as he turned to go into his kayak, he put his hand down
into his pocket and produced one of the spoons. A bright
thing that shone in the sun. The kind the white men use
to put in their cups and dissolve the sweet stuff with. He
gave it to her and said nothing.

The tears came in her eyes, but he pushed himself down
in the narrow hole in the kayak and she took hold of the
stern and lifted it up so he could pull out without scratch-
ing the bottom against the stones.

Without a word he set out. And without a word she stood
at the shore and saw him disappear. Then she had to take
care of the meat and keep the dogs away from it.

Polo rowed and rowed. He killed a couple of ducks and
he went on shore to eat them. He took a sleep in the sun.

Many thoughts went through his head, but he had to
let them go. He had to take advantage of the favorable
weather and use all his strength for rowing.

He saw the clouds coming up from the west. But Kook
was the place he hoped to reach and he set across the fjord
to make it.

The wind began to move the water some and after a
while he had quite a breeze against him. Not that it mattered much. He was among icebergs that never permitted
the waves to spoil their majesty. But just the same, when
snow is falling the land is better than the open sea for a
kayak man.

Gradually the wind grew bigger and bigger, like the gale
he endured with the white men—until Polo saw the water
dart like dust over the surface of the sea. It still came in
spells, but he knew it would be more and more, and he certainly felt better when he could see around a big iceberg
the houses at Kook, situated right under the steep cliffs
where the winds were never as strong and where he could
crawl in and wait for the fair weather to come again.

There were three women at the place. Two of them were old, incapable of hunting or even rowing in the boats. There was no question of leaving them behind to do anything, for they were no good even at watching the dogs, for which a widow was left behind. The three women greeted Polo even more cordially than he had been welcomed at the first place he just left.

The widow was Bolette, and she was famous for her energy. Polo endured some of it, since he had to stay until the wind had calmed down.

He delivered what he had of game, some birds. These were a welcome variation in the monotony of fish and dried meat—women's diet when left alone. The women here had seen Polo's folks, Polo soon heard. Their own people had joined them in fact and they had left for the big fjord, planning to be away for some time.

It was such fun when they passed here, the women said. Some dances had gone on, and lots of meat had been eaten. Polo was patient, listening to their talk, knowing that they would talk about everyone in the party and would soon come to his wife. There was no use exposing himself by asking for Kadara. Sure enough, after the more important members of the boat crew had been the object of stories, the women came to his little wife.

"Oh, and then Itukusuk was along! You know he lost his wife last winter and since then he had been living with a couple up north, but now he got a new little woman of his own. She was very bashful and did not say a thing. When she was told to dance she refused and I saw her crying. She evidently thought she had to show some shyness to make him excited. She was just a miserable little thing and it is a pity that Itukusuk should have to take potluck with such a bad sewer. It is the case with men, they are too hasty and never take time to look around and get a real one that could help them out and make nice clothes for them."

It was Bolette who said these things but thereafter she never spoke about Kadara any more. That, however, also was enough. Polo understood from what she said not only that his little wife was faithful to him, but also that she could be easily found as soon as he joined the hunters. Perhaps there would be a fight when he wanted his things back—particularly his wife, since he knew that Itukusuk badly wanted somebody to take care of his skins. But he was a kind man, and he was not likely to do her any harm while he lived with her during her husband's absence. This was merely a matter of handing over a woman to somebody else to take care of while the owner himself was away. Fine, he felt happy, and he sort of liked the husky widow, and the three days he had to stay there at Kook, he enjoyed her cooking and she looked after his clothes, severely putting blame on Gaga's work which she said had almost ruined his kamiks.

He in his turn fixed their house. It is indeed bad to live in a house in the summertime, but they had no tents. The two old ladies too told stories about their experiences, particularly in their younger days, when people had stronger juices in their veins, and the deeds therefore were mightier.

Polo went out several times every day to look for good weather. The widow followed him and assured him of the hospitality of the place. He felt the ease of being looked after as a baby and one day, as he felt the wind almost gone, he decided to leave. She then took up the offensive and told him to clear out, that he needed a wife, that she had spotted him out for a good hunter but that he could do much better if he had a trained woman that could do everything expected from a housekeeper. That would put him

337

way ahead of the other fellows who were fooling around with newborn children and had to nurse them until they came to the age where they were of any help at all.

Polo stood silent for a moment. Not that he had any temptation to go for her proposal, but it always is embarrassing and difficult. He reached down in his pocket and hauled up the last of the two glittering spoons the white men had given him, and which he had anticipated for a welcome gift for the wife. Bolette had been fine and nice, and now he had to disappoint her. No man in the world could help feeling a bit sorry for her. He said nothing but only stretched out his hand and gave her the spoon.

Poor Polo had never had any experiences with women before. He dropped himself into a dark crevasse by this. The widow grabbed the spoon, the sun sent the shine back in her eyes, and she also grabbed for his neck. He felt her nose rubbing his with great violence. Suddenly she gave a jump of joy, she turned back and ran into the house from where he heard noises from the agitated woman herself but also from the two old dames whose tongues never ceased to comment about whatever happened.

Polo had very little time, but he was a hunter used to grabbing situations fast and he did this time. Only he did not hunt, he ran. Down he ran to his kayak and lifted it up and almost threw it down in the sea.

Out he went in the tiny boat. He was just off land as the cheerful widow who now apparently saw life starting all over again for herself emerged from the house, looking to her great distress at what had happened while she was inside. Polo went and he went fast. She yelled after him to come back but he did not even turn around. She then took to the material side of the game and mentioned his kamiks and his clothes left behind. It only made him slow down the speed for a wink of the eye. Then he realized that there were chances for all kinds of kamiks and clothes but not for a clean getaway like this, and he paddled on and soon disappeared from the sight of the women at Kook.

The long day passed and the night was clear so Polo never stopped. When he came to the place where he thought the party had camped, he went on shore and looked around. They had had a couple of seals, and they had been playing. The ravens still feasted over the remains. This showed they had only been there a short time. The women had been picking berries but they were not yet ripe.

Later on he saw a new camping place. Again some seals were eaten and again he left though he felt tired, but he wanted to reach the entrance of the fjord before sleeping.

He passed a place where a big bearded seal was killed and put in stones and allowed to rot so it could be delicious in the winter to come.

Then he slept a little bit. A few hours later he took up the voyage and shortly came to the place he had dreamed about for days.

On the shore he saw the boats hauled up and loaded down with stones, turned upside down, to protect them against strong winds that might blow the light ships away. No people were to be seen, but Polo knew that they were inland to hunt caribous. He had only to follow their trail to meet them and Kadara.

Polo pulled his kayak up on the shore. He carried it way up beside the skin boats.

Up he went through the ravine to the plateau above. Nothing there. He came to the big lake, where sometimes camps were made. He could follow the lake along which were tracks of a fire and some remains of a dead caribou.

Polo stopped and looked around. There was no big camp here. They had only slept here while on their way farther inland. He walked and he went up on several hills, but found no people.

He also saw a couple of caribous, and he understood from this that nobody had been shooting close to here for some days. The animals would have been more scared than what he saw so he figured on a long march. Not a sound was to be heard. He listened for the crack of a gun, but nothing. On again.

He told himself that just as well go and get something to eat, and he happened to shoot a couple of ptarmigans. It is such a nice bird, and can be eaten raw while they are still warm from the life. The liver is delicious, the intestines are like spices and are very good for soup too. Two ptarmigans are just a meal for a man, and he felt comfortable and kept on. He slept in a warm place in front of a big stone, where the sun was his blanket, and he dreamed of his Kadara.

And after a long day more he came to the place. From the top of a hill he eyed the smoke from their fire, and he had only a short hike to go. Soon he arrived at the main place for the caribou hunters.

What a feeling to walk right into their midst! He was greeted with cheers and was fortunate enough to come while most of them were asleep. Nobody had time to regard him as a ghost coming toward them and take a shot at him.

Kadara was not at the place for the time being. She was out with Itukusuk and they had been away for some days. Nobody could say anything about that. A man needed a woman to carry his meat to a proper place to cache it, so it

340

could be fetched in wintertime when dog sledges were the transport.

Polo waited, and after two days his wife turned up.

She saw him at once and her mind turned from sorrow into joy. It was evident on her face, and she rushed forward to greet him.

But Polo stood there without anything to offer her, and Itukusuk had chosen her for his mate, so it was not settled right away.

Ehre the father was rather inclined toward the new son-in-law, undoubtedly a better hunter and also older than Polo. But what to do here?

Polo was not afraid, but the laws of men are based upon strength, and Itukusuk let him understand that he was supposed dead, and his return was to be looked at as a new man was born. And usually no newborn baby had a wife. This might be logical but it was not pleasant to hear

It was of course a sensation that Polo was back. But it might also cause a loss for those who had already divided his property, and were they now to return it? A council was held. Polo never got back a single thing of what he had had. Kadara wasn't asked; she was regarded as belonging to Itukusuk. Poor Polo stood there without saying anything. But as he looked sullen by the conclusion of the meeting, the old man Sorqaq said to him that he was still young enough to enjoy life:

"When you are getting old like me, you will feel it a burden. I would give everything to be in your age, so even without things you must feel happy. Possessions are only to be lost again, and the nice feeling is not to own things, but to acquire them. And the less you have the more joy in getting something, and therefore I consider you happy."

Sorqaq himself had taken the big ax and the butcher knife of Polo.

What young fellow has intelligence enough to argue against old men's wisdom?

Polo sat outside the camp and looked over the valley. A little woman came to him and sat herself beside him, but they did not talk. They only felt alike. Polo could not get back even his wife, due to his long trip with the white men.

"Didn't they give you anything for your help?" She was a clever little girl and thought of gaining new things and looked forward to a way of going on again.

"The white men had nothing left—we used everything we had on board—but promised to give me much after they had been home and looked at their many belongings."

Itukusuk came to them. "It is my wife you are talking with."

Polo said the same thing. But a young man arguing with an older is at a loss from the very beginning. Kadara cried and told him to go and let two of them alone.

Some others from the camp neared them and Polo's bad luck was topped by shame as he showed his position of dependence on Kadara.

Laughter greeted him, and he did not know how to stop it.

Polo had his gun left—nothing else in the world. He offered it to the stronger man to have him give up the girl. Itukusuk did a few minutes' thinking. He knew that the white men might help Polo, as they had some theories about

342

a man's woman and other funny ideas such as can only exist in brains that are not born in this country.

He took the gun, and Polo took his wife.

Polo and Kadara went outside the camp and sat alone in the bright night and looked at each other and forgot the world around them.

Ehre showed a sad face as he heard about this. Wasn't he the father? Why wasn't he asked? Inaluk told Polo that if he had only been paid by the white men, he would have been appreciated, some honor would have come to the family. But here she said was a man that not only did not fight for his wife, but gave the last of the things he had. This meant only that he was a man to feed not a provider to help feed others.

What a change from Itukusuk!

Polo certainly did not have the best possible welcome. He went out in the open with Kadara and with Ehre's gun, that he was now allowed to use on condition that the meat belonged to the house. This meant that again Ehre was the one to decide everything.

Caribou hunting is paradise-on-earth. That is why in heaven men go after caribou the whole time.

But it is a difficult thing too. The men go out from the camp and pick a girl to follow them. Uphill and downhill. The animals are scattered around and in the time of the year when people are out hunting them, they are aware of the slightest disturbance. They must be approached against the wind. Every noise makes them run.

The land is vast and the sun shines. People feel themselves masters of the earth when walking across it for long

stretches. The man leads the woman and tells her what to do. When they spot some caribous from a hill they have to be careful. Each move might spoil the entire hunt, so he has to explain to her the secrets of the game. Often they must walk along passages around the animal to approach them from the right side. Frequently the caribous do a lot of walking too! It is so tantalizing when one is hurrying up a slope to find that the animals are gone farther.

To shoot a caribou is life. In the days of bow and arrow the hunter had to go close to them, but the age of the gun made it easier. The caribou's sight is very bad. Often if the hunter has to cross an open area, he can take an old antler and keep it up like the horn of a bull, and the caribou may not find out. At the moment he shoots, the whole bunch will start up and run. But after a couple of seconds, they will stop and look around. That gives the man a chance for one more shot. If he hits they will jump again and not knowing where the danger is, they may even run across the man himself. The idea is to try and get around so they can get the smell of the man in their nostrils. At the same time, they know and away they are.

Polo did well; he had five deer the first day and he built a little stone hut and spread the skins on top as a roof. Kadara collected grass and made the finest bed that could be thought of. They had a pot, an empty tin from the white men in which had been the food used by those people that require salt for all their meals. Polo went to the nearby creek and got some water, and they boiled the hearts right away and had soup too. The tallow was rich and white. The ribs were spread out to dry and the sun soon made them black and tasty. Polo took off his kamiks and had them laid out in the sun.

How long they stayed there they did not know, because

346

they slept and ate and told each other how they enjoyed being together again, and figured out how to get along in the world as before. The worst problem was the gun. Polo knew that he had to procure all the food eaten in the Ehre house until he could buy a gun of his own. But how could he? What he would catch of foxes in the winter belonged automatically to the housemaster. But why should he worry? He had his Kadara again, and they spent the time under the sun and forgot what was coming next.

One day they heard shooting in a distance, and they saw a bunch of caribous stampeding toward their place. The animals were frightened and ran right across their hut, but Polo had the good fortune to kill two more.

They had nice skins for clothing and sinew for sewing during the whole winter; dried meat for parties and big hindlegs for frozen meat during the winter and tallow to make people feel comfortable in their mouths. Everything that was nice.

Polo realized he had too much to bring it down anywhere. He would build a cache here and go after it by dogs when ice and snow permitted. He worked hard and gathered the stones together. Kadara just looked at him, but her smile made it easier for him. She had been out quite some time with Itukusuk, and she told about how tired she had been packing meat up and down the mountains to where he decided to cache. They had made their cache where other young men had theirs. When they met, they made a big fire and ate together. Often they changed girls to go with them, which caused some giggling or quarreling among the girls, but the summer is for joy and in the long winters people must have something to brag about and make hints at and think about. And the future looks better when memories are full.

But from now on, Polo said to her, she was to go with no
other man than him, and they smiled at each other and
felt cozy and slept some more. A young couple living together with parents-in-law enjoy it when they get an opportunity to be alone!

Polo's kamiks were worn out. She sewed and mended, but
they were not his best, and she asked for the others. At her
age the making of a pair of boots was quite something to
mention. Later on she would be able to make them in one
day, but why didn't he bring them along as spare pairs?
Polo said that he did, but he forgot them at Bolette's place.

"What were you doing at Kook?"

He told that he had been there to ask for her, but wind
had held him up for quite some time, and he had to have
his clothes looked after.

She did not understand why he should have stayed there
for several days. "But maybe you were not in any great
hurry to come along. It certainly did look like you were
eager to get away from the wife you just got. Just to get out
with the white men!"

Polo sent a gaze up in the air but said nothing. Kadara
had her trouble making his soles keep together, and her
pride as a woman was hurt by this.

"And why didn't the woman there give you your clothes
when you went?"

Polo understood she would not see the situation, if he
explained. So he did not answer.

"Oh, I saw the fat widow there. I am aware of the fact
that she must be attractive to visit. She was alone and had
no competition from the two old witches at the place. I can
see why the wind was too strong to paddle in, and that you
forgot everything when you left. Your eyes must have been

348

full of tears so you couldn't see if you had your things or not."

Polo said no, but no is such a little word, and Kadara felt herself master of the situation. And she felt elevated being the talker and accusing him. This took the blight out of her spending so much time with Itukusuk.

The trip was almost over, and they cached their meat. Polo was going to put a couple of tongues in the pot to cook before going.

"Don't you think of my small sisters at the camp or my old mother, that never taste tongues? Oh they will have to dream about such things as long as they are lending out the gun to a man that wants the delicious things for himself!"

Polo put two other pieces of meat in the pot and they prepared for the return.

Not many words were said between them. But Polo went up on a slope and shot three rabbits, a nice variation in the diet. That made Kadara unhappy. She had enough to carry beforehand, and especially as she saw his kamiks. Two big holes in each of the soles. She had to mend them with caribou skins, and whatever else she had. She was aware that he would have to look terrible the rest of the trip, and she would be laughed at by every woman in the camp and all the people would see until she had some new ones made for him.

They arrived at the camp not too well pleased with their moon trip, but after a short time the rest of the fellows came down too. The district was hunted out, and the men decided to go home for the winter place and make their houses in shape to meet the cold season and catch seal for the rest of the fall.

Everybody walked down to the valley where they had to

camp overnight since they could not reach the boats before the second evening. By this time Polo was almost walking on his bare feet. His toes hurt him and on both of his heels were big wounds caused by stepping on the sharp stones. He felt like crawling on his knees on the last day, and he did not have the satisfaction of the burden that was loading him down: his own. It was the property of Ehre he was compelled to carry. He saw Itukusuk shoot some rabbits with his own fine gun, and he saw the women boiling meat in the pots he had given Kadara. It was no fun to think of the return of the winter, unless the white men would stick to their promise and bring him some stuff so that he would have something of his own again.

The last night before they embarked in the boats Polo could hardly sleep. He saw the face of his darling as she sat and looked at the other women bringing forward spare boots and clothes which they had packed inside the boats, knowing well that coming back from the caribou hunting, everything would be worn out and would have to be renewed. Of course, the way women are, they kidded her and shouted to her, "Hey, Kadara, are you lazy, or have you already given your husband the nice clothes you had prepared for him?" Polo could see that every remark they made hurt her like a blow in the face, but he did not say a thing. He only thought to himself that he was innocent in the whole disaster. So was she, he realized, but just the same he felt sorry because she did not have one word to console him and tell them that she did not care, she was only happy to have him back.

They made a place to sleep, packing some grass together, and she lay there with him, asking him about the trip. She realized from his answers that they must have been pretty close to never seeing each other again. In such cases as the storm at sea, Kadara knew that the white people are useless, consequently Polo must have been a great help. "Didn't they give you anything at all when you departed?" she asked him. "It seems to me that white people always have something to offer and since they have given you nothing at all, we had better forget them and not look for any greater reward."

Nothing but two spoons, said Polo. They were white and when the sun fell on them, they reflected back like a mirror, and they were used by the white men during the whole trip.

"Where are they?" asked the wife right away. "Why didn't you bring them?"

Polo made a mistake there. He understood that Kadara was suspicious and he did not dare tell her about the two women who got the spoons, in the mood he was in when he felt their love and could not return it. "The spoons were left at our place to be there if somebody come back while I was absent," he said and lied to her face. She lay there and said nothing and no smile came over her face. Polo said nothing, his mind was occupied by the lie.

The place where they slept was bordered on one side by a row of stones and on the other side by his kayak. She lay there and put her hand on the skin and felt right away that some of the patches were new and put on with a different kind of skin than the original. "Who did that?" she asked. "I did not do this patching and it has been done recently."

"Gaga did it," he answered, and Kadara was right on her toes at the same moment.

"What were you doing at Gaga's place? It is not in this direction. Why did you go there?"

He tried to explain that he did not know where to look for them and he went first to Sarfak and Gaga had mended his kayak and he had had to stay there until it was done. But

Polo was not good at explaining, and Kadara was no big woman for understanding, so he said nothing and she said nothing. She turned her back and looked out over the camp where some of the people were sitting talking, others sleeping quietly, and some children were playing. Everybody seemed free from worry, except herself, Kadara. She had got her husband back unexpectedly, after she had been crying for him when he was believed dead. But now she did not care much at all. Here she was with a man who had been unfaithful to her, the very first moment he came on shore, and now was telling her things that could not be true.

Polo also turned his back to her and could not sleep either. He thought about his dreams when he was out in the motorboat, or remembered the feelings he had when he first came back to the settlement, and about the reception he had gotten.

The next day, the elderly men shouted out for getting in the boats. The big skin boats, three of them, were loaded down in the water with all the property of the people. All the skins, many pieces of meat, everything was loaded. The women went on board and took their oars and, singing their traveling songs, they passed out over the froth. The icebergs were floating and the water was calm as oil. There were a few birds flying along, the more to emphasize the silence and peace after they had gone. It was quite relaxing for Polo to sit in his kayak using his arms and resting his sore feet. There were several men in the kayak with him and every time a seal showed his head to the surface, they all rushed ahead to be the first to put their harpoons in it. They got very few because there were too many men and it was easy for the seals to see them, and as they were traveling they could not spend much time waiting for the seals.

If they missed them the first time, away they went and did not lose any more time.

They now came to a place where they could put up for the night. Kadara was tired, having been at the oars the whole day. And it had not put her in very good humor to have to listen to the many taunts she had to endure from the different girls, asking her which of the husbands she now had was the worst, and how much the white men had sent her by Polo. They slept together without having exchanged many words during the evening. There were so many people that they had to go to different places. Polo and Kadara went by themselves and this made it seem evident to everybody that something was going to take place between them.

Itukusuk took an interest in Kadara and she was not absolutely unwilling to laugh at his jokes and answer him when he made some remarks when she was close to him. But the night Kadara and Polo spent together, they had very little to say to one another. Polo was hoping that a miracle would happen when they came to Kook. But nothing did.

The next day, after a long, long stretch in the boats, they came to Kook where Bolette and the two old hags came running out together and shouting a welcome to them. Bolette saw that Polo was tired. She had not yet given up the fight for him. Bolette was known for her energy and she would not have been the woman she was if it had not been for her ability to stick to her job. She knew perfectly well what had happened between Polo and Itukusuk. For it was, of course, told at once, that the former had lost all his property because he had been considered dead, and the only thing he had left was the gun and this he had to pay to get his own wife back. Now she saw where she would have her way. The party was going to camp for the night. Those who had their homes here at Kook could not receive all of them as guests, but that did not matter. Here in the summertime, when the sun was shining night and day, and the weather was warm, the whole world was the home of the people. Each one slept where he felt like, and all the meals were prepared and eaten outside.

Bolette knew her ways. She waited until she saw the couple sitting alone. She had been a married woman so many times and so long that she could spot a quarrel at any distance. She could see it now and from different hints she could understand that even though it is hard for a man to die, it is not easy to return from the dead unexpected, disturbing all the arrangements that had been made during one's absence. She neared the couple with a pair of fine new kamiks in her hands for Polo, and she smiled all over her fat body as she handed them to him and told him that they were ready now and he should don them right away and give her the others to be resoled. She also remarked that she felt ashamed to see him walking along with such kamiks.

Polo looked at her face and at Kadara's, and he realized that here, once more, was a place where an explosion would do more harm than good, so he just bent forward, took off the old, worn-out kamiks, and gave them to Kadara. She took them and looked at them but not a word came from her lips. She just looked at him and from him to the widow, still smiling and grinning. Anger flared up in the young wife. Here she sat, their poverty exposed to everybody and, on top of this, here comes another woman, a fat elderly witch, who evidently had turned the love of her husband to herself. Kadara took the kamiks and hurled them out in the field as far as she could, and then she jumped to her feet and walked away. But she made a mistake to walk toward where the other people were, which was in the direction she had thrown the kamiks, and she had to stand there and see Bolette hurrying after the kamiks, picking them up and assuring the still-silent Polo that she would put new soles on them, and that he should never again suffer from sore feet if she could help it.

Kadara stopped and asked, "What have you to do with those kamiks, and who gave you permission to pick them up after I have thrown them away?"

Bolette could not help smiling. With her most pleasant smile she took from the pocket on the inside of her kamiks, a beautiful spoon, glistening and shining in the sun. She patted it with her hand and polished it with her sleeves and in a soft voice said, "Ah, this is so fine, and I am so happy that Polo gave it to a poor woman when he visited her and had such sewing to be done, and when I would not take any payment from him."

Polo went up on the hills and sat there the whole night, looking out over the froth, and listening to the laughing and screaming of the people. They were playing and dancing and singing, as people do after being on a successful hunting trip together. Before anybody was up, Polo was down in his kayak and away from the shore, as he did not want to have a scene like the one he had witnessed the night before repeated, especially as he felt that the audience would not be just one person, but Bolette would be sure to manage to have the whole crowd listening and expose him, and what the results would be, it was impossible for him to foresee. His only refuge was his kayak and the big sea, where he could be alone in his boat and there were no women to follow him.

Polo had two seals floating beside his kayak when the

other boats came up to the iceberg, back of which he waited for them. He had his catch taken up in the boat and now he caught the sad eyes of Kadara. She looked at him but he did not care to answer a question that was asked from her eyes. He had been out getting a change in diet, as he was tired of caribou meat. They all cheered him and some of the girls, when they heard it, began making remarks. "Oh, my mouth is watering for some seal liver," "Oh, I was dreaming of seal liver last night and fresh, warm blubber that has never been cooled off." "Couldn't we have some seal liver?" A certain feeling came over Polo when he heard Kadara say, "Where is my knife? Hand me my knife, I am going to open one of the seals and take out the liver so you can all have some." She was now the wife of the hunter, the one who could offer delicious things to her fellow oarsmen. Soon they saw all the girls with their mouths, and even their whole faces, smeared with blood from the warm, delicious liver, and shining from the blubber they cut out from under the skin of the seal and ate along with the liver. Polo felt happy in heart and it seemed as though an understanding had come between them. They were husband and wife and could serve their guests.

After the meal was over, the girls took up their oars again and their boat songs sounded over the water. The men, who were surrounding them in their kayaks, joined in their songs, and life was happy.

After a while Polo saw that something was the matter and asked one of the men why they were going that way and taking the short route home. "The water is fine and the current is flowing this way," the man told him, "and it was decided this morning to row to Sarfak as two of the families wanted to stay there for the rest of the summer." Polo felt as though his spine were an isolated and cool column down through his body. At Sarfak was Gaga, the other woman to whom he had given a spoon, but whom he had avoided as he was so fiercely devoted to Kadara.

As he had expected, Gaga showed up, happy to be relieved from her lonesome dog watch, happy to see and listen to other people, and especially excited by the return of Polo. Her brain was not so big, and her imagination was stronger than her reason, so she got the idea that Polo came back to her, and that he even came back followed by many people as witness to her triumph. In her overwhelming joy she did not see Kadara, and not realizing anything, she went straight to Polo and yelled a welcome to him. She felt so sure of herself as only a person can who has been alone for a long time and has assured herself, time after time, that her wishes will be fulfilled.

Polo stood there. He had no sin to confess or regret, but he was in for an unhappy misunderstanding and, as all the people stood around, when he heard the girls giggling and the men whisper, he could only see the face of his wife, the beloved Kadara, and it did not look too inviting.

The poor Gaga was bewildered. She had been made fun of many times in her jealous life, but she never gave up as long as there was the possibility of success left. Her hand went down to the pocket in her kamik and she brought forth a glittering spoon, shining in the sun and throwing the reflection right in the eyes of Kadara. The latter did not say a word, but she walked right up from the beach and refused to listen to anything. They heard her laughing, but a laughter of desperation, and they saw Polo walk after her, but the faster he walked, the faster she went ahead back of the hills were no one could see them.

The talking was finished and they had to get ready for

357

the night. The boats were taken on shore and turned upside down so there was room for all to sleep under them. When this was finished, the couple came back and, although it was plainly visible that peace was not entirely established between them, they joined in giving the two seals for a meal for everybody. All the pots were put on the fire and the smoke went up toward the sky in the beautiful Arctic night with the sun low in the north and everybody eating until he got the last piece of meat out of his hand and fell asleep where he stood. Kadara was hostess and encouraged everybody to eat, and eat. She had forgotten that the husband who brought the meat was suspected and still had not cleared himself of the accusations against him.

The next morning they set out on the last stretch. It was only a short distance to the home settlement. As they put the boats out to sea, poor Gaga came running with her spoon. She had spent the whole night crying and now she wanted to see whether or not it was a joke and if Polo had not meant to take her for the rest of his life. What else would make him come to her place and give her two seals to eat, and a marvelous spoon to look at and feel a doubt about?

Again Kadara grew cold and she sent him a look and he understood that whatever explanation he could offer, he was only a husband who died and lost everything and he did not see what the future could bring that could restore his dignity and happiness. At any rate they rowed, and rowed, and now an island emerged up from the sea in front of them. But, what was that? As they came close they could see people walking on shore. Now they could see that they were tall people. It was the white men from their headquarters up north and their motorboat was anchored in front of the place. Polo's hopes grew bigger. Maybe the white men had not forgotten him. Perhaps they would keep some of the many promises they had made him when they fought together out at sea and when he got that seal that saved them all.

When they came closer, the white man greeted them in his funny language, and shouted to them if they had seen Polo and did they know where he was. With a big spring, Polo pushed himself forward in his kayak. He was as proud as he could be that everybody heard that he was wanted by them, and that they came down here just to find him. Now once more he felt the blood running fast and as though he were a live being again. The white men sent him boxes of food, a gun, and all kinds of household utensils. He stood there on the beach, the wealthiest man in the tribe.

Then the white men came to him and asked him to show them his wife, the little Kadara he had told them about. It took him no time to get hold of her, for she stood by his side and smiled and felt that she and Polo belonged together and nothing could come between them. The white men asked him if he would not like to move up to their place and stay with the expedition as long as they were in the country. If he would be as helpful as he was before, they would reward him liberally and give him a place in their house, and of course his wife too.

"What did you think when your husband did not come back? Weren't you worried, or had you given him up entirely?" the white men asked Kadara.

She felt so embarrassed that she could not answer and Polo finally found his voice and answered, "Oh no, a real wife never worries, she just sat home and waited for me to come back. She trusted that nothing would happen to any of us."

VI. The Big Strike

AT FIRST he had the desire to scream and yell; then it was as if he felt inclined to cry; but he did nothing but sit down without any thought at all in his head. His brain didn't function at all. This was the big strike, the real wonderful thing he had never heard about but in stories and never seen but in dreams. Of course he and the boys had talked so much about it, they had hoped, but none of them had really ever believed it could be possible. Yet here it was!

And he was entirely alone. He could have shown his delight in any way without being embarrassed—and yet he did not do a thing. He just sat quiet and looked at a tiny mosquito that sucked blood from his hand—and he let it. He smiled faintly without meaning anything. Now he was rich, finally he was situated in a way that he could never miss anything in the future. This was IT, and he was the one who had found it.

He hardly heard Roger tramping through the forest. Only when he was quite close, Norman woke up and came back to earth and began to feel happy. He shouted and called his friend but he did not do it in a wild and exciting way, as he had wanted.

"Roger, Roger, come here. Hurry up! We got it. I found it. Look here. Just take a look. The color, I tell you, the metal, the gold! Look at the yellow tinge! We got it, my boy!"

Roger was much wilder than Norman; he really did some screaming and squealing. He cried out to the trees, to the valley, to the world, that here was gold for everybody. "Come on and take what you want! It's here to be sent for. Ha, ha, nobody hears me, nobody comes but us! Nobody but us, Norman, you and me!"

After a while both of them calmed down and decided to take a closer view at the strike. They filled their pans with what looked most promising and ran down to the brook to wash it out.

They got gold in small nuggets, light-grained gold, and the gravel was very easy to separate. Norman hurried back after a new panful. Then Roger finished and went for more. He came back fast and washed and washed, and it did not take a long time before both of them had a small pile of nuggets on a stone right beside them. After a couple of hours they were a bit tired and could speak reasonably.

"I never heard of the bedrock being so close to the surface. We will only have to strip the soil and those trees to get at it!"

They started at once and worked with axes, picks and shovels; it took some hours, but then they had had more dirt to work with, and down they went to wash and wash. They kept on, until the sun stood high in the sky the next day. By then they were too tired to keep going and stopped. They had toiled through the light Arctic summer night. They had forgotten the mosquitoes and never gave food

361

a thought. They had only felt the starvation for gold, and they did what was possible to satisfy it. During such a spell no other desire is to be found in one's body.

But suddenly they sensed that they were dead tired, so they could hardly manage to start a fire and make some food and coffee. At once after the meal they fell asleep and only woke up after a long dreamless time.

It was Norman who was the first one to speak.

"But how are we going to get hold of the other two boys?"

It just dawned on Roger that he had entirely forgotten the two fellows, Peterson and MacLean, who had gone ahead to prospect some other places.

The four young men were friends and partners. They had been together to procure an outfit to take them up to the wilderness of the Canadian Arctic, looking for a quick way to get rich. They had sworn to each other to stick together. When they had no more grub to go along with, they all took jobs at mines and worked there, saved and saved until they thought they could go on and then out again on their own. Placer mining does not require any great outfit, and they were all of them young and full of hopes.

Now they had separated, as nothing looked too promising around here. Still, Norman intended to sink a shaft right here at the little brook, and Roger intended to look around while he waited for him. They had two canoes by this time, and Peterson and MacLean went ahead—all of them intending to send for the rest of the party if something turned up. What they had in mind was to get jobs for the winter to come, since they regarded that as the only possibility just now.

But here was the real big strike. Here it was; the bedrock was, so to speak, out in the open, and the pocket was filled with gravel mixed to such an extent with nuggets and dust, that none of them ever heard of anything like it.

The two of them were safe. No other human being was nearer than a couple of hundred miles; they were sure of that. Therefore they placed their free gold on stones exposed to the sun without any effort to protect or conceal it. The two men had the entire world to themselves.

They spoke about how to get hold of the fellows. Better go after them at once. Of course Peterson and Mac wouldn't travel very fast, as they would prospect all the way. So they could be reached in good time. Then they intended to split in two groups. Two of them were to return and build a hut to stay in for the winter and keep on washing and digging. The others should bring what gold they already had down to places where they could sell it. They, of course, would not bring their metal to nearby stores and thereby show everybody that they had struck it rich. That would be the same as giving everything away. No, they would go far away to places where nobody knew of them. Maybe all the way down to the coast. There they would change their nuggets and dust into real cash money and return with that. They were also going to buy provisions of all kinds—dynamite, ammunition and food, new clothes and tools. They also wanted to distract people's attention from what they were doing by buying some trappers' materials, perhaps saying they were tired of gold hunting as it gave no revenue, and that they would go into the fur trade.

That would keep people off their tracks, and all four of them might work day and night in shifts at the mining. During the winter they intended to keep the ground thawed out by fire. They had lots of fine things to do, and then they could quit and go out with their profits.

But at first they would stay a day or two more here and

363

wash on. They could easily bring along with them what they had. They had the biggest of their two canoes. So why not work a little more? They also told each other that it would feel nice to stay over a couple of days when they reached a place with a saloon and meet some folks. Only they assured each other that they should be careful not to drink too much, which would probably make them talk too freely about what they brought. But they also promised to watch out and warn the other fellow if anything looked dangerous.

So they went on. The mine—small as it still was—seemed to have everything. The biggest nuggets were such that they could pick them out with their fingers. The smaller pieces and the mere dust were easy to get out from the gravel; they did not have to use mercury, which took a longer time. Besides, that wouldn't do for such big shots as these men. The dumps, in fact, were thrown aside to be worked over later. And soon they were assured that they had enough gold—so much in fact that they hardly could travel with the weight of it.

Again they had a long, long sleep, and when they woke up, Norman said that he had figured out how to go out and buy provisions of all kinds without being found out. He had made up a wonderful plan, and he wanted to have Peterson along. He was smart and would know how to fool anybody who might intend to follow them back.

He had decided that only when all of them had washed so much out that none wanted more, they would open up and register their lots and sell them. Then they could get outside and nevermore take a hand to a shovel or turn the earth upside down to get money.

Roger asked Norman what he would reckon as sufficient to quit.

"Oh, I guess we will find that out! I want to go home

and open up a fine little restaurant where people can come and eat everything they want. Canned beans won't be served, nor beans of any kind; aside from that, anything people want they can have."

"Well, I am going to buy a nice farm. I know of one at home. And a girl, I tell you, that has been waiting for me. I am going to show all of those people who never thought I would amount to anything. Yes, a farm with cows and horses. Also vast fields, with grain, and me sitting on a tractor and driving around cutting hay! No more paddling canoe for me, no more of this serving yourself as meals for mosquitoes. That will all be over!"

They both had empty bags made of moosehide, and they filled them with real gold. They had bought those bags two years ago, but most of the time they had been stuffed with dry beans or something like that. They had often been ready to throw them away, but that would be the same as giving up entirely. So they had always put the gold bags into these bags when they carried them. Now they would do the same thing. Nobody could know, you see!

The bags were delicious to look at and wonderful to feel, round and smooth with the most valuable of all metals inside. They talked about spreading the tailings and taking down the small headframe they had made on top of the shaft, but why do that kind of masquerade? Nobody would ever come here and find out. So why bother?

Their canoe also needed a look-after. That took another day. But then the large boat was tight. They liked to feel safe in their vessel, and they paddled away in high spirits to fetch their friends.

Two days they paddled along and made good headway. They had to look out along the river, as their fellows might not have gone far, but after two nights' sleep they found a camp and two gold seekers were there. Roger and Norman asked if they had seen anything of their friends, and they learned that they had been there about a week before. The two men themselves were coming along, since they had heard about a rush farther down the river, and they intended to follow it up. But they had just the same morning shot a big moose, and they intended to dry some of the meat for winter provisions; as soon as they could load it in their canoe, they would follow after.

"This part of the country is hopeless, we think!" they said.

Roger said that they were convinced of the same, and therefore they left. "What do you know about the passage downward."

"Well, in two days you will reach a place where some other water flows in. The current is rather nasty there in the rapids. Some can take it, but others have to use the portage. We did. It takes you across a mountain, and some mountain too. But our canoe is not suitable to stand much, and we will have to carry it on our backs again, with all our dried meat. But we want to take it all along, it will fetch good prices down below the rapids."

Next day was rainy, so the voyage was not too wonderful. But prospectors can't stop because of the weather. They had to reach their friends, and now it was late in August, so if they were to return with provisions before freezing, they had to use the days.

"I think we will have to postpone the holidays until next year!" said Roger, and Norman agreed.

Downriver they went. Some places the current was quite strong, so they had to look out for stones lest they tear holes in their canoe sides. Other times they passed through lakes where they had to paddle to get along. And all the time they were looking to both sides for signs of their friends. In short, they did not travel as fast as expected and planned for.

They slept nights in their wet clothes and only cooked meals when it was absolutely necessary. They were very tired, but that was what they were used to. They kept awake by talking about the future. They also told each other about how happy their friends would be when they heard that all their trouble was over for good. And again they spoke about what to do with the money. That was what worried them most. During the nights Norman decided that he, after all, didn't want a restaurant. He would travel around the world at first, see something, live in big hotels and sleep until noon every day and eat at least four times a day. Mostly he wanted to travel without doing any work at all.

Finally they could feel that they came nearer the rapids and when they heard the roar, they went ashore and ascended a cliff to take a look. It did not look too promising, but by looking up the steep path people before them had made by carrying canoe and belongings around the rapids they agreed that that did not look too inviting either, particularly since their canoe was so heavy and unwieldy. They realized that it would take them several days to pass what they could do in half an hour, if luck was with them.

They decided to take the risk and try it. Everything was to be tied down, and they spread their little tent across it all lest the spray might wet it.

Roger took his gold pokes and tied them to himself under his shirt. Norman saw it and did the same. If they were to lose their canoe but came on shore safe, they would at least have money enough to go on.

But even if they lost their gold, they would not cry. "We

know where to go and get more of the stuff. But just the same let us play safe!"

Norman sat fore and Roger aft, and they started. Both had their paddle in the hand and they knew how to use them. Both were very clever and strong, and they knew they had to be both to make it. When they had passed this rapid, they had nothing to hurry about and in half an hour it would be all over.

The spray almost blinded them, and the speed prohibited them from looking ahead. But they knew what they were up against. Norman saw a stone peeking up, he got out his oar and pumped hard, and they passed it safely. Roger could see they were going sidewards, so he took a hard pull on his paddle and got the canoe lined up. They could only occupy themselves with what they saw at close range; the roar of the water was too great to allow them to shout at each other. So neither of them could later tell how it happened or how long a time they had been in water, or if they had run up against one stone or many stones.

The only thing they felt was that they were floating around in the water in circles, that sometimes their heads were above the surface, sometimes they were submerged. Soon they forgot everything, for they realized that they had no canoe any more. But even that didn't bother them— they just wanted to stay alive!

There were some people in a little settlement below the rapids, and they had observed the two men in the boat. Quite a few had tried the same thing. Some had good luck but others didn't. The men had seen that this was a rather large canoe, and that the two boys understood their business handling it. Everybody went out to look at the show; it was in a way exciting—human lives were at stake.

Everybody jumped to the beach and pushed their boats

out to help, and they succeeded in getting hold of both of the unfortunate boys and dragged them up on land. And here they lay winking their eyes against the sun; after they came more and more to life, they looked around and realized.

"Well, that was that!" Roger said. "Bad luck this time!"

Norman looked at him but did not open his mouth. Both of them let their hands move up and down to find out if something was fractured and both of them felt the gold pokes inside their shirts. The heavy metal had not dragged them down because of the rushing current. They looked at each other; they knew that there was plenty to buy a new boat and thus everything was all right.

They got to their feet, the water poured from them. They took their boots off and emptied them and spoke to the people around.

Both boys took it calmly. They did not want to appear too downhearted, and the people from the place did not like to embarrass them with questions. Out in the wilderness one always must let people tell what they want to have known. Never pump anyone!

"Come inside and have a drink to warm up a little!" somebody said. He was running a sort of tavern combined with a store where he sold provisions and ammunition to people. The entire population—it was ten men—followed of course, and it did not take a long time for them to learn that Roger and Norman were in a hurry to catch their two fellows.

These had just passed here about a week ago after having passed the rapids successfully; they had slept here for two nights before they went on.

"But now I presume you will have to build a new craft to go on with, for your own canoe is lost," said one of the men. "It drifted downstream while we tried to get hold of you boys. And what kind of outfit do you need?" It was kind people who asked—men who wanted to be helpful.

"Well, I think we can pay for a new boat or canoe, if anybody has such a one for sale. We also are in need of a gun and some provisions; in fact we have nothing now. Oh, if we only had kept away from those stones," said Norman.

"I don't think it was stones you ran into. It must have been a big tree; there are quite a few of them, their branches and roots catch hold of the rocks in the narrows!"

They sat there for a while and got something to eat. It was nice to rest, and anyway they would have to wait until next day to buy an outfit.

It had started getting dark nights and it was always nicer to spend the evenings inside. There were a couple of brothers among the men, and they had looked at each other when Norman said that he had gold to pay with. They all knew for sure that Peterson and MacLean had had nothing like that when they passed. They had paid by skins to get ammunition and food; gold was not in their possession, nuggets or dust.

The Hardisty brothers had something in mind, but they did not tell anybody.

The next day it was found that Norman and Roger had plenty of gold. They paid everything asked for, and their gold was someway peculiar—light-grained gold, different from what was known around there. Gold of course is gold, but there can be a slight difference in color and shape of the nuggets; so to speak, each place has its own pattern.

Norman and Roger bought quite a lot. They said, of course, that they intended to trap the next winter to get something to keep alive by. But it was easy enough to see, when the two guys poured out from their pokes, that they had no fear of going hungry in years to come.

They bought a real wooden boat to replace the canoe they lost; they got the best clothes to be had there and provisions of all kinds, so they could meet what Canada's hard winter usually offers.

But no sooner had the two of them left than Nick Hardisty called his brother aside. They went out of earshot and talked together.

"Those two guys have got it!" said Nick.

"Do you think I've lost my eyes and my brain?" said Bob. And then they figured out what to do.

The two men had arrived in a canoe, and their fellows had gone ahead. These two, Peterson and MacLean, had been loosemouthed enough to tell that they had left their friends about five days' travel up the river. And they had also said that they could follow the same river the entire way and row all the time.

No map could have been drawn easier to follow to find the place. So the very same evening Nick and Bob told the rest of them that they intended to go fishing, and they had in mind to try above the rapids.

The rest of the boys followed them with their eyes. It was quite a job for the two brothers to haul their clumsy boat across the rocks, but the Hardistys seemed to amuse themselves by it. In fact, they said that they felt no inclination to sleep—they preferred to haul and drag the entire night.

Next morning they started carrying provisions and tools across. But it did not look like fishing gear. They also brought pans and pickaxes and shovels.

"Are you going whaling?" cried Carl Trace after them. "It sure looks like you intend to chop up the whales and melt the blubber in the pans to produce oil!"

The two brothers did not answer. They just smiled idiotically and muttered that nobody could know anything for sure. Each of them said that his brother was a bit crazy, but it was better to please him than to listen to his growling!

Away they went. But no sooner had they disappeared than the entire population, which now was eight men, divided into three groups. Two of these had three men and the third one just two. Common to all of them was slyness, and each tried to get away in the least conspicuous way from the rest of them.

It smelled as if a gold strike was in the air. Everybody had noticed the stuffed gold bags Norman and Roger had carried with them. There was something funny about it!

"Please don't do anything too openly!" all of them whispered to their partners. They were all so cautious . . . so cautious. At night they gathered in the store where they could also buy a drink. It was just a blockhouse with but one room; but it was what was demanded at the place and no more. The trading goods hung down from the ceiling on hooks, the whiskey was placed in a barrel under the landlord's bunk. On the middle of the floor stood the stove, made out of an old iron kerosene barrel, and five men sat around. All of them were unusually friendly that evening; they smiled at each other and asked if somebody wanted their seat and so on. They all said that they might get in mind to go hunting for a change, and they all offered a good-by drink and advised the rest of them to stay home, as the weather did not look too promising. And so on.

That kind of acting is dear to every prospector. He likes it, and they all feel real happy such days. Nobody can tell if the big strike is right ahead. They all knew that their partner was preparing for the race. They all knew, too, that the man next to themselves knew just as much as they did and was doing exactly the same thing; but nobody would be the first to talk openly about it.

By and by they retired. They all complained about being sleepy and tired and hankered for some rest. After a while only three of them were left. One from each group, and they watched each other like birds of prey.

Meanwhile the rest of them hauled and dragged canoes and boats across the mountain. The sweat poured down their bodies, their arms and legs clacked, their lungs could hardly pump air enough into their bodies. But nobody gave up. Soon the last three men also left the hut.

They looked up in the air and assured each other that they were very sleepy and desired a long and undisturbed rest.

As soon as they believed the other two were out of sight, they started running. They jumped the best they could, and thus it happened that they all reached the lake above the rapids almost at the same time, and there they saw the two Hardisty brothers paddling merrily and fast upstream. They had an advantage, but that could be run down. Three canoes took up the challenge. They all saw the others, but nobody told the rest of them that they could just as well have omitted the acting. In fact they did not speak to anybody; they had entered a race for the gold they really did not know anything about. The paddles were hurled down in the water and pulled back in great speed; everybody rowed as if his very life was at stake. A peaceful arrangement could have saved them all much sweat; but such things do not take place in prospecting.

Nobody thought of sleep. The only rest was to take a breath between two strokes of the paddles.

The next day the three canoes had reached the Hardistys,

Nick and Bob. They looked a bit disappointed but said nothing. Their idea was that even if they now were not ahead of the rest of them, those who caught up with them were almost exhausted, so they could get away at their own ease. But soon all four crafts were rowing together. Then someone cried that it might be nice to make camp and take a rest; why not stop up and talk a little about it? They all answered that it was a swell idea. But none of them liked to be the first one to go ashore, so they all rowed on.

Three days passed by. It turned dark early but they all rowed on. The sun rose and they all rowed on. It started to rain and the water refreshed up their faces a little. They took a bite of bread or a spoonful from a tin can while they paddled along. They put their hands down in the river and took a drink that way.

The next day they spied a canoe right ahead. It was the first two men Norman and Roger had met. They too had seen a glimpse of a gold poke in the canoe of their visitors, because at that time they had still not been smart enough to tie their gold up under their shirts. But this was enough. The two strangers had heard from Peterson and MacLean where their fellows were to be found so they knew exactly where to go.

And thus happened what so often has been heard about but not often seen. Twelve men passed up the river and already from out in the water they saw the trailings the two first guys had left behind. Nobody thought of tying up his boat. They all stumbled out and hurried to the shaft where Norman and Roger had worked. From here it was that all the gold came they had seen samples of down below the rapids. As fast as if they were cats, the men jumped around and staked their marks down. Some swearing and a tiny fist fight, a couple of uppercuts and some knockdowns of course. But this was nothing to what has taken place elsewhere. Nobody tried any shooting; no revolver was even drawn. No use for such violence here, as they were only few people, and here was space enough for all of them.

And late the same evening, they had all hauled their canoes on shore and chopped some trees down for fuel for a big fire; they all sat cozily and friendly and talked about the events of the day.

After that they examined the place, and nobody was disappointed. They all hastened to get some samples, and then together they all took an easy ride down to the registration office and told the official that they had opened a new valley. All the lots were staked and occupied. The valley did not contain more than these twelve men had the right to, according to the law.

But whoever believed this? Not one soul, so a rush was started in no time, a new race was on. This time with bigger and better outfits, because it was more than two weeks' voyage. Some came with horses, some in big boats. Some smart guys established a transit station at the rapids, and before winter set in, there were not less than three stores, several saloons—everything anybody could hope for in a gold town.

They had to work hard in the valley but it gave marvelous profits. It was of course heard about outside. Agents for big companies arrived, and soon all the lots were in one hand—a big company with many millions as investment capital. The stocks were sold and resold, and all of the twelve original prospectors were big capitalists who did nothing but sell and buy bonds and stocks, and soon were known all over as Canada's smartest men.

But Norman and Roger were on their way after Peterson

and MacLean without knowing a thing of what was going on. They went for the boys, and they were right on their heels time and again. But luck was against them. The two who had gone ahead often took big jumps to find something that could give them all food during the winter to come. Roger and Norman rowed until the river froze up, then they had to walk. Sometimes snowstorms stopped them, but finally just before Christmas the four friends reached each other and joined in a little town not far from the coast.

All of them were enthusiastic over the meeting, but as they found each other in a public place in the midst of many people, it was impossible to say everything at once.

But Peterson and MacLean were too excited about a rumor of an immense rush far up in the country. Everybody had heard about it, but it was too late this year to go up there. One could in the early spring with a motorboat force the river until some rapids where one had to carry everything across some rather bad mountains. But it was told that soon a cable track along the rapids would be established, and it might not take a long time before a real city would grow up around the mines.

"I really think there might be some jobs to be had for us up there," said MacLean. "It can't be so very far from that place where we parted this summer. Well, that is life; if we had only known about it, we might have been the ones to make the big strike. But let us now hope to get a nice little job. Maybe it'll at least keep us alive for some time."

The Future of the Arctic

I AM ONE of the last surviving explorers of the Arctic, and as I look back over a life filled with adventure and excitement in the old days of the Far North, some thoughts occur to me about the times that are to come.

I started my life as an explorer in Greenland, working with Knud Rasmussen. At that time the only manner of transportation was dog sled in winter and skin boats or kayaks in summer. Such transportation took a great deal of time and caused endless difficulty. But no one complained, because there was nothing else available.

There was a lot of excitement the day the first sailboat came to us for use at Thule. The wind was going to bring us from place to place! The natives were excited and so were we. Then a few years passed, and power boats were introduced, with all the mystery of propeller and motor. In a short while—less than we expected—the Eskimos handled them better than we Danes!

During the early years at Thule, one or two boats visited us in the summer. The rest of the time we were totally

377

and completely isolated. Then came the wireless, later the radio, now there is television. Before we knew what was happening, the Arctic had become a part of the world.

It was as if Arctic man had been waiting in sleep, resting until the white men had worn themselves out inventing things and making life easier. For as soon as Western inventions were introduced, the Eskimos seemed to awaken suddenly and operate them better than the whites. They took part in all kinds of management, operated the radio and Morse key with unusual ability, and surpassed all other societies of the world in the speed with which they became "mechanized."

One of the first men to tell the amazing story of the Arctic, the progress there, and the degree to which it was coming under man's control was Vilhjalmur Stefansson. It was he who told the remarkable story of *The Friendly Arctic*, who captured in beautiful and moving terms the glorious record of those men who changed the unknown and terrible Arctic into a wonderful place to live.

In former days the civilized world had only heard about the Arctic from explorers whose principal stories were to make heroes out of themselves and announce their own doings and pose as victorious conquerors of unthinkable terrors. Vilhjalmur Stefansson undertook great travels in the Arctic and made intensive studies of it down to the last detail so that he could finally sit down and follow its development with greater understanding than anyone else in the world. He took clippings from everywhere, nothing was too insignificant to escape him, and he acquired a view of the Arctic world so complete that he could understand everything and give his readers a picture of all that really happened up there.

I admire Stefansson though I haven't always agreed with

378

him about everything. He was the very first man to teach about the land up there and show how human beings could take advantage of it.

In the first place, he showed, we must get away from the idea that the Arctic is a bad place to live because of its terrible weather. Nowhere in the extreme north does the temperature go lower than in certain parts of the U.S.A. or Siberia. People in Montana or North Dakota suffer much more from the cold than any Eskimo or Lapp.

It is true that there is darkness in the wintertime. I have lived for many years in Thule where we have four months without sun. But I have never seen a time that we could not manage. And perhaps we did the important things better than other people whom tempests and gales keep at home for good parts of the year.

The Arctic could in fact be made a vacation resort on the basis of the good weather usually prevailing up there. Weeks can go by—and do time and again—without wind enough to blow out a match! I have never spent any time in any southern latitude with so much fair weather as that. Strange as it may seem, the heat makes people suffer much more in the Arctic than the cold. The summer is hot and the sun burning, and the mosquitoes terrible in many places. When the winter comes people always feel happy.

It was the airplanes that opened the Arctic to the world. Now travelers can go all over in the North in no time at all. Flying conditions are said to be better there than anywhere else. From now on the Arctic is opened up, and progress can never be kept back.

It was an American, Professor William Hobbs from Ann Arbor, Michigan, who first called the world's attention to the fact that the weather in Europe was "made in

Greenland." He sent an expedition up there to confirm his theories and his ideas were so well established that during World War II the Germans sent up expeditions to forecast the weather conditions so that their generals might make their plans.

Americans fought such German technicians with their protecting armies. The famous Arctic explorer Bernt Balchen was put in charge and his guidance of the American army up in Greenland stands out as one of the most daring phases of the Second World War.

Everyone can see by looking at a globe that the Arctic is between those points in the world where people are living in greatest numbers. Transportation therefore has to make terrible detours or come right across the Arctic. The blessing of this is that the route across the North Pole is just what the pilots want. No high flight above mountains is required. There is no fog, very little bad weather—and, above all, the distances are shorter. People may talk about the darkness in the wintertime—lasting six months at the very North Pole; but in our days darkness is no hindrance to planes.

Of course precautions must always be taken, more so up there than any other place in the world, since no automobiles or trains can rescue wrecked planes. In this regard I am thinking of emergency airports, repair shops, hotels and depots. Furthermore, the regular routes must have a well-distributed network of weather stations, as well as scientific stations of other kinds. On all these accounts it is easy to see why flying will bring many people up to the Arctic—that in a very few years the population inside the Polar Circle may multiply beyond what can possibly be imagined.

For the outside world the Arctic is also of great scientific importance. Meteorological science has advanced beyond the stage where it attracted the laughter of the public. Nowadays scientists know laws totally unexplored before. But as no man would ever think of furnishing his house with heating plants without knowing how his house gets cold, it is essential to know how the part of the globe situated around the Poles is absorbing the heat which the tropics produce. That is what the meteorologists need to-day. Stations to send weather reports of all kinds to everywhere in the world are already in full swing and more will come.

Transport on sea is also developing. From days of old there have been two big routes tempting explorers or kings and merchantmen looking for an easy way to the riches of India: the Northwest Passage and the Northeast Passage. In 1905 the Norwegian explorer Roald Amundsen sailed the Northwest Passage, taking the route north of Canada to Bering Sea from the Davis Strait. The water proved to be very shallow and it took him four years to accomplish the feat.

Later on Vilhjalmur Stefansson found another route which he thought useful, but he did not try it. And still later Captain Larsen of the Royal Mounted Police of Canada took his ship, *St. Roch,* not only through the passage from west to east but back again. This time the voyage from Baffin Bay to the Mackenzie River's mouth lasted sixteen days.

If this route will ever have any practical use I am not aware of it. Up to now very little is produced along the waters of the Northwest Passage to justify any speculation in that regard.

But it is different with the Northeast Passage—the waters

north of Siberia from the White Sea to the Bering Strait. Here the Soviet Government has spent immense sums of money and time and energy to investigate whether this route can be depended upon during the summer.

There is every reason for Russian experiments like this. Not only could the interior of Siberia be made open through the four big rivers flowing out to the Polar Sea, thus taking advantage of the resources of the largest country in the world, but also the way to the Soviet districts in the Pacific would profit immeasurably by an easier route than that around India to the south.

To explore the conditions and possibilities of the route, not only an expedition but more than sixty-seven permanent scientific stations are kept up by the Russians. Every little detail is examined.

Just think of what this is going to mean: the greatest wood country in the world, the minerals of the Siberian territory, farm products, fishery products, salt from the newly found deposits at Nordvik—all of which may be taken around from Kamchatka instead of bringing them from the Black Sea through Suez by way of the Caspian Sea. The Arctic waterways ought to be opened up, just on account of those products alone. But the Arctic can also produce much more: there is a vast country up there with fertile soil that has never been exploited.

Nowadays many different seeds are known. Using some of these seeds under scientific planning the farmers in Alaska could (and actually do) produce grain and compete with the outside world. In Lapland the farmers move farther and farther north every year, bringing with them the advantages of science, and in Siberia I have seen the most modern farm methods in use right up to the Polar Circle.

Aside from farming, there is a huge meat supply that

can be had from the reindeer of the North. It may not be known that reindeer taming is the oldest trade of all between man and domesticated animals except dogs. Up to now only very little has been done to develop reindeer farming in the North. A somewhat unsuccessful experiment was made in Alaska but that did not disclose any fault with the idea itself.

Dr. Stefansson also talks about musk-ox farming. I am not familiar with the possibilities here. But I have no doubt that all the grass of the Arctic can be used and the quantities produced can compete with anything in the world. People would be surprised to learn about the varieties of vegetation of which the Arctic can boast.

Everybody knows too about the gold in Alaska, the copper in Canada. And many think that the northern countries are rich in minerals in such quantities that along with modern transportation and modern need for goods, millions of white people can profitably live there. At present there is some possibility of finding oil around Point Barrow, the northernmost point of America, and this suggests that this settlement will be a city of importance before long.

Up to fairly recent times white men—except the gold miners in Alaska—came to the Arctic mostly to hunt the game that produced oil or skins, or brought big fleets to the north to fish. Fishing was a gamble, frequently a bad one, but today the scientists have made it a less risky business. Zoologists and the oceanographists work together. The tests of sea water taken up from different depths of the water can tell the fisherman if there is any possibility or not for a catch of fish. In older days one simply tried and tried and tried and had to depend on luck. Now it can be figured out ahead of time where to go and expect fish, and where not.

Modern science can also predict if it is going to be a bad "ice year" or not. The currents of the sea are known and all details, even the most insignificant, can be put together and be used to protect the traveler in the Arctic.

Many people say that the Eskimos, Indians, Lapps and other northern people were much happier when living in primitive state. That is the kind of thing, in my opinion, which lyric poets like to write and sing about—mainly because they have not seen the Eskimos starve and suffer, because they never saw the Eskimos when they had no means of fighting nature or tools to tame her.

But give an Eskimo a gun and a steel knife. Let him have matches to light his blubber stove. Let him be able to cook his food in an iron pot and give him some variation in food so he can keep more healthy. Believe me, he will never ask for the old-time conditions again any more than any of us pray to be put back in the caves and be fitted out with primitive tools or be required to swing from the trees.

The people of the Arctic are like all other people in the world. They have possibilities for great development, but they unfortunately came rather late to them, or at least later than the rest of the world, because of their remote locations. But it will take no time before the Eskimo will learn from other people and use his country to his best advantage.

A man who has been able to earn enough to keep himself and his family alive and safe in the most remote country in the world, without help of any kind but only with what he could himself make, and on places where no other nation so far could manage to go along without help from outside—that man has proved his skill and energy and strength and resourcefulness. I have no doubt in my mind that he will get his share of the future of the Arctic.